SCENT OF YESTERDAY

My journey from lotus roots to sugarplum dreams

A memoir by
Jaya Kamlani

Editor & Designer
Minal Cherie Kamlani

SCENT OF YESTERDAY

My journey from lotus roots to sugarplum dreams

Introduction   **v**

PART I

Lotus Roots   3
Blooming Years   23
Stage Fright   35
War Memories   41
My Labyrinth   49

PART II

Hello America   61
Spellbound   75
Hum Dono   87
Pearls of Motherhood   103
Tricky Forks   109

PART III

Frost to Sunshine   117
California Cruising   127
Saudi Affair   131
Polynesian Christmas   137
Don't Let Life Pass You By   143
A Closed Mind   145

Photo Gallery   **165**

PART IV

House of Tomorrow   177

Two to Tango   181

The Roads I Traveled   186

Alien No More   187

Yin and Yang   193

PART V

Pound of Knowledge   201

Memory Lane   205

Ashes to Birch   219

Mother Becomes Child   233

Pearls of Life   238

Southern Escape   239

Farewell   255

Acknowledgements   **261**

Notes   **263**

Introduction

Born by candlelight in August 1947, Jaya Kamlani (née Mirchandani) and her family are among millions displaced by the Partition of India. In *Scent of Yesterday*, she transports readers to post-British Raj Bombay with sweet and spiced vignettes of her youth — from riveting family tales and convent school capers to forbidden love.

In 1969, Jaya gets an opportunity to study in America. With newfound freedom, she weds against her family's wishes and launches a career in the New York advertising industry. She later takes a leap into technology and fights the Silicon Valley glass ceiling, while enjoying simple pleasures with her family. After retirement, she reflects upon her role in the world and writes about it.

Scent of Yesterday is a prequel to Jaya's first book, *To India, with Tough Love*. Her spirited candor and ceaseless determination inspire others to overcome their inhibitions and embrace the unknown. Readers will also cherish music, dance, and local culture of yesteryears.

Jaya Kamlani is an English Literature graduate of St. Xavier's College, Bombay, now known as Mumbai. She presently serves on the Board of Directors for Atlanta: City of Peace, Inc. (ACP) in Georgia. Learn more at www.jayakamlani.com.

PART I

Lotus Roots

My mother was also the man of the house.

From the early 1930s to the 50s, my father's job sent him overseas to Japan and Nigeria, where he managed the offices of an Indian textile exporter. Back then travel abroad was only by sea. His passage from Bombay to Japan took three weeks; to Nigeria it took five weeks. We saw him during his three-month vacation every three years.

With my father away, Mummy stopped by the school to pay the fees and check on our progress. One evening, when Kiku returned from school, she stepped out of the kitchen in her white sari and confronted him. "Where were you today?"

"At school."

"No, you were not. I stopped by and spoke with your teacher. Tell me, where were you?" She gave him a hard stare.

"Bicycling with my friend, outside the school," he confessed, his head hung low.

My mother's jaw tightened. Her dark almond eyes grew larger. She followed him to the bedroom across the kitchen, cornered him, and gave him the spanking of his life. She struck him now with her slippers, now with her hands. I stood by the bedroom door and watched the scene, my seven-year-old body shuddering with every blow tossed at my brother, then fifteen. Like an embattled boxer in the ring, he tried to shield himself, but in vain.

Later, I learned from Kiku that he had gone to see a movie with his classmate.

"But you told Mummy you were out bicycling with your friend."

"If I told her I had gone to the movies, she would have beaten me even more."

My mother's heart was the kindest, but when she was in a disciplinary mood, it was prayer time. I would see many such prayer-time days of my own during my school years.

A few months later, on a Sunday in November, my sister Kamal and I were talking on the balcony when we saw two men step out of a taxi and enter the building. One of them had bloody clothes and a bandaged face and head. *Who was that man?*

Minutes later, the doorbell rang. My mother answered. There in front of her stood the two men who stepped out of the taxi. She stared at the tall bandaged man, whose limp body leaned on the other man and let out a cry. "Mangha! What happened to you?"

"He was riding a motorcycle and skidded on a banana peel," said my brother's friend.

I watched the scene unfold from behind my mother in the corridor. My father, who had returned from his business trip, stepped out of his room. He stood there, speechless. Mummy pulled herself together and led the way to Mangha's bedroom.

While helping my brother into bed, his friend explained that Mangha was rushed to the hospital, where he received several stitches.

As my mother wiped her eyes with one end of her sari, he put his comforting arm around her. "Don't worry, Mummy. He'll be all right soon." My brothers' friends also called her *Mummy*.

For a whole month, my brother lay in bed with stitches across the crown of his head, his face, and his chest. Our family doctor, who lived in the same building, came by to nurse his wounds. I heard her tell my mother that Mangha had narrowly escaped death. The stitches were only an inch away from his heart and his brain.

When I returned from school, I stood by the bedroom door and watched my mother sit on a burgundy upholstered wicker stool while she talked to my brother and fed him liquids from the spout of a silver milk server. In a few days, he switched to drinking through a straw. When she was done feeding him, I dragged the stool to the glass curio cabinet and climbed up to turn on my brother's favorite station: Radio Ceylon. He only liked Western music. That afternoon, a smile lit up his wounded face when Frank Sinatra's "Three Coins in the Fountain" played. His eyes welled up when the lyrics reached a high note. Mangha was then nineteen while I, seven.

Many years passed before I learned the real story of my brother's accident.

"I remember that day well. It was November 14, 1954. I was a daredevil then," Mangha confessed with a blush on his aging face. "My friend and I rented Royal Enfield motorcycles for one hour and we raced down the street. I lost control and hit the concrete wall of Ruia College. My friends rushed me to the hospital and Jatin brought me home."

"But your friend told Mummy your motorcycle skidded on a banana peel."

"He did not want to scare her with the real story."

I don't know how many banana stories my brothers told our mother.

Ours was a large family with three sons and three daughters. We lived in the suburban town of Mahim, across the train station, on the third floor of a sixty-plus apartment building. I was the fourth rung down the Mirchandani ladder. My sister Hari and brothers Mangha and Kiku were older than I. Although I was named Jaywanti, meaning victory or victorious, the elders in my family called me Baby. Perhaps my mother thought I would be her last child, until my sister Kamal and brother Suresh were born. However, that did not make any difference. They still called me Baby at home.

All through my school years, I was the youngest student in class. That's because my first grade teacher at Victoria School told my mother I was way ahead in class and recommended I skip second grade. So I hopscotched to third grade and would wind up graduating from high school at age fifteen. High school then ran through eleventh grade, followed by four years of college.

After graduating from fourth grade, I came down with typhoid. When conventional medicine and homeopathic cures failed to relieve my fever, my mother took me to see a faith healer. Once a week, she had me sit on a rug while she circled chilies over my head and whispered something under her breath. She also gave me herbal medicine to take every day. With each passing day, I felt better.

On my last visit, the faith healer handed me a silver capsule amulet on a black string. "Wear this for a whole year. It will ward off evil."

After having spent four months in bed, I returned to school. Every morning, my mother had me open the amulet and fill it with incense ash from the home shrine. I was now in fifth grade and attended Canossa High School, a Catholic convent school. The cook no longer had to escort me. Unlike the primary school, which was over a mile away, this one was located half the distance from home.

Dressed in white-collar royal blue uniform, white tennis shoes, my hair braided and tied with white ribbons, my books packed in a small steel case, I walked to school with my sister Kamal and neighbors Meena and Sheila. Along the way, we passed eclectic shops and tea cafés. My mother insisted we never walk to school alone. She was concerned about the rowdy street boys — the catcallers and the eve teasers.

School hours ran from eight-thirty to four. The day began with assembly and prayers of *Our Father* and *Hail Mary*. The first class of the day was Catechism for Christian students and Moral Science for non-Christians. A short assembly with prayer also followed the lunch hour. I said so many *Hail Mary*'s during my school days I must have chanted them in my sleep, too.

Studies carried a heavy weight in our family. Since I had missed the entire first term of fifth grade due to typhoid, my schoolwork suffered a setback. My mother hired a Catholic tutor, Mrs. D'Mello, who stopped by for an hour on weekday evenings to help my sister and me with our studies.

When Mrs. D'Mello complained of neck pain, my mother, who was no chiropractor, gave her neck such a twist that my poor tutor slumped in the chair holding her head in a dizzy spell. "Oh, Mrs. Mirchandani. . . my head, my head." Ten minutes later, she regained her equilibrium and returned to my books. Not much studying got done on such days.

For Christmas, Mrs. D'Mello sent our family a tray filled with delicious treats: round rum cake with marzipan icing, decorated with tiny edible silver beads, frosted green leaves and red roses; colorful miniature fruit-shaped marzipan; strawberry shortbread cookies, and a few slices of fruitcake. For *Diwali*, the Hindu New Year, my mother sent her a boxful of *mithai* of milk and nuts and some delicacies. For Easter, Mrs. D'Mello sent us cream-filled chocolate eggs, and my mother returned the tray filled with homemade delights.

A couple of times, the tutor challenged my sister and me to see who would receive better grades. Kamal, about two years younger than me, prevailed both the times. So she received pearl earrings from Mrs. D'Mello the first time, and a lovely piece of dress fabric for the second challenge. I think my mother may have been behind-the-scenes on the challenge and the gifts, to encourage us to do better in our studies.

My mother would often say, "Baby, I think someone has cast an evil eye on you. . . Baby, you used to be so good at your studies before you fell ill. . . Baby, I should have never let you skip second grade in school. I should have never listened to your class teacher." Whatever the reason for my falling back in studies, she asked the tutor to spend more time with me.

Trouble was that Kamal was very competitive and she would taunt me. "I am smarter than you. I got better grades than you. . . I got pearl earrings from Mrs. D'Mello and you did not."

That would make me feel very bad and I would walk away. Once I told her, "Kamal, you are only book smart." That led to an argument.

"But Mummy loves me more than you."

"So what?"

"She said even though you are fairer, I have better features than you."

"So what?"

A few days later, Kamal sprang on me again. "Mummy said if you do anything wrong, I should tell her about it."

"Okay then, I will not tell you anything anymore."

"Mummy said you are adopted."

Oh, that really hurt! I walked into the room where my mother was ironing clothes. "Mummy, am I adopted?"

"No. Who told you that?"

"Kamal said I was adopted."

"Don't listen to her. You were born in Sindh. Dr. Kishini Gurbaxani, who lived in the neighborhood, helped me deliver you."

Sometimes Kamal and I got into sibling rivalry, but usually we got along well. She was the talkative one while I was the quiet one. I hated to get into fights.

Due to his feeble health, my father retired from his overseas job at fifty-two. He tried to start a copper wiring business in Bombay and rented a small office in the city, but his plans did not take off. So, two of my older siblings had to quit college to support the family. Hari clerked for the Indian railways while Mangha sold Olivetti typewriters.

Now that my father was home, he took over my mother's task of checking on my school progress. One afternoon, while my sixth-grade class was in session, Mother Gina sent for me. I hurried down the flight of stairs to the principal's office. There in his glossy champagne sharkskin suit was my father, deep in conversation with the nun. They were discussing my grades. One thing led to another. Soon my father was complaining that I do not listen to him. So Mother Gina had me go down on my knees and apologize to my father. And my father had me apologize to her. I was mighty glad when at the end of the school year, the six-foot austere nun was transferred to Italy, and a pleasant Mother Colombo arrived to fill her seat. Then I discovered that she could be just as unforgiving as Mother Gina, and even stricter.

At lunchtime, I walked home with my sister and neighbors. One afternoon, however, Kamal was more than a little late. My neighbors left while I still waited for my sister. When she finally joined me, she told me her class had been detained. The school had just installed a narrow gate for middle-school students, so they could exit in an orderly single file. But this process, as efficient as it was, took the girls forever to get out.

"I thought you might leave without me for lunch. So I jumped out of the class window."

"*You* jumped out of the window?" I looked at her in astonishment. The window was some ten feet off the ground.

"Soon everyone was climbing out of the window. Suddenly, Mother Trezzi walked in. By then four of us had already jumped out. . . Don't tell Mummy or Dada."

An encounter with Mother Trezzi usually spelled trouble. The tall blue-eyed nun reported the incident to Mother Colombo, the principal. When class resumed after lunch, the teacher summoned the four girls to the front. The principal walked into the room and asked the four to collect their things and leave. She also asked them to bring in their parents the following day, to collect their school dismissal certificates. This was no suspension; the four girls were going to be expelled from school.

Distraught and shaken by the turn of events, the four girls came to see me during recess that afternoon. I tried to calm their fears and suggested they go apologize to Mother Colombo, hoping the nun would forgive them since they were among the top students in a class of fifty-plus. But, she did not. Instead, the nun reminded them to have their parents pick up their dismissal certificates.

That evening, Kamal worked up the nerve to break the bad news to my father. At first, he lent his ear. Then his jaws tightened, his face grew stern, and he flew into a rage. Wagging his finger at her, he scolded, "You deserve it. I'm not coming to your school. You can get your dismissal certificate, stay at home and do menial work." He stormed out of the foyer to his bedroom while Kamal stood there, scared and worried.

Later that evening, Mummy tried to reason with Dada and urged him to meet with the principal. After much persuasion, he finally agreed. The following day, the girls and their parents met with the principal.

When I discussed the incident later with Kamal, she said, "My friends' parents were mad at the school for causing so much pain to their kids, but Dad was furious at me for causing so much trouble. He had me kneel down and apologize to Mother Colombo. She said Dad was the best parent." The girls were sent back to their class and asked to sit in the last row.

Our father, the disciplinarian, had saved the day for the four girls.

❧

Our large family lived on modest means, but there was plenty of love within the four walls of our home. We were not wealthy, but like many middle-class families we employed a live-in cook and part-time servants. Labor was affordable and available in plenty.

Our doorbell chimed all day long. The cobbler mended footwear outside the building lobby. Peddlers stopped by to sell bread, eggs, and fresh produce. The *dhobi* picked up and delivered fresh laundry. The *dabbahwallah* picked up hot tiffin lunches and delivered them to my siblings at work. The florist delivered flowers for the gods' *puja*.

When modern gas stoves came on the market, my mother tossed out the old stoves that used liquid kerosene or coal. But the new cooking range that was hooked to a propane gas cylinder had only two burners. So she bought a couple of electric stoves. They had no temperature controls. Their curly heating wires, which were exposed, often snapped from overheating.

When I returned from school one evening, I found my mother repairing the electric stove. There she sat on the bed in her white sari, her dark hair bundled above the nape of her neck, a locket hanging from a gold chain around her neck, two gold bracelets dangling from her right arm, and big diamond studs sparkling on her ears and nose. Screwdriver in hand, she loosened the two ends of the coiled wire and out sprung the burnt wire from the labyrinth of the white ceramic plate. Replacing it with a new one, she tightened the screws and plugged the stove into the outlet. As the electric eel glowed in the grooves of the round ceramic maze, she smiled triumphantly. *Voilá!* My mother, the great improviser.

Some days a man would stop by to shine old pots and pans. He started a small fire on the street, rubbed dirt and ash on the old utensils, and placed them inverted over the blaze. Then he fanned the flames with a large leather air pouch that huffed and puffed like a human mouth. In ten minutes, our old pots and pans were sparkling again.

Once a year, an old gray-bearded man stopped by our home to renew our cotton-stuffed pillows. He sat in the enclosed verandah outside the apartment, with a cotton-fluffing tool that resembled a giant bow. He scooped out the cotton, piled it in a corner, and pulled at the long bowstring against the matted cotton. *Ping! Ping!* Fuzz flew all over the verandah, down the stairway, and some clung to the old man's long beard. When the cotton thrashing and pillow stuffing was done, he sewed up the pillowcases. *Voilá!* The pillows were all plumped for the night.

The barber made house calls on Sunday mornings. The cook announced, "*Sahib*, the barber is here." My father put down the newspaper and stepped out into the adjoining verandah. The cook brought out a chair for him.

I stood by the door and watched the barber slip a smock on my father and pat shaving cream on his face. Dipping a short fluffy white brush into a mug of warm water, he stroked the lather on my father's face. He gave him a shave and trimmed his gray thinning hair while he entertained him with local gossip. When he was done, he removed the smock, brushed away the scattered hair from the nape of Dada's neck and handed him a mirror. My father looked in the hand mirror from all angles, gave his nod, paid the barber his dues, and reminded him to return the following week for his shave. Impeccable grooming was essential for Indians of my father's generation.

One day, the barber stopped making house calls. So my father went to his shop for a haircut and gave himself a shave at home. Due to his fragile health, his hands were not steady. Sometimes he nicked himself with the razor and walked around the house with a tiny Band-Aid on his cappuccino-toned face.

With so many vendors and people knocking on our door, my mother always cautioned everyone at home, including the cook, "Don't answer the door without first looking through the peephole."

Then one night at the dinner table, my mother told us of a robbery that had taken place in the building. Someone had knocked on a neighbor's door and stolen things from their cupboard at knifepoint. The following month, another robbery took place. Concerned that the cook did not heed the warning, my mother and Mangha decided to teach him a lesson. Dressed like a bandit in black pants, a long fake mustache, and a dark blanket thrown around his shoulders and head, my brother slipped out the side door and knocked on our main door.

The thirty-some year old cook, in his undershirt and loin wrap, stepped out of the kitchen. Forgetting my mother's caveat, he answered the door without looking through the peephole. There in front of him stood a tall mustached man.

The cook's eyes popped. He froze. The man pulled out a knife from under his cloak and thrust it into the cook's stomach. The blunt edge of the blade sprung back into its sheath upon contact.

Not realizing it was a fake knife, the terrified cook scurried to my mother's room screaming, "*Memsahib, Memsahib*, there is a thief at the door. He has a knife."

I held back my laugh, as I had watched my brother rehearse and had seen the whole act.

Just then, Mangha walked into the bedroom, threw down his dark cloak, pulled off his fake mustache and flaunted his faux knife. He looked the cook in his eye and said, "From now on remember: never answer the door without looking through the peephole. Next time, the robber may have a real knife."

The cook's hands trembled as he gave a nod. "Yes *Sahib*. Next time, I will look through the peephole. I promise I will. I promise."

He kept his word for a while, and then it faded away with time.

Our home was always bustling, but the street scene fascinated me even more.

I could spend hours in my balcony and never get bored. I watched commuters spill out of the train station, gypsies stop by with dancing monkeys, acrobats do cartwheels and balancing acts, tightrope walkers perform high wire stunts, jugglers toss bowling pins, fire-eaters jump through fire hoops, musicians serenade us on their accordions, and even teenage boys from the building who entertained us with their kite-fights and amateur cricket games.

This evening, it was the snake charmer who amused us. The music of the flute flowing in from the street was enough to lure me away from my studies. I put away my books and rushed to the balcony. There he sat, cross-legged on the dirt road, the lean barefoot piper wearing a soiled white shirt, loincloth, and turban. He piped on his flute, then leaned forward and gingerly lifted the cover of a round wicker basket. Out sprung the head of a cobra swaying its neck to the music.

Within minutes, a small crowd gathered. The flute melody so sweet, it even mesmerized the cobra. It slithered out of the basket onto its master's lap and curled around him as if he were the trunk of a tree. Gliding higher, as if enchanted by some magic spell, it paused on the master's shoulder and held up its majestic head. All at once, the snake charmer was transformed into the mystical image of Lord Shiva — the destroyer of life — with the cobra at his beckoning.

As the music reached a crescendo, the cobra now perched on the master's turbaned head, swayed its neck. Spellbound by the pageant, the audience applauded and tossed coins into the wicker basket. I rushed to the cupboard in the bedroom, told my mother I was taking some change, tied it in an old handkerchief and hurled it from my third-floor balcony. It missed the target. Someone in the crowd retrieved it and tossed it in the basket. Untying the knot of the kerchief, the snake charmer looked up at me and tipped his forehead with his hand. The money he collected from the crowd would feed a small family that evening. Later, I learned the snake charmers remove the venom from the snakes before they take them on road shows.

It was a regular circus out there, on the street where I lived.

When the real circus came to town in summer, tents went up on the vacant land by my school. My mother took Kamal, Suresh, and me to see the high wire trapeze acts and animal feats. We laughed at the clowns and savored mouthfuls of pink cotton candy. It was no *Barnum & Bailey Circus*, but for a schoolgirl the *Three Ring Circus* was a delight.

When we returned home, my father asked "Did you like the circus?"

"Yes Dada, especially the elephant," said Suresh. "He was so big."

"How big was he?" asked my father.

"Bigger than you, Dada."

My father could not stop laughing.

We had no refrigerator and therefore no cold drinks for summer. When a flatbed ice-truck stopped by the building, my mother summoned the cook to fetch a block of ice. The cook ran down the three flights of stairs with an empty pail and returned with a block of ice covered with sawdust. Washing off the dust, he placed the ice in a towel and pounded it with a hammer. Then he emptied the crushed ice into a couple of large pitchers and poured rose essence, sugar, and water to make refreshing rosewater drink for the family.

Other times a watermelon truck stopped by and the cook ran down to get our family a huge cold melon, which my mother cut up in slices. The juice dripped down my chin as I took a big bite of it.

When I heard an ice-cream van with clanging bells come down the street, I took some change from the cupboard and ran down the stairs to get myself a chocolate-coated or an éclair ice-cream bar before the neighbors came out and the ice-cream man ran out of my favorite.

At times a man wheeled a pushcart carrying an array of bottles with eclectic syrup flavors and an ice shaver. He shaved the ice, clumped it into a big ball, and pierced a long stick through it.

"What flavor will you have today," he asked.

"Strawberry," I replied. "Pour plenty of it." The ice *gola* provide relief on a hot summer's day.

My summer days were fun-packed. Back then there was no television in Bombay. Going to the movies was a once-in-a-blue-moon treat with my older siblings. But, there was always someone to play Charades or Bingo with in the apartment building. I rented a bicycle, played badminton, hopscotch, or skipped rope with neighbors. Some days, Kamal and I played word games. Our favorite word was "Constantinople," as we could construct numerous words from it. Other days, Mummy joined us for board games: Ludo [Parcheesi], Chutes and Ladders, and Monopoly. When alone, I read Enid Blyton mystery books, played solitaire card game, worked on a hundred piece jigsaw puzzle, or did the hula hoop twists. My mother also kept me busy with needlepoint projects like embroidering pillowcases, cotton tablemats, even a quilted tea-cozy cover that kept the teapot warm. One summer, I cross-stitched pretty blue dolls on my pink skirt that I wore with a blue sleeveless top.

The oversized ceiling fans spun all day long at our home. When it was too hot to go out, Mangha and Kiku spent the afternoon playing table-tennis at home. They converted the long teak dining table into a ping-pong table, ran a little net over its center and clamped it down by the sides. Within minutes, they were jumping around the table as the little white plastic ball danced all over the net. When it bounced off the table and skipped on the floor, I fetched it for them. They were happy to have me around, as they did not have to chase the ball.

One afternoon, we played cards in my brothers' room. A few rounds of gin rummy followed by a classic poker game, called *flush*. Mangha and Kamal, both poker-faced, waged their chips 'blind' on their unseen cards, even raising their stakes to drive the others out of the game. Kiku and I chickened out after a couple of rounds. Mummy, who sat cross-legged on the bed, sometimes indiscreetly pulled out a card from under her knee. Aware that we had watched her in the act, she smiled and declared she had a winning hand. We let her win, like you would let a child win a board game. Suresh, the youngest of the six-pack, did not participate. He sat beside Mummy and watched her play.

My father did not enjoy playing cards. Instead, he entertained us with stories of yesterday while he cranked the ice cream machine that sat in an oak barrel packed with ice and salt. The first one who dropped out of the game took over the cranking task from him. When the card session folded, we indulged in scoops of delicious pink vanilla-flavored ice cream.

Like my father, my maternal uncle Bhagwan also worked overseas, in Singapore. Every two years, he would spend a few days with us en route to his home in Pune. He showered us with imported gifts. This summer he got a bag of gold coin chocolates for my younger siblings and me, a bright red Max Factor lipstick and a perfume bottle for my sister Hari, and a white chiffon sari for my mother. Sometimes he also got my mother a small brandy bottle.

My uncle was a great storyteller. Some stories had us belly laughing, others held our suspense. This evening, he told us about the smugglers.

"There were many businessmen on my plane. When we landed at the Bombay airport, the customs officers asked them if they had anything to declare. With a straight face, they said they had nothing to declare." Gesticulating with his hand, and a very apprehensive tone in his voice, he continued. "So the officers opened their bags, pulled out their clothing one by one, and ran their fingers along the hems of their pants, even the sari falls. What do you think they found?"

"Gold coins," I said.

"More than gold coins. They found imported watches and diamonds stitched into the hems."

"Did they arrest them?"

"They threatened to arrest them. But, the men pulled out whiskey and rum bottles, gave them to the officers and told them to keep it. The people in the customs department get their imported liquor free, sometimes even [wrist] watches."

Uncle sipped on his tea, ate some fresh fried spinach and onion *pakoras* that my mother had just made and continued with his story. Some smugglers would hide diamonds and gold nuggets in the insoles of their shoes. Others had false bottoms inserted in their suitcases where they concealed things. Some smugglers got away; others who got caught bribed the officers.

I was delighted when our relatives from Pune or Delhi spent their holidays with us, even if it meant we had to share our beds or sleep on bamboo mats.

Some evenings after dinner, Mangha turned on Western music on the radio and taught us ballroom dancing. His fondness for music and dance rubbed off on me. I was not quite ten when I learned to foxtrot and waltz, rumba and samba, jitterbug and cha-cha. In time I learned to twist and jive and even picked up a few tango strides.

Sunday mornings were *Binaca Hit Parade* time, when Mangha tuned in to Radio Ceylon for two hours of Top-40 Western hits. The disc jockey would roll his tongue and talk fast like a rock-n-roll singer, and I would hear him say, "And now it is *Binaca Hip Hooray* time." Forever after, Sunday mornings were hip hooray time for me. My brothers had two books filled with song lyrics. When a song played on the radio that was in the book, I flipped to the page and sang along, as I did this Sunday morning with Doris Day's "Qué Sera Sera." My mother hummed along from the kitchen.

I was thrilled when Mangha brought home record albums from a friend. We played them on the RCA-Victor *His Master's Voice* gramophone, a music box that always needed cranking. When my brother was out, I placed Pat Boone's LP on the turntable, cranked the lever, lifted the mechanical arm of the gramophone, and placed the needle gently on the record. Then I sat back and sang along "Be Faithful Darling." Halfway through the record, the speed of the temperamental gramophone got slower and slower, as if struck by some malaise, and Pat sounded as if he were chanting a Sunday psalm. Faster and faster I cranked. Now, he sounded more like a chipmunk as he sang "Love Letters in the Sand." I went into stitches, laughing.

A couple of years later, I sang Pat's "Be Faithful Darling" for my ninth grade class of sixty. Music and dance lifted my spirits.

Some years later, when Mangha visited our relatives in Delhi, he brought home an automatic Garrard record player and several albums from our uncle's Rhythm Corner music shop. The music box needed no cranking. It could even hold seven records and entertain for hours with uninterrupted music.

∽

After the six-week summer vacation, schools reopened with the arrival of monsoons. The showers brought much needed relief after the sizzling days. Oh, how it rained from mid-June to mid-September. The parched earth smelled so fresh and sweet as it drank in the first raindrops. Monsoon clouds then whirled in from the Arabian Sea, ushering with it gale winds, whipping rain, rolling thunder, and lightning bolts. Soon raindrops turned to puddles and puddles merged to form pools. Tadpoles swam briskly in muddy waters and beady-eyed frogs croaked on little rocks. In a matter of hours, the storm crested and the shallow pools converged into a stream. Soon the storm drains got clogged. Before long, there was a monsoon lake out there, outside my building.

The monsoons also ushered in a swarm of mosquitoes. One monsoon season, when the bloodsuckers had taken over the town by storm, my mother had the cook put up mosquito nets over our beds for the night. To keep us from coming down with malaria fever, she had us rub coconut oil on our legs and arms.

"Why Mummy?"

"Because mosquitoes cannot bite your slippery legs."

She also encouraged us to eat spicy pickles during the monsoons.

"Why Mummy?"

"Because mosquitoes are attracted to sweet, not spicy blood," she said.

Waterborne diseases are common in India, especially during the monsoon season. Every evening after serving us dinner, the cook tied a thin muslin cloth over a large brass drum and poured water over it. The muslin cloth served as a filter. He also filled two large terracotta vessels with drinking water. The water stayed cool in the vessels all day, but it had an earthenware taste to it.

One rainy morning, I was running a little late. Kamal and my neighbors had already left for school, so I walked alone. Within minutes, the rain came down in buckets. In the distance, I heard the school bell ring.

If I run I can make it in time for assembly. But, who wants to run today? Today, I want to frolic in the rain, so Mother Trezzi will send me home to change again, like she did the last time I got wet.

I pulled down my hood, unbuttoned my pastel blue sleeveless raincoat and ambled merrily down the sidewalk outside the convent. All at once, the wind picked up and whipped through my hair. The gust also swept a black umbrella from an old man's feeble hands and sent it flying down the street. The old man could not chase it. He got drenched like me.

Now that I was tardy for my Moral Science class, I slipped in through the teacher's gate in my dripping wet uniform. And there in the foyer was Mother Trezzi, lending her ear to a student. Gingerly I tried to walk past her, but the blue-eyed nun with thick black-rimmed glasses had eyes even in the back of her head. She stopped me in my tracks. I tried to explain, but she was in no mood for excuses this morning. To my dismay, she did not send me home to change. Instead, wagging her finger at me, the nun in white warned, "The next time you are late you will have to get a note signed by your parents."

Then she directed me to the school custodian's office where I was asked to change into a matronly dress that ran down to my ankles. All eyes were on me as I walked in the classroom in a long dress. As punishment, I was told to pick up all pieces of paper strewn on the school grounds during break. That was the last time I played in the rain in my school uniform.

Sometimes the clouds wept relentlessly for days at a stretch. *Indra*, the storm God, emptied the sky but flooded the streets of Bombay. One such evening, when the weeping clouds calmed and an evening sun broke through the gates of heaven, I found myself gazing at a beautiful rainbow in a kaleidoscope of colors, beginning and ending where the humble earth meets the seductive sky. I returned to my math homework, but found it difficult to concentrate. So I tore out a sheet from my notebook, folded it over and over until I had a paper boat. Ripping out some more sheets of paper, I made several boats and labeled each of them with a friend's name in colorful crayon.

Slipping into my raincoat and black rubber boots, I called out to my mother who was in another room, "Mummy, I'll be right back." Then I hurried down the stairs onto the flooded street with the stack of paper boats, before she could stop me to ask where I was going. During a heavy downpour, storm drains often got clogged with trash and the streets got heavily flooded. I waded through thigh-high murky waters and let the paper boats sail downstream. Some floated merrily; others capsized.

About an hour later, I returned home and hung my raincoat on the antique coat rack in the foyer. Mummy stepped out of the kitchen, took one look at my soaking dress and scolded me. "I told you never to play in the dirty water. Go change into some dry clothes before you come down with a cold."

Slipping out of my wet clothes I changed into a dress over a cancan skirt. Then I grabbed my hula hoop and stepped out into the enclosed verandah for some hula twists, first on my arm, then on my neck and waist, then on my leg.

Two days later, after the floodwaters had receded, the boys took to the street for a kite-fight in the sky. From my balcony, I watched them prepare for the event. Two boys stood about fifty feet apart, each holding a large wooden spool; a third boy rubbed glass paste on the kite string as it traveled in slow motion from one spool to another, air-drying along the way. The glass paste made the string strong enough to hack another kite in the sky. Within minutes, paper kites in a spectrum of colors sailed in the sky; some with short tails, others with long ones.

"Give me some slack," shouted the kite flier to his partner, who then loosened his grip on the spool. The spool spun and the string unraveled fast and furious. Pushed by the monsoon winds, the kite soared like a bird in the sky, dancing and spinning in circles as it inched up closer to another, each kite trying to claim airspace. The kite strings tangled. The boys on the street tugged at their strings. Minutes later, one kite came floating down, then another, until only one or two ruled the sky. Little boys ran down the street to grab the felled kites. A colorful kite coasted down outside my balcony. I reached out for it, grasped it by its string and saved it for my little brother, Suresh.

The kite-flying season in Bombay runs through the monsoon season. So does the mango season, when we had sweet, pulpy Alphonso mango with dinner.

A month after the monsoons bid farewell, the *Dusserah* festival rolled in. As always, this October my father bought us a bagful of fireworks for the occasion: sparklers, whistlers, crackers, and colorful fountains. In the evenings, we got together with our neighbors and lit them on the terrace, adjacent to our apartment. Some shot off in the air, others spun and bounced all over the place, still others hissed, crackled, or popped.

All week long, the boys in our building worked on assembling a twenty-foot figure of the ancient evil King Ravana, who had abducted Lord Rama's wife, Sita. They stuffed it with straw and fireworks and draped it in black cloth. On *Dusserah* night, they gathered on the street, set up the effigy on a platform, and set it ablaze. From our balconies we watched the evil King go up in flames as the explosives crackled, whistled, and flew in all directions.

Ten days later, we celebrated *Diwali*, the Hindu New Year, when Lord Rama was crowned King of Ayodhya, according to the epic, *Ramayana*. Schools were closed for the entire week. We wore our best clothes and my mother spruced up the house with the finest linen and lace tablecloth. She made delicious sesame seed and nut brittles for the family and exchanged boxes of sweets with neighbors, friends, and relatives.

To welcome our guests, we hung a *Happy Diwali* gold banner over the front door that Kamal and I made. We also asked a neighbor to decorate the outside entry of our home with folk art, *rangoli*. After she had drawn the outline of a geometric design on the tiled floor in white rice powder, she filled it in with a spectrum of colors. My sister and I pitched in. For an entire week, at night we lit red-clay oil lamps around it and also on our balcony. On Diwali evening, we prayed to Lakshmi, goddess of fortune and good luck, and welcomed her to our homes.

After dinner, from the balcony I noticed the distant hills to my right were decked with a very long string of lights.

"Who lives on those hills?" I asked my mother.

"The Gods."

I always believed my mother. So whenever I looked towards the hills, I closed my eyes and prayed for my family and for all the families of the world.

Blooming Years

In the late 1950s, Kiku left to pursue mechanical engineering studies in Baroda (now Vadodara). The following year, Mangha, who sold typewriters in Bombay, left to take a sales job in Calcutta (now Kolkota) to sell printers. The two of them would be gone for a few years, although Kiku would come home during his long breaks.

The only radio in our house sat over a curio cabinet in my brothers' room. The glass cabinet displayed tea sets, dinnerware, glassware, silverware, three large glossy exotic seashells with my older siblings' names inscribed on them, and a face with a hat and smoke-pipe chiseled into a pale coconut shell.

The bottom shelf of the cabinet flaunted Mangha's silver-plated athletic trophies from his school days, which I polished when they got tarnished. One morning, I found my mother trading them for large glass jars with a peddler woman at our door. The woman tipped her hand-scale as she placed silver trophies in one tray, weights in the other while she bargained with my mother.

I walked up to her, grabbed my brother's trophies from the scale and said, "These are not for sale. You can have my old frocks instead."

But the woman was not interested in my dresses. She asked me to lend a hand to place her glassware-laden wicker basket on her head. Then she walked away mumbling to herself. As I returned my brother's prized possessions to the bottom shelf of the curio cabinet, my mother threw a hard stare at me for ruining her deal. She wanted the large glass jars to store tangy pickled carrots and cauliflower, shredded carrot jam, and mango preserves.

Several months later, when I returned from school, an empty bottom cabinet shelf stared back at me. Goodness gracious! The trophies were gone. Only last week I had polished them all. Mummy must have traded them for glass jars. Still, who was I to judge her frugal ways? She had to find ways, to make ends meet for a family of eight. Besides, Mangha was working in Calcutta these days, a thousand miles away. He would not know his trophies were gone, until he returned home. By then, he might not care. He would be gone for four years.

My mother would also save newspapers and sell the stack by weight to a man who stopped by our home once a month to collect them for recycling. When I went shopping with her, I watched her drive a hard bargain with the vendors. "Never pay the price they quote you," she would say.

The bottom shelf of the curio cabinet also held lovely Japanese folding hand fans. They lay there folded like passionate books, with red and black tassels hanging at the ends, waiting to be opened. Black silk and filigreed plastic fans, bamboo and rice paper fans, decorated with flora and women in colorful kimonos. When I was forlorn, I shut the bedroom door, opened the glass cabinet and reached for the fans that my father had brought home from his business trip to Japan. Then I put on some lovely music, sat on the edge of the bed, tossed my head back and fanned my cares away, like the fancy bourgeois English ladies in a parlor on a hot summer's day.

On the bottom shelf also rested my father's mahogany English pipe that had once given him many hours of piping pleasure. Every morning and evening after tea, he would read the newspaper and then pick up his pipe. He would pack the pipe with sweet-scented shredded tobacco leaves, kindle and stir it with the end of a matchstick to keep the sparks going. Then, inhaling a few carefree puffs, he exhaled leisurely until the tobacco turned to ashes.

Displeased by Dada's smoking habit, Mummy complained the bedroom reeked of tobacco. So my father halfheartedly switched to the local cigarettes and the inexpensive slim brown, high nicotine-content Indian *bedi*. His good old faithful friend — the English pipe — found a niche beside the colorful Japanese fans in the curio cabinet. Now my father lit a cigarette with his silver butane lighter and blew spiraling smoke rings.

"Dada, how do you make those curly rings?" I asked.

"Curly rings? Ah, that's a secret my dear," he said with a puckish grin.

Ours was a corner apartment with three sides open to fresh air and light. No paintings or ornamental decor graced our whitewashed walls, but everything at home was crisp and clean. The many windows of our home were usually thrown open. Puffy clouds floated above the white café-style curtains: a sly cat here, a werewolf there, an old sage here, Aladdin's magic lamp and flying carpet there. My mother was a stickler for cleanliness and sparkling white linen. The white cotton curtains that got yellowed from nicotine irked her.

My father did not eat breakfast until he fed buttered toast to the birds on the balcony and someone in the family had performed the morning prayers at our home shrine. Due to his frail health, I did not want him to skip his morning meal. Since my mother was busy in the kitchen until lunchtime, from the age of twelve I performed the twenty-minute holy ritual before I left for school, so my father could have breakfast. I cleaned the gods' portraits and statuettes, adorned their foreheads with freshly ground sandalwood paste, garlanded them with marigold and lily flowers, lit the incense and oil lamp, and recited prayers for our Hindu Gods. Every morning I performed the holy ritual until the day I left for America at the age of twenty-one.

On religious or Full Moon days, my family prepared ample of food. My father and two servants then carried a few pots of cooked meals to the shacks down the street where they served the poor.

We had no modern day conveniences. Like most citizens, we used public transportation. We had no telephone. We used the pay phone in the building lobby. We had no elevator in the building, but plenty of services available at our door.

We had no oven or electric can opener. No food processor, blender, or toaster. A manual can opener and grinder served our needs. Bread was toasted on a grid, placed over an electric stove. With a government ration card, our family of eight was permitted four quart bottles of milk a day. Since we had no refrigerator, food was cooked three times a day and milk purchased twice a day from a nearby government kiosk.

During my spare time, my mother kept me busy with household chores, such as shelling peas, cleaning rice and lentils, pulverizing meat in a grinder. At times I helped her with the ironing.

Making butter from milk was one of my chores. Peeling the seal from the quart-size milk bottle, I replaced it with a long-stemmed corkscrew plastic stopper, which served as a churner. For the next twenty minutes while I talked to my parents, I shook the glass bottle vigorously. Since the milk was not homogenized, the cream rose to the top and clusters of it clung to the coils of the stopper. Mummy then scooped out the whipped cream, blended in a few drops of yellow food coloring and a pinch of salt. *Voilà*! The delicious homemade whipped butter was ready to be spread on toast. She then floated the butter in a bowl of cool water to keep it fresh, replacing the water each day until the butter was gone. A couple of days later, I had to jiggle the milk bottle again.

Sugar, rice, and wheat were also rationed. When neighbors ran out of a rationed item, they borrowed a cupful of this and a cupful of that, but they always returned the borrowed staples the following month. Flour was not purchased from the store. Instead, our cook carried a tall metal box filled with whole wheat kernels over his head to a nearby mill shop. There they were stone-ground for *chapattis*, Indian tortillas. I had watched the milling process myriad times, as I passed the shop everyday on my way to school. The miller emptied the grain container into a large funnel-shaped metal silo and turned on the electric switch. As the hopper spun, the kernels traveled down a metal chute and onto a large flat circular grindstone. Another circular stone then came down and rotated in the opposite direction. The wheat was ground and the flour sifted as it traveled down another metal chute and filled the empty box.

Every couple of years, our cook visited his family for two months in his village up north. This time, however, he went on an extended sabbatical to purchase a small piece of farmland that his wife and young son could tend to while he was away. Before his departure, he left us with an eighteen-year-old substitute.

Like our old cook, the substitute cook could not read or write. As a thirteen-year-old ninth-grader, I took it upon myself to teach him English. With my pocket money, I bought him a small black slate, white chalk, an eraser, and a beginner's English book. I spent many evening play hours on our balcony teaching him to read and write the English alphabet. Soon he graduated to the next level English book which had short sentences, such as "See Pat run. . . Pat can run." I also taught him to speak in English. He learned such phrases as "Open the door" (*Darvaaza kholo*), "I am hungry" (*Bookh lagi hai*), "I am thirsty" (*Pyaas lagi hai*), and "I want water" (*Pani chahiyai*). He absorbed the language like a sponge, as if it filled some void in him.

Sometimes he got the words hungry and thirsty mixed up. When I told him "I am thirsty," he brought me buttered toast on a tray.

"*Humko pani chahiyai.*" I want water.

"Sorry, *Memsahib.*"

He took the toast away and returned with a glass of water on the tray.

"Thank you," I said and drank the glass of water while he waited. After I was done, he took the glass away.

When I returned from school one day, the young cook handed me a small brown paper bag. "Baby, this is for you." He called me *Baby* because everyone in the family called me so.

"For me?"

He gave me a coy smile.

To my surprise, I found six pairs of lovely colorful hairclips in the paper bag.

"You can wear it on your hair," he said. "You taught me English. Thank you."

Moved by his kind gesture, I was at a loss for words. I had expected nothing in return. After a few months, our old cook returned, and his substitute left to take another job. Before he left, I told him not to give up on his reading and reminded him that if he studied hard, he would get a better job. He would not have to work as a servant.

The importance of educating the poor is something I learned from my parents. Besides giving our old cook his regular salary, each month my mother also gave him additional money to get his son educated at a private school in his home village. My parents believed that education opened doors to opportunities.

After nine years of serving us, our old cook returned to his village to tend to his family and farm. A couple of years later, he paid us a visit accompanied by his now grown-up son, who had graduated from high school. With one arm around his son's shoulder, he introduced him to my parents and said in Hindi, "Mummy, Dada, my son is not going to be a servant like me. He is going to work as a clerk for a company in Bombay."

My parents shared in his moment of pride and joy.

⁂

Once when I brought home a bad report card that needed my father's signature, he raised his eyebrows, gave me a disapproving look, and asked my mother to fetch him a ruler. I prayed Mummy would not find it, but with three school children at home, there was ample supply of fountain pens, pencils, protractors, compasses, erasers, and even rulers. My stomach knotted when she returned to the room and handed my father a twelve-inch wooden ruler.

"But, Dada, I really studied hard for my test. I really did," I implored.

"Were you studying hard or was your mind wandering?" A phrase he often used when I received a bad grade and had to get my paper signed by him.

For a fleeting moment my gaze strayed off the ruler.

Whack! The jarring sound of the wooden ruler hitting the dining table shattered the silence in the room and gave me goose bumps. Startled, I looked up.

"But, Dada, I … I got …"

"I don't want to hear any excuses today," he scolded, with thunder in his voice. *Indra*, the storm God, could not have been angrier. Brandishing the ruler, my father inched towards me.

I retreated. "But Dada, I got so nervous during the exams, I forgot everything I studied."

He came closer. "Put your right hand out."

I stood still. Without tearing my gaze away from the ruler, I extended my right hand and held my breath. As the ruler sliced through the air, I quickly swung my hand away and held it behind my back.

"Put your right hand out, I said," he retorted.

Stretching my right hand once more, I closed my eyes, and turned my face away.

Whack!

Shaking my hand to ease the stinging pain, I walked away fighting back the tears. As I was leaving the room, I heard Mummy tell Dada, "Why did you have to hit her so hard?"

It was then that my father began to take interest in my studies and took over the task of tutoring me from Mrs. D'Mello. He had me maintain a vocabulary journal, add ten new words to it each week, and tested me on them. He took up my English, geography, and history studies. I also joined a math tutoring group. As I buckled down and plunged into my books, he seldom hit me with the ruler. When he did, he asked for my knuckles, not my entire hand. The wooden stick did not hurt as much on the knuckles.

In a matter of months, my grades improved. My father became kinder and stopped using the ruler on me. Sometimes I found him reading my history and geography textbooks even when he was relaxing. He realized it was not that I did not know my study matter, but that I got nervous during the exams and forgot my material. One day he asked, "Baby, how many times do you read your questions on your exam paper?"

"One time, Dada."

"You must read your question three times before answering it."

I gave him a nod.

"How many times will you read it?"

"Three times, Dada."

My mother made sure we did not leave for school without breakfast. "You cannot concentrate on your studies on an empty stomach," she would say.

"Baby, what will you have for breakfast today? Porridge, cornflakes, egg-and-toast, or *loli*?" she asked.

"*Loli*."

"Masala *loli* or plain?"

"Plain with milk and some *chai* in it." I did not like plain milk. It had to be flavored.

Once when Kamal left for school without having breakfast, my mother had the cook take it to her class. My sister was so embarrassed that she never skipped breakfast again.

Despite her kind and caring heart, my mother was stricter than my father. When Kamal and I got into an argument, she would send us to separate rooms, saying "Divide and Rule" — a remnant phrase of the British Raj era. She had no problems disciplining me, either. I did not know she had such strong hands until she unleashed her fury on me.

I tried to avoid getting both my parents upset at me at the same time for it spelled double trouble. A few times, they threatened to ship me off to a boarding school, "far away from home" they said, the mere mention of which sent a chill down my spine. I did not dare ask which one, for fear it might become a reality. *Tom Brown's Schooldays*, my eighth-grade textbook, had left an indelible impression on me — a story about a little boy named Tom who attends one such school. He is constantly bullied by senior students. Every night before bedtime, they would toss him like a pancake on his bed sheet. So, Tom trembled as it got closer to bedtime.

On several occasions, when my mother packed my bags for the boarding school I cried, I pleaded, and promised to study harder. This time, however, it seemed she was serious. She called the building watchman — a Nepalese *Gurkha* in a khaki outfit — to help carry the suitcase down to the lobby. I locked myself in the bathroom and wept profusely.

"*Memsahib*, where are you going?" I heard the Gurkha ask Mummy in Hindi.

"I'm not going anywhere. Baby is going to boarding school. She is not studying." She spoke loud enough to make sure I heard every word of it in the bathroom. She asked me to step out. I broke into heavy sobs.

"Let it be, *Memsahib*. Baby is crying so much. Next time she will study harder."

That evening, the building watchman was my savior.

Another time, my mother told the cook, "Soon we will not need you."

"Why, *Memsahib*?" asked the cook, caught off-guard.

"Baby will not be going to school anymore. She'll take over the cooking and cleaning."

I always took my mother seriously. The fear of being beaten like Kiku, or sent to a boarding school, or taking over the servant's chores haunted me through all my school years. Both my catholic school and my parents were very strict, so I grew up much disciplined.

On Wednesday mornings during my high school years, Mother Edna let me skip my Moral Science class and attend Novena services with my catholic classmates at the nearby St. Michael's Church. I bought myself a white-laced veil and a pastel blue rosary for the occasion. At the church, I dipped my fingers in the holy water and made my sign of the cross. Slipping into a pew, I went down on my knees, sang hymns, and listened to the pastor read from the Bible. I also learned about the confession box from my friends. Being a Hindu and attending Christian church services taught me respect for all religions.

Couple of times a week, we had physical education classes. The five-foot, middle-aged burly drill sergeant wore a whistle on a string around her neck. After cranking the school gramophone to the right speed, she had us do physical exercise to the melody of the "Blue Danube" on the school grounds. As the music blared through the trumpet, she sent a shrilling note with her whistle, then called out, "Heels up. Arms in front. Arms up. To the sides. Attention!"

What a pity to waste such lovely music on physical exercises when we could be waltzing to it instead. One, two, three . . . up. Ah! Those dance steps flow much better with the Blue Danube music than these silly arm stretches.

All at once, I felt something rub on the back of my leg. Instantly, I was brought down to earth from my waltzing dreams as the drill teacher lifted my uniform with her cane to check if I was wearing the long blue bloomers under my royal blue uniform. Bloomers were required for the physical education class.

Then tapping the ground with her cane she repeated, "Heels up. Arms in front. Arms up. To the sides. Attention!"

When the music stopped, the needle lifted and returned to its cradle. Now she placed "Colonel Bogey March" record on the turntable. It was marching time. The sergeant blew the whistle. "One, two, three, four. Hup, two, three, four. Forward march. Left. Right. Left, right, left."

The bell rang. The class broke up. The drill sergeant blew her whistle once more. "You are not dismissed until I say so."

The class returned to attention.

"You are now dismissed."

❧

Kiku had by now completed his engineering studies. He was back home and working in the city. One day when I was in tenth grade, he said to me, "Baby, you're a big girl now. You need to clean the hair off your arms and legs. Bring a sheet of paper and write a letter to *Femina*." He dictated a letter to the magazine, requesting their advice.

The magazine recommended using hot wax, which could be purchased from Bellezza. Another letter dictated to order the hot wax.

When the package arrived in the mail, Kiku opened it and read the instructions. That Sunday, he told my mother to heat the wax container in a pot of boiling water and cut up some old clothing into strips.

I sat on the edge of the bed while Kiku spread the warm wax with an applicator on my leg and placed a piece of cloth over it. Twenty minutes later, he pulled the rag off my leg with one long *swooooosh*.

"Ouch!" I screamed in pain.

"You think you can look pretty without any pain?" he chuckled.

The hairy fuzz was gone, but my leg stung. It turned tomato-red. With one leg cleaned, it was time to submit the other for treatment.

"Mummy, the wax has hardened," said Kiku. "Can you re-heat it?"

My mother reheated the wax. The process was repeated. When it was done, she said to me, "Baby, go rub some coconut oil on your arms and legs."

The following weekend, Kiku repeated the procedure on my arms. My legs and arms remained silky smooth for almost a month, then the fuzz reappeared and the agonizing process relived. I could not imagine how other girls waxed their limbs every month.

Getting my arms and legs waxed became a family affair. Mummy warmed the wax. Kiku spread it on my limbs and did the honors of pulling the hair from the roots. Hari cleaned up the mess. Kamal watched the scene.

"Next year it will be your turn," Kiku told Kamal.

A few months later in my last year of high school, Hari got married and my mother handled the entire act. During my college years, I switched to shaving my legs. It was much better than having to go through torture each month.

A simple but sweet vanilla childhood was mine, memories of which linger, like the scent of my old favorite perfume, *Ma Griffe*.

Stage Fright

I would give almost anything to take a flight back in time to my days at St. Xavier's College. The college with the stone façade, arched portico and Gothic architecture returns to me in my dreams, flashing faces of friends whom I have not long seen, teasing me of days that will not come again. I see myself in the quadrangle, hanging around with a group of friends, watching boys and girls go by. Then we stroll into the canteen in the clock tower building, where we chat over *bhel* and Coke.

During my freshman year, a student from the junior class asked me to participate in a fancy dress competition she was organizing for the College Day program.

"Does it require rehearsal?" I asked.

"No. You only have to wear a costume and walk on the stage."

"I'll get back to you," I said. But, I did not. My mother never wanted me to participate in any school or college events. She feared it took away time from my studies.

Several days later, when I ran into the program director, I made up an excuse. I told her I could not participate since I had no costume.

"There are plenty of costumes in the Green Room," she replied.

"Where is the Green Room?"

"By the stage. I'll see you there at two. I have a class to attend." She scurried away.

Going from an all-girls' convent school to a co-ed college was not an easy transition for me. Besides, my mother had always forbidden me to even talk to the boys in the building. So I grew up much too shy. To overcome my bashfulness, I decided to participate in the College Day program, even if my mother objected to it.

That afternoon, I met with the event director in the Green Room, a small room where costumes were hanging on racks. A full-length oval mirror stood at one end and a couple of large storage chests sat by a wall. The director asked me to look around and pick a costume.

A long black Victorian evening dress caught my eye. "I'll try this one."

"Pick a matching hat to go with it." She opened a trunk filled with an assortment of colorful hats: felt, straw, and fur hats; Cossack and Texan.

I picked up a broad-brimmed, feather-trimmed black hat and gently dusted it. It complemented the Victorian evening dress. "Do you have gloves to go with it?"

She rummaged through the accessories in the other trunk and pulled out a pair of long, black satin gloves and handed them to me. Stepping into the dressing room, I slipped on the lovely Victorian gown. The gloves practically covered up my arms.

As I walked up to the large mirror, she said. "It looks perfect on you. You look like Audrey Hepburn."

I savored the compliment.

"That's settled. You'll wear this gown on College Day. I'll keep it aside for you with your name tag on it."

"How many others are participating?"

"Twelve, including you."

Twelve had a nice ring to it, like one big family.

On the evening of the event, before our pageant team paraded on the open-air stage in the quadrangle, the organizer paired me up with Harry Gill, a junior student. We were both donned in Victorian attire. The others in the pageant wore Indian costumes; one wore a plaid Scottish skirt.

Gill and I moseyed down the stage, both of us in black: he in his tailcoat and top hat, I in a long Victorian dress, a broad-brimmed hat, and satin gloves. Singing was not supposed to be part of the act, but on that starry night in December 1963 I felt a spontaneous urge to sing. Slipping my arm into Gill's, I strolled down the stage and sang a few lines of Cliff Richard's "The Young Ones," a popular song at the time. I let him think I was bold. He did not know I was painfully shy. Deep down, I was trying to break free from my cocoon after all those years at a convent school.

Before the college program ended, the organizer came up to me and said, "Jay, don't change into your clothes. Not yet."

"Why not?"

"You have to go and receive your prize."

"What prize? I have to catch a ride home with a friend or else there will be no more late nights out for me."

"Don't worry. I'll arrange another ride for you," she said, brushing aside my anxiety.

When my name was announced on the microphone, I walked up to the stage to collect the one and only prize. I cast a fleeting glance at the front row in the quadrangle where rectors in white cassocks and faculty members were seated. There in the front row was Father John, and beside him Father Macia. This time, with renewed vigor and confidence I sang the entire "Young Ones" song for an audience of hundreds.

That night, as I walked in the door at home with a long gift-wrapped box, my mother asked, "What's this?"

"Mummy, it belongs to a friend," I lied. "I held it for her during the college event and then could not find her. I'll give it to her tomorrow."

If I had told her the truth, I would have received an earful of sermons. She might have even grounded me for a few days, as she had done only months before. I shook the box before putting it away wondering what could be in it. Alas, the suspense would have to wait until another day.

Several days later, when my mother was out, I tore open the wrapping of the box. To my surprise, it was a large oil painting kit with thirty-some tubes of oil paint and a set of brushes. Pity I could not paint. I passed the gift on to a young girl for her birthday.

Who would have thought, forty-seven years later I would be asked to sing the same song, at an alumni luncheon in honor of Principal Father Frazer Mascarenhas, during his visit to New York. To my surprise, Harry Gill would also be there. It would be my first encounter with him since that memorable College Day when we walked on stage in our Victorian attire. By then, he would be a gray-haired lawyer practicing in Connecticut, and I, no longer sweet sixteen.

One evening after dinner, when Mangha joined me on the balcony, I said to him, "You have to talk to Mummy. I'm in college now, but she still treats me like a kid. She does not let me wear makeup. She does not let me go to the movies with my friends. She does not let me do anything. She is too strict."

A few days later, my brother said, "Baby, I spoke with Mummy. I've asked her to take it easy on you. But you have to understand her situation, too. If she is strict, it is because she is protective of you. Remember, she wants the best for you. . . By the way, do you have enough spending money?"

"Yes, I always make do with the allowance Mummy and Dada give me."

My brother went to his room and returned with a twenty-rupee note — almost half my monthly allowance. Handing it to me, he said, "Here's some extra money for you. If you need anything, you come see me."

"Thanks Mangha. Thanks for listening."

At moments like these, I reminded myself how lucky I was to have an older brother who understood a sixteen-year-olds' needs. Although I appreciated his kindness, I never took advantage of his generosity.

Over time, as my mother eased up on me, I went with my friends to discos for weekend jam sessions, and we danced to the music of the Beatles and The Rolling Stones.

In my junior year, with English Literature as my major, I enrolled in the college's Literary Club and decided to participate in the club's first debate of the year. When my name was announced, I sprang to my feet and walked up to the platform. Oops! I tripped on the wooden stairs. Pulling myself together, I took center stage. My nervous eyes swept over sixty-plus heads, mostly male.

The crowd waited for me to begin. A hiss here, a whistle there broke the eerie silence. My pulse quickened. My stomach churned. My heart pounded like the beat of a bongo drum. My opening lines forgotten, with trembling fingers I unfolded the sheet of paper.

Booing and cooing filled the large classroom. I got that sinking feeling, as if the platform was also caving. I held onto the podium before it too might fall, thereby exposing my frailties and all. Gathering pluck, I cleared my throat and started reading my speech; a speech I should have recited from memory.

"Louder! Louder!" jeered the daunting boys, thumping their fists on the desks, as if waiting for me to trip again. It was a wild jungle out there.

I'd better get out of here before they throw things at me.

Speech unfinished, head bowed, teetering on high heels I hurried off the platform. That week, I dropped out of the Literary Club. I could not face the rowdy boys again.

After the debate debacle, I thought I might never return to the stage. But, I challenged myself to sing a couple of Hindi songs at the Sangeet Mandal programs and was told I should sing louder as they could not hear me in the back rows.

Then in my junior year, Professor Kenny, Director of the History Society of which I was a member, asked if I could perform for his upcoming social event. I asked him what he had in mind.

"How about an Indian dance?"

Determined to overcome my stage fright, I obliged and decided to dance to the "Jhanan Jhan Jhanake Apni Payal" song from the movie *Aashiq*. My neighbor had the music record, so I practiced at her home. Since I had not seen the movie, I made up my own dance steps.

On the evening of the event, except for the stage lights the college auditorium was in the dark. That helped, as I could not see any faces. Dressed in a long flowing gold-trimmed white satin skirt, I pretended I was dancing for myself and was pleased when the audience applauded at the end.

The following week, Professor Kenny handed another dance performer and me twenty rupees each, as a token of appreciation for our participation. With that money, I bought myself a small pink clutch purse.

When a friend from my Alliance Français French classes invited me to a youth social event in the city, sponsored by the YM/YWCA, I took my sister Kamal along. It was a fun-filled evening with a cheerful crowd. I did the cha-cha dance to *Baby Elephant Walk*, and rocked to Bill Haley and the Comets' *Rock around the Clock*. "One, Two, Three O'clock, Four O'clock rock. . . We're gonna rock around the clock tonight."

With music blaring, everyone dancing, I twisted the evening away with Chubby Checker singing "Come on Baby, let's do the Twist." To my surprise, my dance partner and I received the one and only dance prize: two cans of condensed milk each. When I came home that night, I handed the cans to my mother and explained to her how I got them. By now, she had eased up on me.

The next morning, I smiled to myself as I watched my mother open the can and drop a spoonful of the sweet condensed milk in her cup of tea.

War Memories

September 1965. Monsoon season had ended and the sky was swept clean of clouds. The commuter train I took home from college that afternoon stopped short of Bombay Central station. Ceiling fans slowed to a halt, and the humidity became insufferable in my *chooridhar-khameez*. I fanned away the oppressive heat with my notebook and hoped the train would start rolling soon.

A grating siren began to wail through the city. This was not a factory call announcing a change in labor shift. This siren roared like a voracious lion: thunderous, ominous, and continuous.

Fifteen minutes later, the train pulled into the station. The two other women in the first-class ladies' compartment slept through the pandemonium. I rushed to the doorway, grabbed the pole, leaned out and looked on either side of the station. No smoke. No fire. The station was deserted except for a police officer in khaki uniform. Baton in hand, he peeked into each train car as he walked down the long stretch of the platform. When the officer approached my car, I inquired about the siren.

"Ma'am, Pakistani warplanes were seen flying over the city."

"Here? In Bombay?"

He gave me a nod.

"Is it safe for me to be on the train?"

"Yes ma'am. Please stay in your seat. The train will depart as soon it receives a signal." Then he moved on to inspect the next coach. Meanwhile, planes screamed through the air. I wondered if these were Pakistani planes or Indian military aircraft chasing the rival planes out of town.

After the blaring siren ceased, the train rolled out of the station. Twenty minutes later, I arrived at the suburban station of Mahim. With jangled nerves I crossed the street, hurried past the cobbler and the building watchman in khaki who gave me his salute and up three long flights of stairs to the comfort of my home. When the cook answered the door, I rushed to my father's bedside. Dressed in white tunic and pajamas, he was reading the *Times of India*. He put aside the newspaper and lent me his ears, as I spilled the news about the planes, the train, and the siren.

"Pakistani planes, here in Bombay? Baby, you're imagining, my dear. We're very far from the border."

I walked into my brothers' bedroom and turned on the radio. "Dada, it's on the news," I called out.

Within minutes, my father joined me. Over crackling airwaves, we listened to the news bulletin. It confirmed Pakistani planes had been seen flying over the city. Then an alert signal was relayed and people were advised to follow broadcast instructions the next time they heard the alert.

The next morning, the corridors of my college were buzzing with news about the air raid. I had just turned eighteen and was a junior student. Trouble began the month before when Pakistani troops marched into the northern Indian state of Kashmir. The dispute over the jurisdiction of Kashmir had been brewing since 1947, when the country was partitioned into India and Pakistan.

For weeks following the air raid, the city of Bombay was on high military alert. Every time a plane flew overhead, we wondered if we should run for cover. Curfew was imposed from dusk to dawn. The roads and train stations were then eerily serene. When the clouds masked the moonlight, a blanket of darkness shielded the town. From our third-floor balcony, I spied on the handful of policemen discreetly posted outside the Mahim train station.

Travel and communication between India and Pakistan came to a screeching halt, and Lata Mangeshkar's haunting patriotic war song echoed through the streets and corridors of Bombay as she sang of the sacrifices made by heroes and martyrs. *"Aye meré watan ké logo, zara aankh mein bhar lo pani. . ."*

Paranoia spread through the city. Fearing another air raid, my mother stockpiled provisions. When we ran low on flour, rice, or wheat rations, my mother complained about purchasing them at exorbitant black market prices.

As required of all homes in the city, Kamal and I masked the windows of our home with dark opaque paper, so war planes could not spot any lights. Dinner was usually served at eight, but on these blackout evenings we dined in the fading daylight. When evening fell, the city became a landscape of darkness. The servant lit a single hurricane-style kerosene lamp in the enclosed hallway, which guided us through the night. Sometimes my sister and I would entertain ourselves with finger puppet shows that cast shadows on the foyer wall. Before bedtime, we all gathered in my brothers' room to listen to wartime news on the radio. This nightly ritual went on for seven weeks until the war ended.

For my family, news of the 1965 India-Pakistan war triggered a stream of memories of the 1947 Partition of India. One evening, we sat around the long teak dinner table and reminisced about the large ancestral home we left behind on Jacob Road in Hyderabad, Sindh. Three generations of the Mirchandani family had nested comfortably in the large whitewashed three-story house.

But on August 15, 1947, our heritage on Jacob Road quickly began to fade. India gained independence after two centuries under the British colonial rule and Lord Mountbatten went down in history as the last British viceroy. At the same time, India was partitioned into India and Pakistan. Pandit Jawaharlal Nehru became India's first Prime Minister while Mohammed Ali Jinnah was sworn in as Governor General of Pakistan. The states with a Hindu majority population remained under India, while those with a Muslim majority came under the jurisdiction of the new sovereign state of Pakistan. Sindh was a

Muslim majority state, and my family was not willing to convert to Islam to avoid persecution.[1]

Two weeks after the Partition, on August 29, 1947 I was born at our ancestral home in Sindh. "Baby, you were born by candlelight," said my mother.

"Why candlelight, Mummy?"

"The night you were born, there was no electricity in the neighborhood. There were riots between the Hindus and Muslims. Ammi [grandmother] told the servant to fetch the lady doctor who lived across the street."

Running her index finger on the white oxford linen tablecloth, my mother mapped out the Tilak Incline and Sreghat communities of Hyderabad-Sindh. Pointing to the location of our home, she said, "This is our house. During the riots, Pakistani troops moved into our neighborhood. They camped at the Training College, the boys' school across the street, and at Brahmo Samaj [a religious center]." Moving her finger to the left of our home, she continued, "They moved here to Pigad High School, the girls' school."

Placing her finger to the right of our home, she added, "They even occupied the Civil Hospital. Our home was now surrounded on three sides by Pakistani troops."

My father explained that at the time of the partition he worked in Bombay, a thousand miles away. "When I heard about the riots and killings, I called your mother and instructed her to leave with the other members of the family for Jodhpur [in Rajasthan, India], without delay."

"That night we sat up late packing," my mother continued. "The next morning, I went to the post office to collect the money Dada had wired. Later in the day, I saw Pakistani troops standing across the street. Our only escape was through the back door. So we bolted the front door on the inside, and slipped out the back door."

"Several *tongas* [horse carriages] were parked out there. We hired four of them and told the *tongawalla* to take the back roads to the Hyderabad train station. We were twenty-one of us, our relatives and some family friends," Mangha chimed in.

My mother, my fourteen-year-old sister Hari, my brothers Mangha and Kiku, who were then twelve and eight, and I, a ten-day-old infant, rode in one of the horse carriages, carrying with us bare essentials.

Because of his thriving medical practice, my father's older brother and his wife stayed behind in Pakistan while their only daughter accompanied us. His younger brother stayed back to sell the 1,400-acre family plantation in Badin, although his family and in-laws joined us. His sister was settled with her family in Delhi. Grandmother and her sister joined our caravan. Grandfather had passed away the year before.

"We got to the Hyderabad station early enough and were fortunate to find seats on the train," Mangha recalled of the exodus. "But many who arrived late wound up traveling on the roof of the train. Their baggage was confiscated by the Pakistani police."

"Why did they travel on the roof of the train?" I asked.

"It was a chaotic scene at the train station. No one knew when the next train would leave. People had quit their jobs. They had shut down their businesses and locked their homes. They wanted to get out of Pakistan before things got worse. The ones who stayed behind were mostly *zamindars* [landowners]."

"It all comes back to me now," said my mother, as she dished out egg pudding dessert for everyone. "From Hyderabad Station we took a train to Luni. When we heard the earlier train had arrived with dead bodies, we were thankful we were not on it. From Luni we took a train for Jodhpur." Arrangements had been made for the extended family at a large bungalow in Jodhpur by my older uncle.

After transfer of power by the British to India in August 1947, tensions between the Hindus and the Muslims escalated on either side of the new border. On the heels of the announcement of the Partition of India came the Civil War. On both sides of the frontier, trains rolled into the station littered with corpses. Cities of Lahore and Amritsar burned. Roads were awash with blood. Homes plundered. Women raped. Muslims killed Hindus. Hindus killed Muslims. They forgot Gandhi's words of wisdom: An eye for an eye leaves the whole world blind.

The heightened state of violence led to a mass displacement of people. Some fled voluntarily; others were driven out of the newly carved sovereign country of Pakistan. Some fourteen million refugees on either side of the border, both Hindus and Muslims, including my family, found themselves on the crossroads of life.[2] Clashes erupted at the new India-Pakistan border. More than a million people died.[3] Millions lost their homes and businesses. What should have been a historic moment of celebration of India's independence turned into a trail of bloodshed and tears.

"We were lucky we left for Jodhpur in time," said Mangha as he filled us in on the plight of Hindus who stayed behind in Pakistan. "Had we stayed on for another ten or fifteen days, we would have been persecuted like our neighbors who lived across the street. Who knows, maybe even killed."

Doors of Hindu homes were marked with a red cross. Many who stayed behind in what was now Pakistan converted to Islam; others feigned to be Muslims. They put on a *Jinnah* cap and carried an Urdu newspaper. Sikhs abandoned their turbans, trimmed their hair and shaved their beards, so as not to be easily identified and targeted by Muslims. Likewise, Muslims were persecuted in India. Many of their homes were set on fire. Despite this mass human tragedy, there was a silver lining. Scores of Hindu and Muslim neighbors protected each other in their homes.[4]

Recalling the turbulent times, my mother said, "One day Dada called from Bombay to say we should pack up and leave Jodhpur as soon as possible."

"I heard the situation had gotten worse on both sides of the border and there were lootings and murders," my father explained, his voice mellowed with age. "We could not return home to Sindh. So I told your mother to take a train for Baroda and I would join you at Ahmedabad Station."[5]

"Let me tell you what happened," said Mangha. "On January 30, 1948, after a five months' stay in Jodhpur, our family boarded a train for Baroda while our relatives took a train to Delhi. At Marwar Station, our train was held up for a few hours. When we inquired about the delay, we learned Gandhiji had been assassinated."

The country was in mourning. Alas, Gandhi, who had orchestrated a crusade to liberate India from the British, did not live long enough to taste freedom.

The final destination of our journey was Bombay, where my father had been working during the past year. Due to the mass exodus of Hindus from Pakistan, he was unable to find us accommodation in the city. So we spent a month in Baroda (now Vadodara), and seven months at the army camp town of Deolali, where his friend had arranged a four-room rental apartment for our family. We sublet two rooms to another Sindhi family, who were in the same predicament as us. In October 1948, thirteen months after we had fled Pakistan, we embarked on the final leg of our journey to Bombay.

Meanwhile, on the other side of the border in Pakistan, the Mohajirs — Muslim émigrés from India — had moved into my family's ancestral neighborhood of Hyderabad-Sindh. Fearful for their lives, my father's older brother and his wife locked up the three-story family home and moved to a small bungalow by his medical clinic. His younger brother, unable to sell the 1,400-acre family farm in Badin, joined his family in Delhi.

As I listened to my family's partition story, I could sense their hopelessness, uncertainty, and despair at having lost everything and having to plant new roots. Yet, my family was luckier than many who were displaced, some of whom sought shelter in tent-cities and had to stand in food lines. For my family, Bombay was to be our beacon of hope, a city of new beginnings.

We found temporary abode at the army barracks in the fishing village of Koliwada, built by the British during WWII. After the British quit India in 1947, these barracks were converted to residences for those displaced by the Hindu-Muslim civil war of India. A year later, my family purchased a condominium in the suburban town of Mahim, across from the train station. At 12 Ram Mahal, third floor is where I would spend the next nineteen years.

Years later, as I wrote about my family's partition story, I would learn from Mangha that following the partition, Hindus who wanted to leave Pakistan could swap property with Muslims who wanted to leave India. The government of India had also set up the Refugee Rehabilitation Department to help refugees file claims against the property they had left behind in Pakistan.

"Did we file a claim?" I asked.

"No. Here's the catch. To qualify, all owners had to be present to claim their assets. If even one of the owners was absent, the government confiscated their entire parcel of land. As a result, many absentee landowners found their property tied up in courts for years. Once we settled down in India, we could not claim compensation from the Indian government either."

"Why not?"

"Because one of the questions asked on the claim form was: Do you have any family members residing in Pakistan? We could not lie, because Uncle [father's older brother] was still living there."

"Could it have been claimed from the government of Pakistan?"

"No. The Pakistani government inquired if the property owners had any surviving family members who had fled Pakistan. Uncle claimed all the family members were dead. So he became the *de facto* beneficiary of the family home and the 1,400-acre farm. He got everything while we struggled here in India."

Noticing my brother's agitation, I tried to reason with him. "Mangha, as I see it, Uncle had no choice. If he mentioned he had family living in India, the Pakistani government would have confiscated all the property. He had no choice but to tell the authorities he was the only surviving member of the family. . . What would you have done if you were in his shoes? If Uncle took the risk of staying back in Pakistan while the rest of us fled, he was entitled to grant the property to whomever he wanted. I know we went through rough times. But so did millions of others who were displaced by the partition."

Then I learned that my older uncle and aunt had adopted their only grandson at his birth. When they passed away, the grandson inherited the entire family estate in Sindh. Eventually, the grandson sold the estate and kept the proceeds. This infuriated my brother. "The house and the farm land belonged to all of us. The profits should have been divided equally."

Leaning forward in his burnt orange upholstered armchair, Mangha cracked his knuckles while I sat there thinking of Leo Tolstoy's parable "How much land does a man need?" The Russian farmer's story and his insatiable lust for land had resonated with me since eighth grade. His greed had cost him his life. *Six feet from his head to his heels was all he needed.*

The feud over our family estate in Sindh dragged on for decades, long after the Partition dust had settled. Had it not been for the Partition, we would have led very comfortable lives. Instead, like many others who were displaced by the historic event, we had to live spartan lives, sometimes even on borrowed money after my father's untimely early retirement.

My Labyrinth

It had been a month since the war with Pakistan ended. With curfews and blackouts behind us, the city of Bombay was swinging with parties again.

One evening, Kiku and I accompanied Mangha to his friend's home for a dinner party. After dinner, we all piled into cars and drove up to the Shalimar Hotel restaurant for coffee and dance, where a live band was playing western music from the fifties and sixties.

Mangha could glide across the dance floor with such grace and panache, like Fred Astaire himself, but I was no Ginger Rogers, although I tried. He would often take me to social events in town and dance with me if a live band was playing. We were the only two in the family who loved to dance.

That evening, while Mangha and I danced to *La Paloma* music, a small group of men sitting at a nearby table tossed offensive remarks at me. My brother got furious. He marched off the floor with a couple of friends, went up to the men at the other table and confronted them. A brawl broke out. Profanities exchanged. Someone in the crowd lifted a chair, then another. Had the hotel manager not intervened, it could have turned into a pretty ugly scene. He asked our group of sixteen and the other party to leave. A wonderful evening was ruined by a couple of eve teasers. Mangha and his friend Kishu were banned for a whole year from Shalimar's, their favorite hangout place, even though they did not instigate the incident.

Two months later, I attended a New Year's house party with my brothers. Kiku's friend, Ranjit, was also present. As we ushered in 1966, he asked me for the midnight dance. The last time we had danced was at Shalimar's, when the unfortunate incident occurred. But, this time it was different. Sparks flew as we slow-danced to Percy Faith's lovely music of *A Summer Place*. I was wrapped in my mother's white embroidered sari with my hair piled high into a bouffant while Ranjit looked debonair in his gray suit. The night was young and there was magic in the air.

The following evening, the building watchman called out from the street below. I rushed to the balcony. "Phone call for Baby," he said.

I scurried down the three flights of stairs to the payphone in the lobby. It was Ranjit.

"Kiku is not at home," I said. "Any message for him?"

"No. This time I called for you."

Called for me? The New Year's dance must also be lingering on his mind.

That week, Ranjit and I met for lunch at Kit Kat's by my college. Then we watched a matinee show of *Houseboat* starring Cary Grant and Sophia Loren, at the Metro theatre across the street. We had just settled in our back row seats in the balcony when Mangha walked in with his longtime friends, Ranjit's cousin and her husband. They sat a few aisles down from us. In the dim theatre light, I recognized my brother from his navy blue beret. Only days before, he had shaved his head as his hair was thinning. He was a six-footer and good looking. The beret looked stylish on him. It was uncommon to find anyone wearing it those days on the streets of Bombay.

My first date with Ranjit, and of all the places in Bombay his cousin and my brother had to show up at the same theatre, on the same day, for a matinee show. Then again, only a handful of theatres in the city showed English movies. "Let's leave before the movie ends," I said to Ranjit. "I do not want to get into trouble at home."

At home, my lips were sealed about my rendezvous with Ranjit. I was afraid my parents might stop me from seeing him. My family did not approve of girls in the family going out with young men. Besides, love is not a subject we discussed at home.

Once when I had dated a friend's brother, an engineering student who hailed from a reputable Sindhi family, my parents had warned me never to see him again or there would be no more college days for me. It so happened that my friend's brother had come to pick me up one evening for a party at his home. As I was stepping into the car, I heard my father call out, "Baby! Baby!" I stopped, looked around and saw my father coming down the street. He approached the car. I introduced him to the young man and reminded him that he and his sister had visited our home when Mangha had thrown a party. But, that did not help. My father told me to walk home with him. I was so embarrassed, as neighbors watched the scene from the balcony. The young man and his friend in the car drove away. I never saw him again. It was the mid-1960s when dating was scorned upon in India.

The news about Ranjit would have to wait. I would have to break it to my family gently. I started keeping a small pink personal diary, which I kept hidden in the folds of my clothes in the armoire. I noted the date when I saw Ranjit, although I did not write down his name. Sometimes I noted down a girlfriend's name to throw anyone snooping into my diary off the track.

Ranjit and I continued to meet at places where we would not be seen by any of our siblings or family friends. Often we met at an ice cream parlor or at M.G. Café by Marine Lines train station, where we had lunch in a booth with swinging café doors that offered some privacy. One afternoon we took a chance to meet at the Cream Center, a popular restaurant in town across from Chowpatty Beach, renowned for its mouth watering *cholé bhaturé* — spicy garbanzo peas in tomato and onion gravy, served with deep fried leavened bread. I prayed none of his relatives would walk in for lunch as they lived only fifteen minutes away.

Sometimes, we escaped to the far out suburbs and sat on the big rocks at Bandra Bandstand and watched the waves break on the shore, as the sun gently slipped into the sea in hues of crimson, peach, and mauve. There was no one there but us as the seagulls flocked home. Other times, we took a stroll on the sands of Juhu Beach. When we wanted to be together, we checked in at the Sun-n-Sand Hotel for a couple of hours as we could not hold hands or kiss in public places. It was considered a taboo then.

We were returning from Juhu Beach one evening by train when Ranjit decided to stop by my home and say hello to my brother Kiku. As we got off at Mahim station, I told him to go ahead first as I did not want to be seen walking with him by my family or neighbors from their balconies. Back then a woman could only be seen with male members of her own family. So I hung around the station. Ten minutes later, I walked home alone and found Ranjit talking to my mother. I greeted him as if I had not seen him for a long time and then we chatted about Shakespeare until Kiku got home. My family had no clue I had been out with him that evening.

Another time, I had to keep Ranjit waiting at Bandstand, because my mother would not let me step out that evening. I told her I had to meet my college friend in the city, but she would not let me out of her sight. I had no way to reach Ranjit. When I did not show up for our rendez vous, he called from a nearby telephone. I scurried down the three flights of stairs to answer the phone and explained to him that my mother refused to let me go out that evening.

"No problem. I'll come and see you at your place." Half an hour later, he showed up at our home. Kiku was out. As usual, my mother was glad to see Ranjit and chatted with him, while he kept throwing glances at me and smiled. Although I was happy to see him, my mother did not know she had ruined my plans to watch the sunset on the seashore at Bandstand with him.

A month later, I broke my silence at home. I told Kiku I had been seeing his friend. He gave me his nod and spoke well of him. I was also delighted to receive my mother's approval. I figured she would have no problem convincing my father. I needed one more endorsement, that of my oldest brother Mangha, twelve years older than I. As the oldest son in the family, his word carried much weight. However, when I spoke to him, he asked me never to see Ranjit again. No explanations given. Yet, it was not for me to question why. At our home, we seldom questioned our elders on their decisions. Lucky for Sophia Loren, she did not need her family approval to go out with Cary Grant.

Despite Mangha's objections, I continued to see Ranjit in secret. I could not understand why a young charismatic man like Ranjit, who was good enough to be my brother's friend, good enough to make my mother laugh, was not good enough for me. He came from a well-educated family of engineers, and was of the same caste as I, a Hindu-Sindhi. Marrying outside the caste was then considered unthinkable in India. Perhaps I was fated to have an arranged marriage like my sister Hari. She married a Sindhi businessman from Lagos, Nigeria because their horoscopes had matched.

As Ranjit and I strolled on the sands of Juhu Beach one evening, he caught me off-guard. "Jaya, I will be leaving soon for [West] Germany."

"For business?"

"No. For a training program."

"How long will you be gone?"

"I don't know. Perhaps a year." He shrugged his shoulders. Heartbroken, I kicked the sand while he talked about his plans.

A few weeks later, I bought him cufflinks for his shirtsleeves, hoping he would not forget me in Germany. I was then eighteen and in my junior year at college while he was twenty-three and worked for his father's engineering company.

I went to see him off at the airport in my lemon embroidered organza sari. The plane took off late in the evening and his sister and brother-in-law offered to give me a ride home. Just as we pulled over by my building, I noticed Mangha standing in the balcony. Since I was sitting in the backseat of the two-door coupe, Ranjit's sister would have to step out so I could get off. My brother would certainly recognize her, as they moved around in the same social circle. Then, I would be in hot soup at home. At that point, I had no choice but to tell them that I did not want my brother to see me step out of their car. Ranjit's brother-in-law, who was very slim, slid his car seat close to the driving wheel so I could slide out from behind him.

Once a month, I received a letter from Ranjit at my friend's address, the back of which was signed off with SWAK (sealed with a kiss). The letter took about nine days to arrive, and another couple of days to receive it from my friend. Receiving his letters at home would mean trouble. When I thought of him, I put on Percy Faith's *Summer Place* music record. It took me back to the New Year's midnight dance.

After a few months, his correspondence tapered off and eventually stopped. *Perhaps he had found himself a nice German girl. Perhaps he would not return.* Still, I kept a green tree in my heart, hoping the bird will fly home someday soon.

I would stand on the balcony alone with my thoughts, but the dirt road was paved and transformed into a busy boulevard, with honking cars and British-style red double-decker buses. The gypsy performers and snake charmers did not stop by any more.

Upon graduating from college, I worked as a secretary to contribute to the family coffer. Time and again, my mother would tell me of the proposals she received for me. "Baby, they don't want any dowry for you. They want you only in your wedding sari... Say yes and you will live like a queen... Say yes and you can go to America."

"Mummy, I am not interested in getting married."

"The boy's family wants to meet you. Shall I tell them to come tomorrow evening?"

"No. I don't want to meet anyone. If you call them over, I will spend the night at a friend's house, and you will not know where to find me."

Most of these proposals came from families of young Indian engineers and doctors, who were visiting from America in search of an Indian bride. Eventually, my mother gave up trying to convince me.

In January 1968, Kiku migrated to America where he was offered a job as a mechanical engineer. Two months later, I received a postcard from Ranjit, saying he was on his way home. He had been gone to Germany for almost two years.

That Sunday afternoon I met Ranjit. It was good to have him back in my life. He brought me lovely gifts from Europe: a sheer mustard-yellow cotton blouse and a brocade clutch purse. I did not ask him why there had been no word from him for long. I had learned the golden rule from my brothers: *Ask no questions and you will be told no lies.*

As we walked down Breach Candy Road, we ran into Mangha. He was coming down the road on his Lambretta scooter. The weekend before, when he had taken me to a party, I had casually mentioned to him that Ranjit was headed back from Germany. He responded with a stern "So?" With that, our conversation on the subject ended.

Mangha stopped the scooter to say hello to Ranjit and me. My stomach churned. I was lost for words. Of all the people, I had not expected to run into him that afternoon. His friend, Lal, who was riding with him in the backseat, said to me, "Jaya, I told Mangha to bring you to the luncheon today, but he said you were busy teaching Suresh."

"Yes, I was teaching Suresh for a while in the morning."

While Lal talked to Ranjit, whom he knew well, I stayed mum. I knew I was in trouble now that I had run into my brother.

It was a small world in Bombay then. Everyone knew everybody. I knew my brothers, sisters, and my mother's friends. They knew my friends. Everywhere I went, I ran into someone I knew. No secret places to date unless I went far out in the suburbs like the Juhu Beach or Bandstand.

At home, Mangha did not bring up the subject of Ranjit that night or another night. That made me even more nervous. I avoided talking to him.

Just as we were picking up where we had left off, Ranjit was gone again for three months. This time it was on business to Calcutta (now Kolkata). When he returned, we continued to meet in clandestine. He arranged a friend's bungalow that was empty, where I could have my twenty-first birthday party.

One evening, while we savored ice cream with sweet vermicelli *falooda* topping at the ice-cream parlor, Ranjit announced, "Jaya, I will be leaving soon for America."

I almost swallowed the wiggly *falooda.* "For business?"

"No. For a computer science course."

"How long will you be gone this time?"

"I don't know."

He had been a hummingbird, who had hummed in and out of my life. This time, however, I thought it was forever goodbye. He was all excited about his life's ventures. I was the one who stayed mum.

A few weeks later, on a September evening, I was preoccupied with my thoughts on the balcony when Mangha joined me. "Baby, do you want to go to America for further studies?"

"Me? Go to America?" At first I thought I was dreaming. This couldn't be happening. Then I wondered if it was a trick question. Perhaps he was sending me away to America now that Ranjit had returned from Germany. Perhaps he had not heard of Ranjit also leaving for America. Confused, I hesitated to respond.

"Do you want to go to America for further studies?" Mangha repeated.

I fumbled for words then replied with not much enthusiasm. "I. . . I would love to."

"I'll ask Kiku to make arrangements for you. What do you want to study?"

"Since I majored in English Literature, I would like to study journalism."

My family believed in higher education. They believed it opened career doors for sons and better marriage proposals for daughters.

The next day when I met Ranjit, I spilled the good news. He said he would be staying with his sister in Bloomfield, New Jersey. I told him I would be staying with my brothers in Hoboken, New Jersey. "What a coincidence! Imagine both of us landing up in the same state."

I was one happy peacock, although I did not flaunt my feathers. A miracle had fallen in our laps. Ranjit and I now made plans to meet in America, eight thousand miles away from home. He said he would write to me at my friend's address. Afraid that Mangha might change his mind to send me overseas, my lips at home were sealed.

In the last week of October 1968, Ranjit left for America. Meanwhile, I interviewed with the American Consulate and filed applications for student visa and passport. I visited the doctor for medical clearance and turned in my resignation at Atlas Copco (India) Ltd, the Swedish company where I worked as a secretary for the managing director.

One evening in January 1969, weeks before I was to take a flight for New York, Mangha called me to his room, had me shut the door and take a seat.

"Baby, I want you to withdraw your resignation letter from your company. Do it tomorrow."

"Why Mangha?"

"You're not going to America."

"But why?"

"Tell your manager an emergency has come up at home."

"What emergency?" I feared something terrible had happened. Perhaps my family was in some kind of financial trouble and could not afford to send me overseas. Perhaps it was my mother's health. The stresses in her life had weakened her heart. She had a history of angina attacks and always counted on me when she fell ill.

Then he mentioned he had received a letter from Kiku saying he met Ranjit at a party. "Since Ranjit is also in New Jersey, you cannot go there." Mangha's voice was stern.

My jaw dropped. My spirits sank. Yesterday my heart was singing a happy tune. Today it was broken into smithereens. "But Mangha, it looks bad to turn in my resignation one week and take it back the next," I pleaded, but to no avail.

How I wished Kiku's letter to Mangha had gotten lost in the mail or arrived after my plane had taken off for America. Now, not only had I lost Ranjit forever, I had also lost the opportunity to go to America. Besides, I had not heard from him since he had left for distant shores three months ago. I also had no way of contacting him. I was caught in a Bermuda triangle with three men steering the rudder of my life: my two older brothers and Ranjit. Did any of them care that I was sinking? Why did my brothers want to give me the gift of my life and then take it away?

Mired in despair, the next morning I walked into the personnel manager's office and withdrew my resignation letter. As advised by my brother, I told him an emergency had come up at home and my trip to America had been cancelled. That evening, I handed the resignation letter to Mangha, a letter he had dictated. Everything was done to his satisfaction. With dampened spirits, I resigned myself to my fate.

Ten days later after dinner, while I stood on the balcony deep in my thoughts, Mangha joined me. "Baby, do you still want to go to America?"

"As you wish," my heavy heart sighed. My towering brother held the key to my fate, but I was ill prepared for what followed.

"Promise me you'll never see Ranjit again. Not even in America."

With such a tall order, what choice did I have? "I promise," I said. Without the pledge, my trip to America was as good as dead.

The following day, once again I handed the resignation letter to the personnel manager.

He threw a skeptical look at me. "Are you sure you're going to America this time?"

"Yes, I'm sure."

"What about the emergency at home?"

"It has been taken care of."

My life had become the pink labyrinth I played with when I was a little girl. Just when I got the little silver bead all the way around the maze, somehow it slipped down another path.

PART II

Hello America

It was the second week of February 1969. I was to leave soon for a one-year course at the New York Institute of Advertising. But, riots and curfew ruled the streets of Bombay. When gunfire broke, my mother pulled me away from the balcony and bolted the street-side doors and windows. Later, I learned that a bullet had lodged itself into the bend on the main floor of our five-story building.

Newspapers reported the riots were orchestrated by the local Shiv Sena political party. They lay down on the street and barricaded Union Finance Minister Morarji Desai's motorcade, hoping to persuade him to sign a border dispute agreement with the neighboring state of Karnataka. When the protestors clubbed his sedan, the police arrived, dispersed the crowd, and the minister's convoy drove away.

Violence spread to neighboring towns, resulting in dozens of casualties and injuries. But, the epicenter was on the street where I lived: Tulsi Pipe Road. The riots also kept me anchored at home that week. If the pandemonium did not subside soon, I was afraid my flight to America would be cancelled.[6]

At the crack of dawn on February 12, 1969, dressed in my new orange bellbottom pantsuit, I went to the balcony to take one last peek at the horizon. Save for the crowing of a rooster and an occasional rumble of a train rolling into the station, silence reigned. The birds were in their nests. The streets deserted. A handful of policemen stood on guard outside the train station. On the other side of the station lay Charles Dickens' world. To the left the Dharavi slums, to the right the Jasmine Mill — a cotton textile mill that employed thousands of workers, many from the nearby shanties.

Wrapped in a white georgette sari, her salt-and-pepper hair swept back into a braided chignon and covered with black netting, my mother came up to me and said, "Baby, it's time to leave for the airport. Go pray to God before we leave." I went to the home shrine, lit a sandalwood incense stick, and recited a prayer before departing on my long journey.

My father's poor health prevented him from accompanying us to the airport. As I hugged his lean body at the door, he gave a tender smile and kissed me on my cheek. "Baby, don't forget us in America. Write home as soon as you get there."

"I will, Dada. And you take care of your health."

"Give my love to Kiku and Suresh. Tell them to write home more often."

"I will Dada."

We went down the three flights of stairs: Mummy, Mangha, Kamal, and my friend Veena who had spent the night with us. The cook followed with my suitcase. The curfew had ended just minutes ago at six that morning. There were no taxis outside the station on that day. While we waited in the dimly-lit weathered lobby, Mangha crossed the street to fetch a police officer, who helped us board a train for Santa Cruz Station. From there we piled into a taxi. Due to the riots, Mangha asked a policeman to accompany us to the airport.

My mother got misty-eyed as I hugged her goodbye at the airport. Tearing myself away I walked to the gate, looked over my shoulder to wave goodbye before boarding a shuttle bus to the Kuwait Airways jet.

This was my first flight on a plane, my first long trip far away from home. In all my twenty-one years, the longest distance I had traveled was eight hundred miles to Delhi by train. Now I was flying eight thousand miles to America. Walking down the aisle to my seat, I stashed away my small gym-style carryon bag and my brown velvet coat in the overhead bin. Due to the tropical climate of Bombay, it had been impossible to find a winter coat. Fortunately, I had stumbled upon one at a consignment shop. It was two sizes too big and almost swallowed my small frame, but I needed a warm coat for the New York winter.

Soon the Kuwait Airways jet pulled away from the gate and coasted down the runway. Gathering speed, it lifted off and soared through the early morning clouds. With it surged my spirits, too. I looked out at the drifting clouds and saw the city of Bombay fade away in the distance. There was no turning back now.

As I relaxed in my window seat, a flurry of events of the past week flashed by me: the riots in the city, the goodbye to my family, the pledge Mangha had me repeat the night before my departure that I would never see Ranjit again. Brushing off the unpleasant thoughts, I escaped to my dreams of America.

I wondered if America was as beautiful as I had seen it in the movies: Camelot with ivory towers and fancy stores and gracious manors with manicured lawns and swimming pools. I wondered if young women were permitted to date men. Were they as stylish as Elizabeth Taylor and Audrey Hepburn, and the men handsome like Troy Donahue and Rock Hudson? Sugarplum dreams of New York were already dancing in my head.

I was going to John F. Kennedy's country, but he was no more. The American President was very much liked in India. I remembered the distant morning his assassination made headlines in the *Times of India*. At college, the corridors were abuzz with news of his untimely death. Years later, I would visit the Texas School Book Depository in Dallas — renamed the Kennedy Museum — from where Lee Oswald fired the bullets that killed the president on that ill-fated day on November 22, 1963.

En route to America, I spent four days with relatives in London. The city was dreadfully cold. Traces of snow still hugged the ground. The following day, when passing showers washed away the lingering snow, I went on a sightseeing drive and attended the *Jack and the Beanstalk* performance at the Palladium Theatre with my relatives.

The dollar, which is now over sixty rupees, was then worth eight rupees. With the only eight dollars (sixty-four rupees) I was permitted to carry by the Indian Customs Department, I had to borrow money for shopping. I bought myself a casual wristwatch, some lingerie, and a trendy camel-tone, light winter woolen coat. It fit fine and looked flattering on me. A month ago, I had no coat; now I had two.

I spent an evening with a college friend, who had married and moved to London. Although she and her husband hailed from wealthy Bombay families, as new arrivals in London they lived in a humble one-room apartment.

While we chatted, she asked if I could trim one inch of her shoulder-length locks, since she could ill afford a visit to the hairdresser. As I trimmed her thick dark tresses, we reminisced over our fun-filled college days. The small pair of scissors would not cooperate. I looked at my friend's head of hair from different angles. The haircut looked lopsided. I tried to level it, now on one side, now on the other. We reminisced some more. I kept clipping. When I was done with her haircut, she looked at herself in the small oval wall mirror on the wall. Her mouth fell open. Not one, but more than two inches of her lovely, thick raven hair lay on the newspaper on the floor. Her disappointment was soon forgotten as we chatted over a home-cooked Indian meal, followed by *Shrikhand* for dessert.

The night before my departure for America, I watched television with my relatives. The news report mentioned that due to unprecedented heavy snowfall in New York, John F. Kennedy Airport had been shut down for the last four days. The next morning, I called British Airways and was relieved to learn that my New York bound flight was expected to take off on schedule.

After two hours of idling at the Heathrow airport runway, the plane was finally airborne. The seats on either side of me were empty, so I sprawled out and fell asleep until a tap on my shoulder woke me up. "Please sit up and put on your seat belts. We'll be landing in twenty minutes," said the flight attendant.

As the plane descended, I looked out the window and saw New York City twinkling in a cloak of nightlights. When the jet taxied towards the gate at the John F. Kennedy airport, my eyes fell upon the mounds of snow piled high along the airfield; evidence of the four-day blizzard.

America had once seemed so distant, another world, another planet. And here I was on this Sunday evening, February 16, 1969, at the other end of this planet, where only three weeks before Richard Nixon had been sworn in as the 37th President of the United States.

While I waited to collect my baggage, I reflected back to a distant day in August 1957, when I was ten. It was the day my family and I had gone to see cousin Gulu off at the Bombay docks. He was headed for America, to study engineering at MIT. I remember the colorful streamers flung by passengers as the ocean liner bellowed its horn and set sail. His ship crossed the Arabian Sea, the Red Sea, and the Mediterranean Sea. It berthed in Aden, Alexandria, and Malta, where he boarded another vessel bound for the French port of Marseille. From there, he took a train to London. The last leg of his three-week journey concluded in September with a trans-Atlantic flight to Boston.

Thankfully, I did not have to sail on a turtle of a steamship to America, like cousin Gulu. While my cousin's odyssey from Bombay to Boston took three weeks, the same distance could now be traveled on a jet in a single day. The world had come a long way in a mere decade.

After going through the U.S. immigration and customs clearance, I headed for the lounge where my brothers Kiku and Suresh were waiting. It was good to see them again. Thirteen months before, Kiku had left for America. Eight months later, my younger brother Suresh had joined him to pursue computer science studies. By now, three of us from the family had come to America.

We stepped out in the cold on this Sunday evening. Kiku hailed a cab for Hoboken, New Jersey. Travel weary and eyelids heavy, I leaned my head against the cab window and dozed off until I caught Kiku's fading words, "Baby, this is the Queens Midtown tunnel." After a while, I heard him say, "This is the Lincoln Tunnel. You will go through it every day on your way to school in New York."

"It's too long a tunnel. I hope there are no more tunnels to go through." My tired limbs were ready to fold for the night. The cab driver pulled up outside a five-story brick building on the Stevens Institute of Technology campus. I had dozed off for an hour in the cab.

"We're home," said Kiku.

I heaved a sigh as I stepped out of the warm cab into a bed of soft snow in my high-heeled shoes. "It's frightfully cold here." Unaccustomed to such freezing temperatures, I cupped my naked hands to my mouth and blew warm air into them.

"You'll need to buy a pair of gloves and a hat to keep yourself warm," said Kiku. "You can buy them in New York when you go to school."

While Kiku paid the cabbie, I watched clouds of vapor escape my mouth and dissipate, as I had watched curly rings from my father's cigarette puffs fade away. Just then, Suresh, almost a six-footer with lanky legs, four years younger than I, picked up some snow, rolled it into a ball and threw it my way. "Hey, Jaya! Here's your first snowball."

Oops! Too late to duck. The soft, cold thing slapped my face. Dusting the snow off my shoulder-length hair, my face and my coat, I spat out the slush that had seeped into my mouth. The frost sent my teeth quivering.

Still the same Suresh, who used to pull my braids and run away when he was the size of an elf. Waving my index finger at him I said, "Wait till I get you one of these days."

"We'll see." He threw his head back and let out a belly laugh.

Kiku led the way with my carry-on while Suresh carried my suitcase up the stairs. Since the building was located on a hill, its main lobby was on the third floor. As Kiku turned the key to a door marked 503, I expected to step into a spacious modern apartment of America. When he threw open the door, I entered and found myself standing on a burgundy rug laid out on a white tiled floor. I scanned the room. The soiled white kitchenette tucked to the left caught my eye. *Today I shall close my eyes to it; tomorrow I shall clean it.*

"What do you think?" asked Kiku.

"Not bad. Where are the other rooms?" I expected to see a room for me.

"This is it."

"This is *it*?"

"Let me give you a tour of our dorm."

Dorm? No one at home had told me Kiku and Suresh lived in a dormitory.

Kiku opened a door to an adjoining 5 x 6 foot room. It had a window, a built-in desk and a chair. "This is the study."

Running across on the left wall of the room was a metal rod on which my brothers' clothes hung. An ironing board leaned against the corner behind the door. Sliding the clothes to one side, he added, "There is enough room to hang your stuff here. You can have one of the chest drawers in the living room."

He led me to a small passage by the closet-size kitchenette. A coat closet with a sliding door stood on one side, the bathroom on the other, and a vanity with a large wall mirror outside.

"We'll have to take turns using the bathroom," he grinned. It's a good thing we have the sink outside . . . just like we did back home." Seeing the anxious look on my face, he added, "We'll make do, don't worry."

What a letdown from those sugarplum dreams!

"Kiku, where do we all sleep?"

"Here, in this room."

I looked at him in disbelief. "Three of us, in this room? On the floor?"

"No, not on the floor. This is where I sleep," he explained, pointing to the only big piece of furniture in the room — a divan-style daybed with a burgundy cotton slipcover. He bent down, lifted the bed skirt, and pulled out a collapsible trundle bed on wheels. "This is your bed." He studied my face for reaction.

"What about Suresh? Where is he going to sleep?"

"Don't worry. We have everything under control."

Kiku always had everything under control, except no one at home had prepared me for the humble accommodations in America. I wondered what other surprises were in the hopper.

Turning to Suresh, he said, "Why don't you bring out the rollaway bed from the study and show Baby where you're going to sleep."

Suresh rolled out a flimsy aluminum folding cot from the study and laid it open by the kitchenette. It blocked the apartment entry. The 11 x 18 foot studio room now looked much smaller with three open beds, a chest, a dinette, an armchair with orange cushions, and a floor lamp. Barely any room left to walk. To think I had traded the comforts of home in India for these cramped quarters in America. To think I had traded the sunshine of Bombay for the freezing temperatures of New Jersey. I did not know what I had signed up for.

Pointing to the trundle bed assigned to me, Kiku chimed in, "Suresh used to sleep on this bed. Now that you're here, he'll sleep on the rollaway."

I walked up to the collapsible rollaway. I had never seen one before.

"Don't … Don't sit in the middle," cried Suresh, as he saw me take a seat.

Oops! Too late. The rollaway almost folded up on me. I shrieked.

Suresh doubled over with laughter as he gave me his hand and helped me up.

"What if the bed folds up on you while you're sleeping?" I asked.

"It doesn't fold so easy. You shouldn't have sat in the middle."

"You warned me too late."

"And don't sit on the corners, either."

"Why? What will happen?"

"The bed will jump up on you." Suresh was always a barrel of laughs.

"It's a good thing I don't have to sleep on the rollaway. And it's a good thing that my bed is close to the bathroom."

I changed into my pajamas, opened my small carry-on bag and pulled out two cartons of 555 cigarettes I had bought on flight for Kiku. Like most Indian men, my older brothers loved their cigarettes, especially the imported ones. They could go through a pack as if it were a bag of caramel candy.

I handed him the cigarettes. "Thanks for getting me over to America."

His eyes gleamed. "Thanks for the cigarettes. I'm almost out of my mine."

A candle loses nothing by lighting another candle. Instead, it adds to the light in the room. Coming from a large family, we had not many extras, yet we lacked nothing. We had learned to give and share. With the few dollars I had on me, cigarettes were all I could offer while he paid my way through school, expecting nothing in return.

"Let's go to bed now. I'm tired," said Kiku. "I have to get up early in the morning to go to work in New York. I have classes in the evening on the campus. I'll see you tomorrow night. Suresh is at school all day. He usually stops by for a quick bite. . . Baby, your classes don't start until a week from now. Take it easy until then."

Kiku drew the curtains and then slipped under the covers on the divan. Suresh turned out the lights and got into the rollaway bed. I called out "Good Night" from my trundle bed.

Morning light filtered through the window blinds of the study and streamed into the living room. No rumbling of trains like back home. No honking of cars on the streets. No clanking of pots and pans in the kitchen. No part-time help popping in and out of the house — someone to clean the bathroom, someone to wash the dishes after every meal, someone to wash everyday clothes for the family. No peddlers chiming the doorbell. All was hush in the dorm room, save for the dripping of the kitchen faucet that broke the silence.

My brothers had left for the day. In my deep slumber, I had not heard them move around. Slipping out from under the covers, I rolled out of bed, stretched my limbs, and drew the curtains of the wall-to-wall picture window. The winter sun was up in all its glory, throwing sparkles on the blanket of snow.

The divan was dressed in its maroon slipcover and the rollaway bed returned to the study. Tucking away my trundle bed under the divan, I turned on the radio, sat by the window and took a bite of the toasted English muffin with marmalade spread. Outside, all was serene. My eyes swept across the pristine white landscape, rested on the icicles that hung from the portico eave, then danced over to the sparse footprints in the snow. There in the warm room, I leaned back in the dining chair and drank in the splendor of winter.

A new day in a new country.

Perched high on Castle Point, on the banks of the Hudson River in Hoboken, is the century-old Stevens Institute of Technology campus, the oldest mechanical engineering college in the country. The MSA graduate dormitory where my brothers lived faced the campus grounds. The rear of the building looked out to the Hudson River and the New York skyline.

For a whole week, I hibernated in the cozy den, looking forward for my classes to commence. I sat by the window listening to music, reading the newspaper, watching students bundled from head to toe hurry for their classes, and feasting my eyes on the snowflakes that floated down gently like confetti. At times, my thoughts drifted half a world away, meandering down memory lanes until they rested in a warm place: my home in Bombay, where each year my mother etched progressive markings of my height on a wall behind the bedroom door.

It was the night before my school commenced. While Kiku ironed his shirts for the week, I asked him how to travel from Hoboken to the New York School of Advertising on Madison Ave. "Kiku, let me also have your office phone number in case I get lost."

"You cannot get lost in midtown Manhattan. The streets cross the avenues. They're all numbered. You have to go down only one block to realize you've gone the wrong way. Downtown is another story. You can get lost there. Downtown is where Chinatown is. Downtown is where I work. It has street names, not numbers."

I noted the directions and his phone number.

"I suggest you buy a street map from a bookstore in New York," he continued. "Every train compartment also has a map showing the train stops. Follow the subway map and the street map. Don't ask people for your way around."

"Why not?"

"Because they'll send you the wrong way."

"Now Kiku, why will they send me the wrong way?"

"I'm telling you, if you're looking for one street, they'll send you down another street."

"Has that ever happened to you?"

"Yes. A few times." He let out a chuckle.

"They sent *you* the wrong way?" I threw my head back laughing.

The next morning, I woke up in high spirits, like a little girl on her first day of school. As I came down the hill to catch a bus for New York, I caught a whiff of fresh roasted coffee wafting in the air. A few sniffs was enough to perk me up on this cold winter morning. From the bus window, I saw gray puffs rise from a smokestack of the Maxwell House coffee plant. One-way bus fare to New York was forty cents while cross-town bus in the city another fifteen cents.

One afternoon, on my way back from school, my gaze fell upon an unkempt man at the Port Authority bus terminal concourse. Clad in a black soiled winter coat, ragged dark pants, and a knapsack thrown over his shoulder, he looked prematurely bent for his age. I saw him walk over to a garbage receptacle, rummage through the trash and mutter to himself, until he came upon an unfinished bagel. Brushing the piece of bread with his hand, he took a big bite.

The scene struck a somber chord in me. Until that afternoon, I had not known of America's homeless. Here I was in the richest country in the world, yet there in front of me was a grown-up man searching for food scraps in a trashcan. I stopped, reached for my wallet and found a few dollars to spare. Approaching the man in frayed clothing, I asked, "Are you hungry?"

Head bowed, he gave me a sheepish nod.

"Follow me. I'll get you something to eat."

We walked into a hamburger joint at the concourse. "How about a hamburger and shake?"

The man in the black coat took a seat. "Yes ma'am. Vanilla shake, please."

I left him at the table to order some food. Minutes later, I returned with the shake, some paper napkins and a paper bag stuffed with a hamburger and French fries. "Enjoy your lunch."

"Thanks, lady," he said in a muffled voice. He wiped his face with the napkin and took a big bite of the burger. I wondered when he had last had a proper meal.

It snowed again that night. The next morning, as I stepped out of the dormitory to go to school, the frosty wind slapped my face and sent a shiver through my spine. Pulling the knit cap over my ears, I tightened the wool scarf around my neck and treaded gingerly in mustard high-heeled jitterbug dance shoes. I had only brought a couple of heeled shoes with me from India.

"Watch out for black ice," a student passing by cautioned me.

"Black ice? What's that?" I asked. Since it never snowed in Bombay, how was I to know anything about black ice?

"Melted snow," he replied. "Looks like water, but it's frozen. Be careful, you can skid on it."

"Thanks for the warning."

Skirting around the icy patches by the fraternity house, holding on to every car parked along the curb, I made my way downhill. Where there was no car, I reached for a tree or a wrought-iron fence. It's a wonder I did not skid and go rolling down the hill. The cold numbed my leather-gloved fingers. The chill crept through my knee-length coat, my mini-skirt, my stockings, and into my bones. The hemlines were short that year and the silk and cotton dresses I had brought with me from India were not suitable for New York winters.

By now, I had given away the over-sized warm brown velvet coat to the Salvation Army. It took up too much space in the small coat closet I shared with my brothers. Since I could ill afford to buy pantyhose, I bought the affordable thigh-high stockings and held them up with a garter belt. If one of the pair got a run, its twin was usable, like a sock. I did not yet own a pair of winter boots, as I did not want to burden Kiku with additional expenses. With his modest income, he was already saddled with too much responsibility — paying for Suresh's tuition and mine. Besides, in another month winter would be behind us.

As I tiptoed my way down the hill that morning, I prayed no one was watching me from a fraternity window. Along came a smart aleck cruising in an old blue T-Bird. He stuck his head out of the car window and jeered, "Lady, next time try going down the hill on a sled."

I turned a deaf ear, pretending not to hear him. He went his way, and I mine.

Winter-weary, I looked forward to the first blush of spring. Then I learned about an old American folklore. On February 2nd, if the groundhog sees its shadow when it emerges from the underground, it means a long winter. So it retreats back in its cubbyhole. If it does not see its shadow, then spring was near. Fortunately that year, the groundhog had not seen its shadow when it surfaced after its winter hibernation.

On weekends, I shopped at the A&P grocery store on Washington Street, the main street in town. I was overcome by the tantalizing display of foods, even exotic fare from half a world away. On the shelves sat an assortment of bread loaves ranging from 19 to 26 cents. As I wheeled my shopping cart between the aisles, I was amazed I could buy peeled, shelled, sliced, diced, frozen vegetables. Rice was pre-cleaned; wheat flour ground and sifted. No wonder they did not need cooks in America. Back home, the cook had to take the box of wheat kernels to the miller and get it ground for chapattis.

Carried away by the array of foods on my first visit to the store, I tossed too many grocery items in my shopping cart. When the woman at the register rang up my groceries, I realized I did not have enough money to cover all my purchases. I told the clerk to put away some items.

Then I remembered what Kiku had told me before I left home. "Baby, you cannot bargain at the grocery store or any store here. The prices are posted for everything. Before you buy anything, check the price."

I had checked the prices, but I had no calculator on me to sum it up. I labored up the hill, cradling a brown paper bag piled high with groceries in each arm, stopping at intervals, resting the loaded bags on parked cars to stretch my arms. It's a good thing I had put away a few items. It's a good thing milk was delivered at our doorstep.

One evening, when Suresh returned from school, he said, "Hey Jaya, I'm cooking noodles today. Want some?"

"Any time is noodle time for me, Suresh, so long as I don't have to cook."

I had arrived in a do-it-yourself society and marveled at the way my brothers fended for themselves. They did their laundry, ironed their clothes, made their beds, and even cooked their own meals — tasks they would have never considered doing back home. Over there, the servants attended to these chores.

Hoboken was both a college town and an industrial town littered with smokestack industries. Lipton tea, Maxwell House coffee and the many flavors of Jell-O were all produced in this community, in the shadow of New York. Then there was the Bethlehem Steel plant, and the riverfront shipyard where World War I and II ships were once assembled.

I was uncomfortable walking down the distressed neighborhood of Frank Sinatra's hometown. The streets of downtown were lined with dilapidated brownstone row houses, with a tavern at every other corner. Growing up in India, I had walked past many tea cafés, but no pubs. Bombay had been a dry city during the British Raj days. The liquor ban was lifted only in 1967, two years before I left for America.

To save bus money, on good days I walked down 42nd Street to school on Madison Avenue. But I felt uneasy as many hoodlums hung around Times

Square, and theaters displayed signs for peep shows with half-naked women. So I walked through the garment district on 40th Street, but that was not any better. It was peppered with oglers and eve teasers, like those of Bombay. They stared and passed lewd remarks as they unloaded clothing racks from trucks. However, the scene got better once I crossed Fifth Avenue, an avenue lined with trendy shops.

As time went by, I became familiar with American lingo and my ears tuned in to the New York accent. I seldom saw Indian faces on the streets of New York City, except at Port Authority concourse newsstands, where they sold newspapers, cigarettes, and chocolates. Some days, I stopped to buy a chocolate bar just to say hello to them. When I learned these jobs provided temporary means until they could find professional employment, I felt blessed to have the support of my family in America.

Spellbound

One Sunday in March, alone in the apartment, I turned on the radio, sat by the window and penned another letter home. When Tom Jones' "Delilah" played, in a heartbeat I was back in Bombay, dancing with Ranjit at Bistro's. That was the night before he left for America.

It had been almost a month since my arrival and I had not heard from him. *Was he still in New Jersey? How far did he live from Hoboken? Did he know I was in town?* Abandoning my pledge to Mangha I picked up the phone, asked the operator for Ranjit's sister's number, and learned that he had moved to the YMCA in Newark. I dialed the number at the Y. My heart sang when I heard his voice, but at home my lips were sealed.

The following Sunday, Ranjit and I met at the Newark train station. The cold weather had brought a glow to his face, although his cheekbones were more pronounced.

"Let me show you where I live," he said, as we stepped out of the station.

When his gray tweed overcoat and burgundy scarf came off at the Y cafeteria, my mouth fell open. "Ranjit, what happened to you? You've lost so much weight. Haven't you been eating?"

"Yes, I have." He was not a good liar.

After a meal of hamburger and fries, we walked back to the train station. "Why didn't you write to me after you left for America?" I asked.

"Kiku told me to stay away from you."

"You met him?"

"Yes, at a party."

While we talked about his computer science program, he mentioned that my brother Kiku had made arrangements for his school admission and visa. Now I was totally confused. If Kiku had made arrangements for Ranjit to come to America, why did he and Mangha object to my seeing him? After all, he came from a highly educated and reputable family. His father had been the vice chancellor at the University of Roorkee, an engineering college. There had to be more to the story.

As we took the escalator up to the platform, I remarked, "What a miracle that we both landed up in New Jersey. I guess we were destined to see each other again."

The train pulled into the station. "How about next Sunday?" he asked.

"What time?"

"Same time. Same place."

The following Sunday, after spending two hours on the bus and two trains, with a picnic basket swinging from my arm, I met Ranjit again.

"Smells good." He took one peek in the straw basket, sniffed, and gave me his million-dollar smile. "What have we here today?"

"Meat cutlets and rice pilaf with cauliflower and peas."

"I'm hungry."

Although the sky was spilling over with sunshine, it was nippy. On our way to the park we picked up a couple of soft drinks, then planted ourselves on a bench and ate lunch, which had by now become cold. For over three years, he had flown in and out of my life. I was happy to have him back again.

"How has life been treating you in America?" I asked.

"I have a good job now, but the first few months were rough. On weekdays, I worked at a gas station in Bloomfield, pumping gas. I made good money on tips when I cleaned windshields or checked oil and water for customers. But when it was bitter cold, the chill seeped through my gloves, which were cut at the fingertips."

"Why were they cut?"

"I had to cut them otherwise it was difficult to count the change. Sometimes, I worked with the mechanics in the shop. I changed spark plugs and tires, helped tune cars and fix brakes. I brought in a change of clothes with me. In the evenings, I washed up and changed at the gas station, then took a bus to New York to attend my computer class. A young Jewish lady at the school sometimes shared her dinner with me. She knew I was short on money."

"That was very kind of her."

"After school, I stopped for a slice of pizza and a glass of beer at Port Authority terminal. Then I took a bus to Bloomfield. By the time I reached my sister's place it was almost midnight."

"Did you have warm clothes?"

"No. Just the ones I brought from India. It was a fifteen-minute walk from the bus stop to my sister's. After a month I moved out of there."

"What did you do on weekends?"

"On weekends, I worked at a carwash in town. Those cars, you won't believe how fast they came rolling out after a wash. I had to quickly clean them, because another one was waiting on the tracks."

"Why did you have to work so hard?"

"To pay for my tuition, lodging, and boarding. When I came from India, I brought some trinkets, silk scarves, and silk ties. I hoped to sell them here and make some money to pay for my expenses. I got five dollars for a silk tie. My cost was only one dollar. Some women even paid me more than I asked for the silk scarves."

"They must have felt sorry for you. You've gotten so skinny. I'm going to have to fatten you up with some home-cooked meals on weekends. By the way, how are the living conditions at the YMCA?"

"It's like living in a dorm. It has an affordable cafeteria. They change linen once a week. The only thing I'm not crazy about is the common bathroom. Other than that, it's not bad. There are a few Indians of my age also living there. Before that I lived with an Indian guy in the ironbound section of Newark."

"What's an ironbound section?"

"It's the industrial section of town." Then Ranjit explained the class distinctions of America: the blue-collar and white-collar jobs, the blue- and white-collar neighborhoods.

"The Indian guy I lived with is a Punjabi. . . about my age. His name is Robert."

"A Punjabi named Robert?"

"Yes, he took on an American name. Many immigrants do. They call me Ron here. He worked for the Indian Merchant Navy. One night while they were docked at the New York port, he jumped ship."

"Jumped ship? Why?"

"He wanted to live in America, so he stayed back. He did not return to his ship. He has been living underground for the last two years in Newark, but he has a day job at a factory. On weekends, he performs chores for the landlady. Nice guy. One day I'll take you there."

"How much rent did you pay him?"

"Twenty-five dollars a month. I shared the apartment with him. But after two months of sleeping on a sofa, I found a room at the YMCA."

That's when I first became aware of how far people would go to live in America. They would even jump ship and live underground. Soon I heard of stories where people got married to Americans just to get a Green Card, and divorced shortly after.

Spring made its debut with lovely cherry blossoms. Tulips were in bloom and daffodils were smiling. A sense of lightness filled my life, too. I continued to see Ranjit on Sundays. He was now studying for his Masters program in computer science at Rutgers University in New Brunswick, New Jersey.

One weekend, he took me to the ironbound section of Newark where I met the tall and stout Spanish landlady, but the man who had jumped the ship was not around. He was out on his weekend job.

As time went by, I made some friends. The residents at the MSA (married students' apartments) dormitory were graduate students, most of them married. Their wives invited me to Avon and Tupperware parties, even to a baby shower. These events were all new to me.

On the fringe of the campus down the street from where I lived, stood a four-story dilapidated magenta building, referred to as "India House," where several Indian students and immigrant families lived, huddled together in small one-bedroom apartments. Kiku introduced me to a young couple there. The wife and I soon became good friends. Often we took an evening stroll on the campus grounds. Sadly, our friendship was short-lived. A couple of years later, she died from complications during childbirth.

Before long, summer was upon us. Since classes were held on weekday mornings, I had the afternoons to myself. I used this time to become acquainted with the city. One balmy afternoon, I took the elevator to the rooftop observatory of the one-hundred-and-two story Empire State Building, the city's tallest building at the time. Dropping a coin in the brass binocular post, I got a *Mary Poppins'* view of a world of skyscrapers — some with flat roofs, others with smokestacks. No chimney sweepers danced in my lens though. From a dizzying height, I took a peek at the street below where people moved like ants, and autos looked like children's toy cars.

As I walked down Fifth Avenue, I came upon a Gothic citadel with spires. I went through the heavy bronze doors of St. Patrick's Cathedral and found myself in America's largest Catholic Church. It was graced with baroque arches and stained-glass windows. Dipping my fingers in the holy water, I made a sign of the cross, dropped a token of gratitude in the donation box, lit a candle, and went up to the altar. As I went down on my knees and prayed, I was back to St. Michael's Church in Bombay, where I once attended Novena services with my Catholic classmates on Wednesday mornings.

As I stepped outside the cathedral, a hotdog stand on wheels across the street caught my eye. I crossed over and treated myself to a Polish sausage with sauerkraut and mustard, and then ambled down to Rockefeller Center Plaza, where the piazza turns into a skating-rink every winter. Some afternoons I took a stroll to Central Park, stopping at intervals to browse at window displays of trendy shops on Fifth Avenue. I loved New York. I could live here forever.

Like many young women in the city, I wore my dark shoulder-length hair with a slight flip at the ends. Dressed in a mini-skirt or an occasional bell-bottom pants, Jackie-O sunglasses, and a modest version of clogs, I blended in with the city crowds.

Bellbottom pants, Afro-style permed hair and sideburns were in style among young men in the city. Although Ranjit occasionally indulged in a stylish corduroy jacket, he preferred his conventional straight-legged trousers and sleek Frank Sinatra hairstyle. A head taller than me, he stood at five-foot-seven, and so did not shy away from the popular three-inch heeled men's platform shoes.

Kiku dressed conservatively, but he loved his Elvis Presley sideburns. On the other hand, Suresh wore his hair Beatles-style long, straight-legged cream cotton pants, and a dress shirt to school.

The year 1969 was an interesting year to be in New York. It was a time when the country was experiencing a cultural revolution. A time when women burned bras to make a statement of freedom. A time when free-spirited youth with counter-culture ideals roamed around Greenwich Village. Young men and women in long hair, faded jeans, tie-dye clothing and ponchos gathered at Central Park or Union Square, some strumming on their guitars as if they were Jimi Hendrix, others singing songs by Bob Dylan, Janice Joplin, or Carole King. They sang of love and peace. They called for an end to America's involvement in the Vietnam War. Sometimes, I stopped to listen to their music. On the trendy Fifth Avenue, young men and women in saffron clothing and shaven heads also sang of peace. They clapped cymbals and tambourines as they chanted "Haré Rama, Haré Krishna."

This was the Woodstock era. That August, I watched rock stars on television entertain an audience of almost half a million at the New York festival in Bethel. For three days, music of love and harmony filled the air. Despite the rain, the hippies high on drugs made love and danced freely to the spirited music into the night. The Woodstock rock concert would go down as a symbol of America's counter-culture period in history.

Each day, I opened my mind to the experiences of my new life. However, coming from a conservative family, I could not relate to the hippie culture of American youth and their Utopian spirit. I could not embrace their sexual mores or indulgence in drugs.

As I looked beyond the glamorous and liberal façade, I realized I had arrived in America at a time when the country was torn by social unrest. It was a year when the civil rights movement had gained momentum. It was a year when Gloria Steinem carried Betty Friedan's feminist torch and led the Women's Liberation Movement through the streets of New York. Until then, movie stars with strong personalities like Katharine Hepburn, Elizabeth Taylor, and Jane Fonda had shaped my concept of women in the West. Unlike women in India, they seemed confident and liberated. However, I soon realized that women of America had to also fight for their rights and equal opportunities.

It was also a period of mourning. In the past year, Senator Robert Kennedy and the civil rights leader Dr. Martin Luther King, Jr. had been assassinated, and the three-week "Tet Offensive" in Saigon had resulted in a barrage of American casualties in Vietnam. The seven-year-old civil war of Vietnam had taken a toll on the people of America. The country was besieged by protests on city streets and across college campuses. It was the first war fought in the living rooms of America. Television broadcasting turned the tide of American sentiment against the war.

On Fifth Avenue, outside the main New York Public Library, peddlers sold hard reminders of war. In support of the anti-war movement, I bought myself a black-and-white "Make Love Not War" and peace symbol buttons and pinned them on my dress.

Uncle Sam's posters were everywhere: on the billboards, lampposts, and street corners. The man wearing a long goatee was dressed in the American flag colors: a navy tailcoat, white shirt, red bowtie, blue-and-white striped pants, and a star-spangled white top hat. With his finger, he summoned every passer-by with a message that read, "Uncle Sam Wants You."

One day I asked Kiku, "Who is Uncle Sam? People keep talking about him on the bus. I see his posters everywhere."

"It's the US government."

"You're kidding. Americans must love their government if they call it Uncle,"

Kiku chuckled.

A frog in the well does not know the ocean. There was much I needed to learn about America and its people. Uncle Sam wanted American citizens to join the army to fight the civil war in Vietnam. I was glad my brothers were not eligible for the US draft. Kiku was twenty-nine, a green-card holder, and

Suresh was on a student visa. But, my heart went out to the families whose loved ones were drafted to fight another country's civil war.

The year 1969 was also a defining moment of America's triumph in space. On July 16, 1969, I was awestruck as I watched Apollo II lift off on its journey to the moon. A few days before, Kiku had bought his first black-and-white television so we could watch the historic event. While Michael Collins orbited the command module in space, the lunar module separated from it and astronauts Neil Armstrong and Edwin Aldrin Jr. stepped out. They looked like jumping jacks in bunny suits bouncing on the moon.

Had my trip to America been delayed by six months, I would have missed the grand event, since television had not yet made its debut in Bombay. I would not have heard Neil Armstrong utter the legendary words from space that day. "One small step for a man; one giant leap for mankind." A week later, on July 24th, the astronauts returned to earth.[7]

However, man's landing on the moon also touched a chord in me. Back home in India, each month on full moon day, my family performed the *Satyanarayan puja* — a holy ritual offered to *Chandra*, the Moon God. During my high school years, Mummy encouraged me to fast on this day. When the moon peeked from behind the hills, I broke my fast and had dinner. Only now that man had landed on the moon, I grew skeptical of fasting on this day. Since the moon was within the reach of man, I wondered if there really was a Moon God.

༄

Mrs. Pearlman, founder of my school, got me a part-time job at a small advertising company. It helped me contribute in small ways to my family. After school hours, I stopped at Chock Full O' Nuts for a nutted-cream cheese sandwich — raisin bread with cream cheese and walnuts spread — and a piece of coconut cream or chocolate layer cake and then headed for work. Fortunately, my school, the restaurant, and my employer were all located on the same city block. I made three dollars an hour, which was good money considering minimum hourly salary was then only half the amount. With the money I made, I bought groceries for the family and paid for my personal expenses and commute.

At the office, I worked for two middle-aged Jewish women — Ruth and Sylvia, the company accountants. They brought me up to speed on American culture and the latest news. They were my second memorable Jewish experience; the first being the Pearlmans.

One afternoon at work as I passed Stanley Aaron, the Vice President, I said "Good afternoon, Mr. Aaron."

"Jay, everyone here calls me Stan. I want you to call me Stan."

"Yes, Mr. Aaron."

"That's Stan."

"Yes, Stan." I felt a little uneasy to address him so informally.

In India, I never addressed my manager by his first name. It would have been considered disrespectful. To my astonishment, I discovered that rules in America are different. People here are informal. They call everyone by their first names or abbreviated names. They called me Jay.

Sylvia took me under her wing and became my American Mom. One summer weekend, she treated me to a John Wayne movie, *True Grit*, at the Radio City Music Hall. I spent that night at her home in the Bronx. The next morning, she fixed me a wholesome breakfast of fried eggs, sausages and English muffins with orange juice and coffee. Then we took the subway to the city, where she introduced me to some Indian friends, who were students at the New York University. She went the extra mile to make me feel at home. Whenever I thanked her for her kindness, she waved her hand and said in a light-hearted manner, "Oh Heavens to Betsy! It's nothing." When she told me she volunteered one weekend a month at the Bronx Hospital, I imagined all New Yorkers must be kind and giving like her.

Autumn whisked in. The cooler weather was a welcome change to the sultry days of August. Maple and oak leaves turned to scarlet, copper, and russet. Birch and sycamore paled to yellow before they were shaken off their limbs by a mighty gust of wind.

This October afternoon was unlike any other. I was engrossed in my work at the office when Sylvia grabbed me by my arm and led me to a window that looked down on Madison Avenue along 40th Street. Throngs of people led a parade up the avenue. Some sang and danced, others honked their car horns. Some sailed along in stretch limos, others popped champagne bottles and toasted merrily in their convertibles. Across the street, confetti and colorful streamers, even rolls of toilet paper rained down from the office windows.

Just then the agency's copywriter joined us by the window. "What's all this celebration for?" I asked him.

"The Mets won the World Series."

Noticing a blank look on my face, he raised his eyebrows. "You don't know who the New York Mets are?"

"No. I recently arrived from India."

"They are New York's baseball team. They won the World Series."

"Which country were they playing against?"

"Baltimore Orioles."

"But Baltimore is in America."

"That's right."

"Then why do they call it the World Series if they beat another American team?"

"Because no one in the world plays baseball like we do." Then whistling "Take Me Out to the Ball Game," he strolled out of the room while I continued to watch the victory parade.

The 1969 victory had come to the Mets after many years of losses, so they celebrated it with much fanfare.

By now I was getting familiar with the New Yorkers' candor and their bold sense of humor, with a little panache here, a touch of chutzpah there. Like coconut shells, they were hard on the exterior, but tender on the inside.

With my student visa about to expire in February, I was expected to return to India before then. However, New York was growing on me like sweet, intoxicating dandelion wine. I loved its every heartbeat, its sights, and its sounds. I loved its pepperoni pizza. I had seen the greener grass on the other side. I had woken up to the Maxwell House coffee aroma. I had even regained my love potion. How could I give it all up and return to India where I would be forced into an arranged marriage? I had to do something about my immigration status soon if I wanted to stay on in America. I mulled over this dilemma through all my waking hours.

There were two options: apply for a permanent resident Green Card or for a training visa. Since Kiku was not yet a citizen of America, he could not sponsor me for my residency. Since I was not a doctor, an engineer, or a scientist, I could not apply for a Green Card. Thus, I had only one option left.

Without consulting an immigration lawyer or my brother, I applied for a training visa. I assumed that once I had the visa I could look for an employer to sponsor me. Little did I know the process worked in reverse! Meanwhile, Ranjit had applied for his Green Card and was awaiting news from the US immigration authorities.

Before Thanksgiving holidays that November, I graduated from the advertising school. The Pearlmans gave our class a dinner reception at the historic New York Biltmore Hotel, by Grand Central Station. I wore my brown-and-blue silk sari for the occasion. To my surprise, I was honored as the class valedictorian with a toast.

"Speech, speech," my classmates called out.

Gees! At the age of twenty-two, I did not know how to give speeches, but I tried. Gathering my composure, I gave my impromptu valedictory address.

Fall slipped into winter. I continued to work at the advertising company. Sadly, Ruth died of breast cancer shortly after. My friendship with Sylvia continued for a while. The set of wine glasses she gave me for my wedding gift would last me for thirty years. But the spell that New York had cast on me would last forever.

Hum Dono
(Two of Us)

January 1970. Ranjit's New Year wish was fulfilled. With the receipt of his Green Card, he officially became a permanent resident of the United States of America. He could fly as high as his new green wings could carry him. He could live his American dream.

Later that month, Ranjit and I met at our usual rendezvous. We picked up sandwiches and sodas, walked to the park and made ourselves comfortable on a bench. The winter sun smiled upon us as we shared his moment of joy.

"Jaya, have you heard from the immigration authorities?"

"Not yet. It's been three months since I applied for my training visa."

"Don't worry. Sometimes they're backed up with applications."

He took a few bites of his sandwich and then let the words spill out. "Jaya, let's get married."

Get married? This was the moment I had waited for a long time. I should have jumped from the park bench, thrown my hands up to the heavens, and given him a big hug. Instead, words of worry found their way to my lips. "Ranjit, what if my folks don't approve?"

"Jaya, this is your life. You're grown up now. You're entitled to make your own decisions."

True, at twenty-two I was entitled to make my own decisions. But until my visa situation was cleared, I was at the mercy of my family and the immigration office.

Encouraged by his Green Card, Ranjit said, "Let's go to the city next weekend and get the engagement rings."

On a frosty Saturday in early February, four years since our first date, we went to the diamond district of Manhattan. With his meager savings as a computer programmer-analyst, Ranjit bought me a half-carat diamond ring and a wedding band for himself. Since I had no money to pay for his ring, he paid for both the rings.

"We'll get engaged next weekend."

"But what about my folks?" I asked.

"You can inform them after we're engaged."

"Just like that?"

"Yes, just like that." Ranjit was bold with his decisions. Once his mind was made up, no horse or hailstorm could stop him.

The following Sunday, we met at a diner by the Y. After breakfast, we walked over to the parking lot and stepped into his brand new cream-colored Volkswagen. Opening the glove compartment of his Beetle, he reached for a little maroon suede box, opened it and pulled out the platinum band with the shimmering diamond we had bought the week before.

As he gently slipped the ring on my finger, a thousand thoughts raced through my mind, a mélange of emotions flooded my heart. Sadly, there was no one there to share our moment of joy. The cheerful day, however, ended in a litany of woes. When I got home, I broke the news to Kiku. It was not well received.

"What do you mean, you're engaged? You were told never to see Ranjit again."

The smile left my face. On this happy day, I stood heartbroken and alone. I urged my brother for an explanation, but he skirted my question and continued writing in his notebook.

Then he rose to his feet, picked up his books from the dining table and stormed off to the study. "Mummy and Dada are going to be very angry at you. If they have a heart attack, it'll be your fault."

Wounded by his remark, I remembered my mother's past angina attacks. Even as a kid, I would wake up at night at the sound of her moans coming from the adjoining room. I would rush to her side and attend to her. Then I would wake up the cook and send him to the doctor's home for emergency medicine.

"Kiku, you can break it to them gently," I pleaded in a lighter vein.

I searched my brother's face for reaction, but his silence spoke volumes. Even the snowcap of Mount Kilimanjaro would have melted a bit by now. Still, I did not harbor ill feelings towards him, for this was my brother who had brought me over to America and paid for my tuitions. This was my brother who always came through for everyone in the family. Only now it hurt to think we were at odds with each other.

Hours later came the tidal wave. Kiku called home. The news was not well received by my family. I still could not understand why they objected to my seeing Ranjit. By now, I was convinced my family had someone else in mind for me. I envied young women in America who were permitted to date. While a young man in India enjoyed much freedom, a young woman was expected to be a beautiful rose and an untainted white dove.

The following week, I received a letter from my father. He said that if I married Ranjit, I would have to sever ties with the family. I was shocked. It was so unlike my father to write that. Mired in despair and torn between my loyalties, I lay awake at night deep in thoughts. Two roads had diverged: Ranjit and my family. I loved them both dearly. Which road should I take? Would they merge some day?

I had still not heard from the US immigration authorities. Meanwhile, although I looked for a copywriter's job in the advertising industry in New York City, I settled for a media estimator's job. I needed the money and it was the first job offered to me. It would later lead to a media planning role.

The next time I met Ranjit, we talked about the big day. "How about June?" he asked.

"June is fine with me."

"No, June is too long a wait. Let's get married in April."

"That's next month. We don't have time for arrangements."

"What arrangements, Jaya? You inform a few friends. I will inform mine. We can get married at the Bloomfield City Hall. Later, we can have a small reception."

City Hall? A civil ceremony? A few friends? I had always imagined my wedding to be a grand affair, but given the circumstances a simple ceremony would do.

The weekend before the wedding, we bought some used furniture for our small one-bedroom apartment: an olive-green sofa, two flimsy side tables and lamps from our friends who dropped them off at our home in a pick-up truck. We also bought a student desk and a black kitchen dinette with a white Formica-top from a moving sale. Ranjit and I transported the student desk in our Volkswagen trunk on the first trip. To bring home the kitchen dinette, we took another trip, packed the four chairs in the back seat of the Volkswagen, and tied the table to the roof of the car. Then we took the back roads and drove home at a snail's pace. Afraid the table might slide off the roof, each of us stuck one arm out of the car window to hold it in place.

On the eve of our wedding, we spread newspapers on the living room hardwood floor and unscrewed the chair seats. While Ranjit spray-painted the dinette black to give it a fresh look, I reupholstered the seats in black-and-white plaid cotton fabric with the help of an upholstery stapler gun purchased the day before. The only new pieces of furniture we bought were a cheap double-bed, a pole lamp, and a black-and-white television set.

The big day was here. April in New York is usually a wet month, but this morning the sky was bursting with sunshine. Ranjit was to pick me up at half-past-eight. Suresh left early for school. Before Kiku left for work, he pulled out a new Hoover upright vacuum cleaner from the coat closet and brought it over to me. "This is your wedding gift."

My wounded heart sank. *If he could not accept my marriage, how could I accept a gift from him?* I held back my emotions. "Thanks, Kiku. But I'm sorry I cannot accept it. Why don't you keep the vacuum cleaner for yourself? You only have a sweeper."

A sad look brushed over my brother's face. He had always been a kind and caring brother. Yet, there we stood for a long painful moment, looking at each other in silence.

"You're sure you don't want it?"

"No. Thanks anyway." My heart tore as he put away the vacuum cleaner back in the coat closet. I had never been so assertive with him before. Until now, I had always sought his advice; done whatever he asked me to do.

"Call me at work if you need me at the wedding," he said, as he headed out the door.

At promptly half-past-eight, Ranjit arrived. He helped me carry my only suitcase to the car. Everything I owned was packed in that bag.

As we drove down the highway, I asked, "How much did you pay for this car?"

"It cost me sixteen hundred dollars, including financing. But I only had to put down twenty-five dollars for registration. The rest is financed." Living on credit, our American dream had begun. Back home in India, he would have had to wait two long years for a new car and pay cash for it. Even getting a telephone installed at home was a two-year wait.

We pulled up at an old garden apartment complex in Belleville, New Jersey. While Ranjit unloaded the car and unpacked, I covered the entire ugly bathroom floor with a wall-to-wall carpet. Then we headed for his sister's in the neighboring town of Bloomfield.

To my dismay, Ranjit and his sister went shopping for our wedding party, and I was left to take care of his sister's two children for four long hours: a two-week old infant and a two-year old. This was my wedding day and here I was changing diapers of a little one. My sister-in-law, who I barely knew, said it was "good training" for me. I could not refuse the babysitting, as I did not want to start off on the wrong footing with my in-laws.

The day had not gone well so far. Ranjit and I did not get back to our little apartment until half-past-five. The two witnesses for the wedding — our friends, John and his wife, Vicki — arrived at our home at six. While Ranjit got dressed in a jiffy, kept them company and served them wine, I wrapped myself in six yards of a beige silk sari.

Our friends barely had their first glass of wine when Ranjit announced, "Jaya, let's go before we miss the judge. We have to be at the City Hall at seven."

The folds of the long flowing sari refused to cooperate. It took me a long time to get those pleats right, as I was not accustomed to wearing saris.

"Ranjit, give me a few minutes," I called out. "I still have to comb my hair and put on lipstick."

"You can do that in the car, Jaya."

I never imagined I would have a Las Vegas-style wedding in New Jersey, yet there I sat in the backseat putting on my lipstick and brushing my shoulder-length tresses.

Five minutes past the hour, we pulled into the Bloomfield City Hall parking lot. Taking the closest entrance, we scurried up the stairs and found the courthouse doors shut.

Oops! Wrong way!

"Must be the other entrance," Ranjit called out.

We turned around and hurried down the long flight of stairs. I held up my sari folds, lest I trip on them in my high-heeled shoes.

"Ranjit, I hope we haven't missed the judge."

"Then we'll get married tomorrow."

"Very funny. Remember the judge is going on vacation tomorrow? That's why we had to schedule it for today."

We raced up another long flight of stairs at the other end of the building and found ourselves standing outside the judge's chambers.

"You guys go ahead. I'll be there in a couple of minutes," Ranjit said, as he headed down the hallway.

John, Vicki, and I walked into the judge's chambers, where he sat on an elevated platform. The judge's stern face put me at unease.

"You're late," the judge scolded, as he looked at his watch. "Who's getting married today?"

"I … I am." Looking towards John and Vicki I added, "These are our witnesses."

"Where's the groom?"

"He'll be here shortly, Your Honor."

"He'd better be here soon if he wants to get married today."

Just then, Ranjit walked into the room in his pinstriped gray suit, a white shirt, and a slim maroon tie.

"Who has the ring?" asked the judge.

"I have it, Your Honor." Ranjit reached into his coat pocket and pulled out the gold band. With the marriage vows exchanged, the wedding band slipped on my finger, the knot was tied.

"I now pronounce you man and wife," declared the judge. He made his way down from the platform to congratulate us. "You may now kiss the bride," he said to Ranjit.

Ranjit threw a blank look at the judge and then at me. Stepping aside, he said to the judge, "You may go ahead."

The judge gave my man a hard stare and scolded him, "*You* Sir, are supposed to kiss the bride, not *me*."

Ranjit dropped a light kiss on my lips. I understood his confusion. Perhaps he did not know the protocol of a civil marriage. Perhaps he was a bit nervous. Back then love was considered a private affair in India. The groom did not kiss the bride in public.

Despite the happy ending, I was sad no family members were present to revel in our moment of joy. No henna decorated my hands and feet for good luck. No *shehnai* flute music played in the judge's chambers. No mantras chanted by a priest. No circling around the sacred fire seven times. No vermillion *sindhoor* on my hair parting. No garlands or sweets exchanged. No blessings showered with rice and rose-petals by relatives and friends, as it had been at my sister Hari's wedding. Instead, with a fleeting ceremony and vows exchanged, with two witnesses and a grim judge, we were pronounced man and wife. We had just become another statistical record at the City Hall.

Our friends, John and Vicki, left after the brief wedding ceremony. Ranjit and I headed for a restaurant where we had dinner reservations for two.

"To champagne dreams," Ranjit toasted.

I raised my glass to celebrate the occasion and took a few sips. Within minutes my head was reeling, as I was not accustomed to drinking alcohol.

"Ranjit, I want to hit the sack early tonight."

"No, you can't do that."

"Why not?"

"Because we have to dice the fruit and marinade it in wine tonight for the party punch."

"Who said we have to do that?"

"My sister. I bought the fruit and the wine for the punch this afternoon."

"Easy for her to say. She did not have to sit up on her wedding night dicing fruit."

That night, Ranjit and I sat up peeling and dicing fruit for the wine marinade. The following day, we had a small party for family and friends at our modest apartment. I wore the pretty olive-green silk sari with a gold border that my mother-in-law had sent me through a friend. The honeymoon would have to wait until we could afford one.

In hindsight, a simple civil wedding followed by a small party was the best solution for our situation. It barely cost us a couple of hundred dollars.

Two months later, I received a disheartening letter from the immigration authorities. They had denied my training visa. I was asked to return to India in ten days and notify the authorities of my departure schedule. My heart sank as I handed the letter to Ranjit.

"Don't worry," he said, "they'll not send you back to India. You can explain to them that you're now married to a resident of the United States."

At the immigration office, my fears were laid to rest. The officer asked me to fill out a change-of-status form and return another day with my photographs and passport.

The following month, during the July 4th Independence Day weekend, Ranjit and I drove up to Maine for a belated honeymoon. We had planned to drive as far as Bar Harbor, but due to holiday traffic jam on the highways, it was not possible. Music on the car radio helped us make it through the evening as we listened to David Gates of Bread sing his new release "Life can be short or long, love can be right or wrong. . . I'd like to make it with you."

We got only as far as Boothbay Harbor, where in the still of the night we checked into an affordable motel that had cottages. For the next couple of days, we went into town, treated ourselves to an afternoon cruise, and savored lobster and crab meals.

On the third day of our honeymoon, Ranjit said, "Jaya, let's go home."

"Why? We planned to spend a whole week here."

"Yes, but we have to leave today."

"Something the matter?"

"I have a deadline at work. We've seen all there is to see here."

"Can we stay another day?"

"No. We have to leave today. I have a lot of work to do."

Just as I was warming up on our vacation, we headed home, a four-hour drive back to New Jersey. I would soon discover that although Ranjit loves to travel, he is like a restless sailor. After a couple of days at a place, he gets the urge to move on.

When we got home, Ranjit put on his Gemini charm. "Can you help me with my computer program?"

"Me? Are you talking to me?" He had to be talking to me. There was no one else in the apartment. "I don't know how to write a computer program."

"It's easy. I'll show you."

He marched off to the bedroom and returned with a square-lined paper pad. Then he tore a sheet, wrote a few lines of the computer program and explained the process to me. Handing me a few sheets of paper he sweet-talked me into writing similar processes with minor changes, so the computer program could perform different routines. And so it was, on our honeymoon at home, I wrote my first computer program, not knowing anything else about computers.

That summer, Kamal came to America to pursue graduate studies in finance. She was the fourth member of the family to arrive in the US, all in a matter of two-and-a-half years. She lived a couple of hours away in upstate New York, so I seldom saw her. By now, Kiku had completed his graduate studies in mechanical engineering, and Suresh had two more years to go for his undergrad studies in computer science.

After my marriage, my relationship with my family was tepid at best; with my in-laws, none. I did not know why his family also objected. At twenty-two, it was easy to block unpleasant thoughts from my mind. Life was hectic and I tried not to worry about things over which I had no control.

Meanwhile, Ammi, my paternal grandmother passed away in Delhi, at the ripe old age of ninety-one. She was the only grandparent I had known. The others had departed before I was born. I was reminded of the times when she visited us in Bombay to escape the cold winters of Delhi. In the evenings, she often had me help her chop vegetables for the family's dinner or remove grit from lentil seeds and kernels of rice. At bedtime, while I massaged her back and legs, she had me tell her about my day at school and count my numbers in Sindhi. When I mispronounced, as some Sindhi numbers are difficult to say, she laughed so heartily.

Ammi kept a little silver snuffbox under her pillow. A couple of times a day, she would open the little box, take a pinch of the chocolate-colored powder from it and sniff it. Then she would sneeze incessantly.

"Why does Ammi use snuff?" I asked my mother.

"It clears her sinuses."

One day I came down with a nasty cold. While Ammi was taking a bath, I took a pinch of snuff from her silver box and inhaled it, like I had seen her do. Goodness gracious me! My nose stung as if I had taken a big whiff of red chili powder. I could not stop sneezing. When I finally came around, I hoped my sinus passages had cleared forever. Never again did I go near the pungent brown powder.

At home, my mother kept a thick red guide to homeopathic cures and a large wooden box with tens of slots filled with bottles of tiny sweet pills, all name-tagged. She took it for her aches and pains. When my siblings and I came down with cough, cold or fever, she had us take the sweet pills, too. For injuries, it had to be *Arnica*. We also used home remedies and thus seldom visited a doctor.

As I took the office elevator up this morning, I was taken by surprise when a young man I had known from college days stepped in.

"Yogi, what are you doing here? Do you live in New York?" I asked, happy to see a familiar face from back home.

"No. I'm here on business."

"How long will you be here?"

"I am heading back to Bombay in four days."

I was supposed to get off at the fourth floor. Instead, I rode the elevator with him to the eleventh floor and talked with him for a few minutes in the reception area. Back in 1970, it was unusual to run into an Indian on New York City streets, leave along being on the same elevator.

The commute to work was almost two hours each way. When I returned from work in the evening, I had to attend to household chores: cook, wash the dishes, and iron clothes. I went to bed exhausted.

While we watched "I Love Lucy" show one evening, Ranjit clapped his hands and the television channels changed.

"What's wrong with the TV? We just bought it. Clap your hands again, Ranjit."

He clapped once more. The channel changed again.

"What can I say? You have magic hands, Ranjit. Now you don't have to ask me to change the channel for you every time." But, the temperamental TV did not always switch to the channel he wanted. So either he had to clap several times until he got to the right station or I had to stop whatever I was doing and change the dial for him. It was the Archie Bunker era. Fortunately, there were just a few channels available then on television.

When my Green Card arrived in the mail that October, I was one happy Jaybird. I embraced my new life in America as it meant the world to me.

Meanwhile, with the joint invasion of Cambodia by the United States and South Vietnam, the Vietnam War expanded. Nineteen to twenty-five-year old American men, whose names were drawn in a lottery, were drafted to Vietnam. As a result, war protests continued on city streets and college campuses across America.

In January 1973, with the signing of the Paris Peace Accord, the eleven-year Vietnam War ended. Across the country, American troops were welcomed home by streams of yellow ribbons tied around the trees. Sadly for some, the music had died forever.

That spring, three years after we were wed, Ranjit and I took our first trip home to Bombay. Since I could not take a month off from work, I had to quit my job to visit India. By now, I had worked for Muller Jordan & Herrick, Young & Rubicam, and Grey Advertising in New York.

It was the first time I saw my family since I had left for America. By now, my family had moved from the suburbs to Cuffe Parade in the metropolis of Bombay. They lived about a mile-and-a-half away from my in-laws who lived by Radio Club in Colaba.

It was also the first time I met Ranjit's parents. They were very kind and gracious to me. On the day of our arrival, we visited his father who had been in the hospital for a few days. He was so happy to see us that he insisted on being released that same evening.

"I want to go home today," he told the doctor. "My daughter-in-law has come home for the first time." After some discussion about his medication, the doctor discharged him.

My father-in-law had been going through depression since he had retired. I was sensitive to it. So when he asked me to sit beside him and talk to him, I did. He was a very fine man. In the past, Ranjit had told me stories about his kindness, his sense of ethics and fairness.

He had accomplished much in life. In his early years, he had been a visiting engineering professor at US, UK and Japanese universities through a USAID program. He went on to become the Vice Chancellor at the University of Roorkee (now Indian Institute of Technology Roorkee) in the state of Uttar Pradesh. With the aid of funding received from American universities, he had helped build an extra dorm, an engineering design center and other facilities at the university. He had been a director on the Indian Railway Board and had even launched his own engineering company in Bombay.

While in India, Ranjit and I traveled a bit with his sister and brother-in-law. From Delhi we drove to Dehradun and Mussoorie in the northern state of Uttarakhand. We spent a couple of nights at the Savoy Hotel, a Gothic-style English hotel built during the British Raj days on the hillcrest of Mussoorie. As we walked towards the village, Ranjit pointed at the valley below where he had once attended the Oak Grove boarding school. He filled me in on some childhood stories of his school days. We took a sky lift over the scenic hills and had a memorable vacation.

I am glad for that visit to India. Two years later, Ranjit's father passed away. I never did get to see him again.

Upon our return home, I took up a freelance assignment as a media planner at a small advertising agency in New Jersey. Since I had to take two buses to get to work, Ranjit taught me to drive. It was not easy to take lessons from my husband, especially on a car equipped with a stick shift. Even though I had the gear in forward drive and tried to co-ordinate between the clutch and the accelerator, the silly car rolled back on every hill.

"Gun it! Gun it!" Ranjit screamed.

I pushed the accelerator as far as I could and heaved a sigh. Phew! "Ranjit, one day you will have to buy us an automatic car."

That day arrived sooner than I thought it would. Ranjit traded in his Volkswagen for a new fire-red automatic Opel Manta. Even though it had been five years since he had returned from Germany, he was still partial to German toys. He traded in one German car for another. American or German car, it did not matter, so long as I did not have to struggle with a clutch or wrestle with the gears. Life got easier as I drove the red Opel to work.

In the summer of 1973, the fuel crisis crept upon us like a panther in the dark. Gas prices soared to over fifty cents a gallon at the pump, due to an oil embargo imposed by the Arab countries to protest America's aid to Israel.

Drivers lined up at the gas station on odd or even days, depending on the last digit of their automobile license plates. Some mornings I woke up at half-past-five and drove our Opel to a nearby gas station to find that I was not the only smart one who tried to beat the others to the pump. Many were camped there before me. Some read the newspaper and drank their morning coffee; others listened to their car radios while they waited for the station to open at six.

Talk and more talk filled the airwaves as I waited in line: Arab oil embargo, OPEC and the cartel, stock market woes, recession worries, gas prices, and wartime profiteering by oil companies. The gas line got longer. I turned the dial, leaned back in my car seat, and let the musical notes of Don McLean's *American Pie* fill my ears. The sun rose. Its beams filtered through the trees and threw prisms of light on my windshield. The station finally opened and the cars inched up. When I reached the pump I asked the attendant to fill up the gas tank.

"No ma'am, you're only allowed half a tank."

"Half a tank?" I was disappointed. My Opel had a small gas tank. Two days later, I was back in line for my half-a-tank quota of gasoline.

It did not take long for Americans to abandon their gas-guzzling automobiles for fuel-efficient, sub-compact ones.

That October, war clouds gathered over the Middle East. Egypt and Syria attacked Israel. The six-day Arab-Israeli war ended with a victory for Israel with the capture of the Golan Heights from Syria. Shortly after the Mideast conflict, the gas prices stabilized and I could fill up my gas tank to the brim.

～∽

The following spring, we bought a small home in Middletown, New Jersey on an acre of land with oak, pine, and willow trees. Here we would nest for seven years. The town was then home to many Irish and Italian families.

In the mornings, I dropped Ranjit off at the station for a train to New York City and then drove to work. In the evenings, we watched the unfolding of the Watergate story and the impeachment hearings of President Richard Nixon. August 9, 1974 was a sad day in American history when President Nixon resigned for his role in the cover-up of the Watergate scandal. The American judicial system had proved that no one is above the law, not even the President of the United States.

In the five years I had lived in America, I had watched the Civil Rights movement, the Women's Liberation march, the Vietnam War demonstrations, the Watergate investigation, and the fall of an American president. It made me realize the strength of America's democracy.

Meanwhile, five years after receiving his Green Card, Ranjit received his US citizenship and his American passport. He asked me to hold on to my Indian passport. "You never know when you might need it," he would say. "One of us should retain our Indian citizenship."

Pearls of Motherhood

I quit working when I was expecting our first baby. Since I had experienced a miscarriage a couple of years before, I did not want to take another chance, especially with the long commute. But when I was eight months pregnant, I slipped and landed on my back while mopping the bathroom floor. I crawled back to the bedroom and called my doctor, who said no x-rays could be taken at this stage of pregnancy. I prayed no harm had come to the baby. Later, I would learn I had fractured my lower spine. Living with back pain thus became a part of life.

Spring showers not only brought flowers in our garden, it also blessed us with a healthy daughter. We named her *Minal*, "fruit of labor." In keeping with the American tradition, Ranjit took a box of cigars for his colleagues at work to celebrate the occasion. Although he did not smoke cigars, he would say, "Cuban cigars are the best." Soon after Minal's birth, he even quit smoking cigarettes because I would remind him not to smoke in front of our little daughter, as she might develop asthma.

At twenty-seven, my life was transformed. Deciphering a baby's cry was like unraveling the mysteries of life. When little Minal cried, I rushed to her crib, wondering if she was hungry or in pain, if she wanted to be hugged and reassured or if she was afraid of the dark. I walked her in my arms, gently patted her back, and sang her lullabies. Soon her little head grew heavy on my shoulders, her breath soft upon my neck. Before long, she was sound asleep.

We lived on Ranjit's modest income. He worked in the computer field in New York. If there was one thing I had learned from my mother, it was to improvise. Even though I was not a good seamstress, after we got married Ranjit had bought me a Singer sewing machine from Sears. Over the years, I had altered his pants, turned the collar of his shirts, sewed a few *chooridhar-khameezes* for myself, and curtains for our home.

When Minal was a toddler, I dug up a vegetable patch in our yard and she helped plant the seeds: a medley of tomatoes, green beans, bell peppers, hot chili peppers, peas, corn, and carrots. *Voilá*, I was blessed with a bounty of fresh home grown vegetables, tomatoes that I canned, and vines with pumpkins for home-baked pumpkin-nut bread. There were even a few stalks of corn. No, I did not have a green thumb. I probably overfed the soil with lime and fertilizer, or it was just a beginner's luck. The carrots though did not fare well. The garlic cloves I had planted along the edges of the vegetable patch did not keep the rabbits away. The hungry bunnies chewed up all the carrots.

When Minal was a year-and-a-half old, I returned to the hospital. With a cry of new life, our son was born. We named him *Ari* after Aristotle, the Greek philosopher. It was not so difficult taking care of one child, but quite a challenge attending to two. I don't know how my mother went through life with three times the burden. With one day rolling into the next, I felt like a washed-out rag and often longed for a soothing massage. Minal kept me on my toes all day and little Ari kept me up at night. Meanwhile, Ranjit transferred to Fordham University in New York and switched to an MBA program in finance. Twice a week, he attended evening classes after work. On such evenings, he did not get home until eleven at night.

Many young mothers lived in my neighborhood. I learned to crochet from them. Often we gathered for tea along with our little ones. It was a good support group. As seasons turned, Minal and Ari learned from *Mister Rogers'*

Neighborhood and *Sesame Street* educational television shows. They also learned their ABCs from the lime green alphabet blanket I had crocheted for them, with upper case alphabets sown in pink wool and lower case in yellow. The blanket lasted over twenty years. The children used it as an afghan when they watched television.

Now that we were a family of four, we needed a bigger car. We replaced the red Opel with a second-hand hunter green Pontiac Grand Prix. At times, I fed dinner to the children on the hood of our car while they watched neighborhood teens go by on roller-skates; other times, they ate on the bench-swing in the shade of an old willow tree while I recited Mother Goose nursery rhymes to them. When it rained or snowed, I read them Curious George stories. Some weekends the family picnicked at a farm-park by a lake. On long weekends, we indulged in family vacations. And when we were in a music and dance mood, I put on a Polka record and we danced to the *Pennsylvania Polka* and the *Beer Barrel Polka* music.

Happiness also came in bright colored Legos. The children and I spent hours building entire towns with blocks that fit snugly into each other, each block needing another to grow, much like people need each other for growth. We built schools, skyscrapers, houses, and barbershops. We put together entire communities with fire houses, parks with people, and cars on the streets.

As the seasons unfurled, so did my two lovely buds.

෨෧

One winter, I took the children to visit their grandparents in Bombay. They had a very pleasant time. My family catered to their whims and fancies. My mother played with them while my father told them stories.

After two memorable months when I returned home, Ranjit said, "Jaya, one of these days you have to get back to work. We can't manage with one salary."

"But the kids are too young," I pleaded.

"You don't have to work in the city. It's too long a commute to New York. Besides, you have been away from the advertising world for several years now. Why don't you take some classes in computer science and find a job locally?"

I was disappointed I had to get back to work when the children were so little. I could not see myself bringing up two children, cooking, cleaning, and working outside in a demanding career. On the other hand, women in India could count on their families and had plenty of domestic help readily available to them.

I signed up for the computer classes, hoping they would be rewarding in the long run.

With Ari barely out of diapers, I dropped the children off in the mornings at Mountain Hill School, a Montessori school in Middletown, and then headed for my classes or the computer lab at the Brookdale Community College in Lincroft.

Back then in the 1970s, IBM computers were the size of oversized refrigerators with blinking red and green lights. Data processing was done on the main computers and data storage drives were as big as the washing machines. All computer equipment was stored in freezing air-conditioned rooms.

I learned about bits and bytes and how information is stored in the computer's registers. I learned how to code a program in different computer languages. Class assignments were keyed in on punch card machines, one line of code per card. Five hundred lines of code generated five hundred punched cards, and one thousand lines spat out one thousand punched cards. The stack was then turned over to the computer operator, who fed it into a card-reader and then through a compiling machine.

Once I was on my way to turn in my 2 x 6 inch pack of cards when someone bumped into me around the corner. The stack fell on the floor. I went down on my knees, gathered the cards, and had to rearrange them in sequential order. It happened to most programmers at one time or another. After that episode, I always secured the stack of cards with a rubber band. Technology has since come a long way.

Even though math and science were not my forte, I plunged myself in the computer field and worked with hexadecimals and learned to convert ASCII characters to EBCDIC code. Figuring out why my computer program did not work was like deciphering Morse code. I had to run through a series of numeric EBCDIC codes to get to the root of the problem.

Once Ranjit showed me a pocket-sized computer he had assembled from scratch. It had computer chips, hard-wired printed circuits, tiny transistors, and an LCD display. He even got it to function to the computer code he had programmed. I was impressed.

In keeping with the do-it-yourself tradition of America, he also painted our home while I pitched in with the trimming and cleanup. He repaired plumbing or electrical fixtures, even though we sometimes had to eventually call the plumber for an emergency trip. At least he tried. Armed with a set of screwdrivers, wrenches, a mechanic's flashlight and spark plugs, he sometimes stuck his head under the hood of our green Grand Prix and gave the old car a good tune-up.

His sense of confidence rubbed off on me. I also began to trust my own wisdom. This Baby was all grown up.

Tricky Forks

In the spring of 1979, I got a job as a computer programmer in Holmdel, New Jersey, where I went through an initial three-month intensive training program. The take-home assignments kept me up until the early hours of the morning. Since this was my first job in computers, I made little money. After paying for the children's all-day nursery school and after-school care, I paid out more than I brought in.

When I discussed this with Ranjit, he said, "Jaya, even if we have to dip into our savings, we'll do it. Once you have a couple of years of experience under your belt, you'll make good money. Keep a low profile at work and learn as much as you can." I followed his advice.

Soon life became overwhelming. I had to get the children's lunch boxes ready the night before. In the morning, I fed the children, got them ready and dropped them off at the nursery school, which was in one direction and my job in the other. I had to be at work before eight for the training program.

I had barely completed the three-month program when I received a call at work from Ranjit. He said he was calling from Cabrini Hospital in Manhattan.

"What are you doing at the hospital?"

"I got sick on the bus."

"Did they tell you what's wrong with you?"

"They think I've come down with hepatitis."

"Hepatitis!" The phone almost fell off my hand. This was no time for crisis.

That evening after work, I picked up the children from school and hamburgers from Roy Rogers for dinner. While they ate in the back seat of the car, I drove into Manhattan to visit Ranjit. With the rush hour traffic, it took me almost two hours to get to the hospital.

At the hospital, the nurse advised us to keep our distance. "He could be contagious."

"I saved the Jello-O dessert from my dinner for you," Ranjit told the children.

"What kind?" asked two-and-half year old Ari, clinging to my skirt.

"The kind you like. Strawberry Jell-O."

The nurse went to the lobby, returned with the Jell-O dish and a couple of plastic teaspoons and handed them to Minal. The children stepped out into the hallway, sat on a bench and shared the dessert.

The next day, the children and I went to the doctor's office for gamma globulin shots. Ranjit came home after ten days. His recovery took another month. Now when I returned from work, I had to attend to the children and a recuperating husband. Besides, my new job was very challenging. Headaches and neck pains weighed me down. The fall I had suffered earlier in the bathroom gave me chronic backaches. Frequent visits to the chiropractor did not bring lasting relief.

One evening, I wept profusely as I listened to an old Indian song by Mukesh, "*Aansoo bhari hain yeh jeevan ki rahein*" (The roads of life are full of tears). I felt as if an Indian genie was slowly chipping away at my American dream. I had to confront my ghosts. Removing the cassette from the tape recorder, I unraveled the long yards of magnetic tape and threw it in the garbage. Then I opened the kitchen drawer and pulled out more tapes. One by one, I tossed them in the trashcan. No more would the melodies from the past haunt me. For years thereafter, I did not play Indian music, but the lyrics somehow found their way to my lips. Another time, another place, they would have caressed my soul, but today they only ripped at my heart.

Having lived a sheltered life in India, never did I imagine life in America could be so difficult. Where is the "Yellow Brick Road" of America? The only roads I had crossed so far were the meandering, rocky roads. I had seen better days, but those days seemed so distant now.

Ranjit suggested I send the kids to my family in Bombay for a couple of months. At first, I was reluctant, but finally gave in. That August I called my family. I told Mangha about Ranjit's illness and my predicament. I asked him if I could send the children for a couple of months to Bombay.

"Sure. No problem. The children will liven up the house." He instructed me to request a special stewardess to be assigned to the children when booking the airline tickets on Air India. She would take care of Minal and Ari through the flight and the transfer in London, and hand them over to my brother at the Bombay airport.

On the evening of their departure for Bombay, Ranjit and I drove the children to New York's John F. Kennedy Airport. At the Air India ticket counter, I requested permission to board the children and get them seated while Ranjit waited at the airport lounge. I handed over the children's passports and tickets to the flight attendant.

When it was time to say goodbye, four-year-old Minal refused to take her seat. She held on to my skirt and wept. Two-and-a-half-year-old Ari, in his royal blue overalls, looked at his sister with sadness and wondered why she was crying. Placing his little hand on her shoulder he looked at her and said, "M'aal, don't cry." Those words, that scene, stayed forever etched in my memory.

I held back my emotions, draped my arm around my daughter, hugged her tight and said, "Uncle Mangha will pick you up at the airport, sweetheart. You'll see Nani and Nana. There are many children in Nani's building."

Her tears did not stop. Brushing them gently away, I said, "I'll write to you and talk to you on the phone. And when you come home from your vacation, we'll have lots of fun."

I pulled out my lipstick from my purse. "Minal, sweetheart, here's my lipstick. I want you to hold on to it and bring it back with you when you come home. Will you do that for me?" I hoped it reassured her she would return home.

She held on tight to the lipstick in the small fold of her hand and nodded.

"Now let's see that big smile of yours."

A lump rose to my throat as I saw the sad look in her dark eyes. To think we had come to America for a better life. Then I remembered my father's comforting words. "Don't worry, Baby. This too shall pass."

Watching the scene on the plane was a middle-aged woman, fair of face. "Why do you have to send them off on their own? Why couldn't you go along with them?" she snapped at me.

Here I was almost down on my knees, hugging the children, and the woman scolded me as if I had taken her prized jewels. These precious jewels were mine. Couldn't she see I was having a difficult time parting from them?

I wanted to cry out, *Lady, shut up! You don't know what I'm going through. You think if I could, I wouldn't go along?* Instead, I buttoned my lips and swallowed my grief.

Just then the flight attendant walked up to me. "Ma'am, you have to leave now. We're taking off in five minutes."

With dampened spirits as I hugged the children one last time, silent tears gripped at my heartstrings. Tearing myself away, I walked down the aisle to the exit door without looking over my shoulder. Minutes later, Ranjit and I watched the plane race down the runway, then soar and disappear into the night sky.

Now I returned from work to an empty house and silent walls. I missed the children's laughter and chatter. I missed their sunny smiles and bear hugs. I missed packing their lunchboxes with peanut butter sandwiches and juice and "I love you" notes I scribbled with smiley faces and valentine hearts in colorful crayons on paper napkins.

The chronic pain in my neck and back continued. So did the twice-a-week visit to the chiropractor. Some evenings after work, I went to the neighborhood spa and relaxed in a hot tub; other times I stopped by at a friend's for coffee.

When Billy Joel's song "Just the Way You Are" played on the radio while I cooked, I penned another letter to the children. "Minal, I'm listening to our favorite song on the radio. . ."

One September evening, on my way home from work, I stopped at the neighborhood bakery. The cheesecake with the blueberry topping under the glass counter looked tempting. *It shall be my dinner tonight.*

Once home, I opened the irresistible bakery box and dug my fork into the luscious dessert. The blueberry and cream cheese flavors burst in my mouth and tickled every taste bud of mine. Another forkful and my thoughts sailed to distant shores.

The morning must have dawned in Bombay. Minal and Ari must be up and about.

Another forkful.

The children must be having breakfast and telling my mother tales of America.

Another forkful.

Mangha will take them to his club in the evening and treat them to kebabs and ice-cream.

Another forkful. The delectable cheesecake was almost half gone when I heard a car pull into the driveway and the garage door roll up. In a flash, I dumped the rest of my dessert into the garbage can and placed a newspaper over it. Ranjit would not understand why I gobbled down half a cheesecake for dinner. This evening, however, my taste buds were satisfied, my appetite filled, and my emptiness numbed. Opening the refrigerator, I pulled out two containers of leftovers of rice-with-peas and lamb-and-potato curry and heated them up for Ranjit.

After having spent two months in Bombay, Minal and Ari returned. On a clear afternoon in early November, Ranjit and I went to receive them at the Kennedy airport. The lounge doors flung open and an Air India flight attendant in a silk sari walked in with Minal and Ari. We rushed to hug and kiss the children. The stewardess checked our drivers' licenses for identification before releasing them and their passports to us. After retrieving their baggage, we headed home. The children must have been very tired, for they fell asleep in the back seat of the car. The next day, after a good night's sleep, Minal and Ari were energized and recounted memories of their two months' stay in Bombay.

Soon, life was back to normal. The children returned to their nursery school and the walls of the house echoed with laughter again. Ranjit, who had recovered by now, was back to work. The two months had helped me regain my equilibrium.

PART III

Frost to Sunshine

That winter Mother Nature unleashed a heavy snowstorm. Rhododendron and azalea shrubs were blanketed in white. Pinecones and acorns fell off our trees in profusion. Bundled in coats, hats, scarves, mittens and boots, the children and I stepped out into the soft heap of snow. As we tread gently through the front yard, more flakes floated down on us and concealed our footprints.

Dragging large metal snow saucer sleds behind them, the children trekked up the street outside our home, and then came sledding down the knoll with the other little ones from the neighborhood. When the morning grew old, the children put away their flying saucers and tossed snowballs at each other, throwing a couple of snowballs my way, too. Then we packed and piled huge snowballs until we had put together Frosty the Snowman in our front yard. We gave him a carrot for his nose, little black toys for his eyes, Ari's red wool cap for his head, and Minal's red wool scarf around his neck. With that, Frosty came to life.

The sub-zero temperatures stayed with us for many days. When the children returned in the evenings from school, they gave Frosty a big hug. After twelve nippy days, the winter sun melted the snow on the rooftops, the streets, and in our yard. When the children returned that day from school, Frosty was no more. A melted mass of snow with a red wool cap and scarf remained in its place. The children were heartbroken. They had just lost a dear friend.

❦

By now my relationship with my family had begun to thaw. Kamal had married a fine Caucasian man and was living in Connecticut. Kiku had married a nice Punjabi woman and was living with his family in California. Like me, the two of them had love marriages, yet they were not told they would have to sever ties with the family, as I had been told.

In the summer of 1981, the children and I visited Kiku. When I returned home, I convinced Ranjit to move to Silicon Valley. I gave him my best sales pitch on how the valley was thriving in the computer industry and he could easily find a job in his field.

"Ranjit, the California weather is so good you will never have to worry about shoveling the snow."

I finally convinced him to move to the West Coast. With a for sale sign posted outside our home, in the spring of 1982 we moved to California. We left our furnished home in the hands of a real estate agent, who rented our property without our approval and pocketed the cash.

The agent told Ranjit over the phone our property was difficult to sell. This went on for about six months. Frustrated that our home could not be sold, I asked a friend to have her real estate agent check on it. She found some people living there and beer bottles and garbage strewn on the lawn. When Ranjit learned about it, he was furious. He took a flight to New Jersey and found that our home was rented to drug dealers, who had trashed our place.

Disgusted by the corrupt agent, Ranjit relisted our home with another agency. He also got the movers to move our furniture to California, as in the interim we were living with rental furniture. In the process of packing and cleaning up the garage, he asked the movers to check if there was anything in the crawlspace by it. They found drugs packed in plastic bags stashed away in a dollhouse my daughter once played with.

Within weeks of relisting our New Jersey home, it was sold.

As New Jersey transplants, we were rocked not only by California's earthquakes, but also by Silicon Valley home prices. We bought a small ranch home in Fremont on a jacaranda tree-lined street that bloomed with pretty mauve flowers in spring. The lofty home prices meant I had to continue working. Fortunately, the children's elementary school was one short block behind our home. Juggling the demands of work and home was not easy. Being up before the break of dawn and turning in after the clock had made its midnight run had become my way of life.

One night while I tucked Ari in bed, he said, "Mom, my friends' moms always pick them up from school. Why don't you pick us up, too?"

Guilt pangs nudged at me once more. Holding back my emotions, I sat by my seven-year-old, his hand in mine, and said to him, "Ari, don't you ever forget, you and Minal are very precious to me, but we need the money. So I have to go to work."

"Dad can go to work and bring the money. You stay at home and pick us up from school. Then you will not need babysitters to take care of Minal and me."

"But Ari sweetheart, we need more money than Dad brings."

Picking up his small stuffed dog, I made it dance while I sang him Patti Page's song I remembered from my childhood days, "How much is that doggie in the window, the one with the waggily tail?" It brought a smile to Ari's face. Stroking his hair, I placed a gentle kiss on his forehead, bade him good night and turned off the lights.

Before bedtime, I usually read the children storybooks. Some nights I read to them from *Amar Chitra Katha*, a children's comic book series with folklore and legendary tales from the Indian epics. Other nights we made up our own stories, each of us tagging on a line to move the story forward.

One night, when I was not well and could not read to the children, Ari said, "Mom, you lie down and I will read you a story today." He tucked me in bed and pulled the comforter up to my chin. Then he sat on the carpeted floor by my bed and read me a story from his Curious George book. My heart melted. When Minal did not feel well, he would tell her stories about dogs that got into trouble.

On a rainy day afternoon, when the sun hid behind the clouds and rain-drops drummed down like gumdrops from heaven, I prepared hot chocolate with marshmallows for my little ones and kindled a log. There by the crackling fire we sat while I read them a book of Tutankhamen. They sipped on their hot drinks, lent me their ears, as I leafed through the legend of Egypt's King Tut, crowned at nine, buried at eighteen in the Valley of the Kings, a Valley of the dead.

"How did he die?" asked my curious munchkin, as the fire crackled in blue and amber.

"From a head injury," I replied. "And all the people of Egypt mourned his death."

"Where is the Valley of the Kings?" asked Minal.

Far in the desert, in a town called Thebes by the River Nile, is the Valley of the Kings, where tombs of ancient pharaohs lie, I explained. They rubbed the king's body with oil, wrapped him like a mummy, and placed him gently in a wooden chest. Then they covered his face with a golden mask, sealed the coffin and painted his figure on it.

"Why?" asked Ari.

"So people could tell who was buried inside." Then they placed his casket in a tomb, filled it with treasures, and built a pyramid over it, I portrayed.

As the rain beat on the windowpane, to my children I explained the mysteries of afterlife: the people of Egypt believed the king's soul would one day return, find the casket with his painted face and quietly enter his frame. Then King Tut of Egypt would come to life again.

The children were so rapt by King Tut's tale they had me read the book time and again.

August rolled in and with it *Raksha Bandhan*, a day when a sister ties a *rakhi* string on her brother's wrist. He in turn gives her a gift, implying he will always protect her. In keeping with the Indian tradition, Minal tied the decorated string on Ari's wrist and exchanged sweets; Ari gave his entire weekly allowance to his sister.

The next morning, when he took off the *rakhi*, I told him to put it away in his dresser.

"Why, Mom?"

"For good luck, Ari."

He stashed it under his clothes. Each year Minal tied the love band on her brother's wrist, and each year he gave her his allowance. And so the brother-sister bonding continued.

Some days when I returned from work, I found Minal all dolled up in my two-inch heeled shoes and a silk scarf. She romped around the house wearing my reddest lipstick, bluest eye-shadow, and deepest red nail polish. She loved to play grown-up, even loved grown-up music. When she was seven, I bought her the children's musical album *Annie*, but she exchanged it for an Olivia Newton John record.

Minal was a precocious child and was enrolled in the gifted children's program through her elementary school years. She loved to read books, listen to music, and work on art projects. At eight, I taught her to draw flowcharts. At nine, she maintained my accounting books for my consulting practice. At ten, she wrote a ten-page research paper on West and East Germany and typed it on the computer, a project I had assigned to her during the summer holidays. For reference, she pored over home encyclopedias and books at the public library. It was the mid-1980s. IBM and Hewlett Packard personal computers had just made their debut in American homes.

While Minal typed reports on the computer, eight-year old Ari found a way to use it in a different way. One day when I returned from work, he drew my attention to the beautiful flowers placed in a glass of water at the kitchen window. "Mom, that's for you."

"Thank you, sweetheart. Where did you get these beautiful flowers from?"

"From the neighbor's garden. I picked them when I was returning from school."

In the past, the children had sometimes surprised me with wild yellow flowers they had picked from the fields by the school. "Ari, you can pick flowers from the fields or from our yard, but not from the neighbor's yard. Okay?"

He lowered his head and nodded.

"Now go write one hundred lines: *I will not pick flowers from the neighbor's garden.*"

"Mom, do I have to?" He gave me a hound dog look.

"Yes Ari, you have to, my dear. The sooner you get started the better."

"Mom, how do you spell *neighbor*?"

I got a piece of paper and wrote out the sentence for him.

An hour later, he walked into the kitchen and said, "Mom, I'm finished."

"So soon?"

I glanced at the pages he handed me. "But Ari, this is typed. Not handwritten."

"Remember Mom, you showed me how to use the computer. So I typed two lines and repeated them."

"Next time you will have to write it, not type it. Okay Ari?"

He gave me a reluctant nod.

I got the dinner cooking, put on some music and did some mending. While Santana's *Black Magic Woman* played this evening, I ironed suede knee patches on Ari's pants and reinforced them with hand sewing. Iron-on patches on his pants, even his jacket, became his signature style. It was cheaper than replacing the clothing every three weeks and quite stylish, too.

Ari was accident-prone. One year, his arm was in a sling. The next year, his leg was in a cast. The third year, I received a call at work from the elementary school secretary. "Mrs. Kamlani, your son Ari has fainted. He's not breathing."

"What happened?"

She explained that while Ari was playing on the school grounds, he was hit by the tetherball on his Adam's apple and he passed out.

I panicked. "Rush him to the hospital. I'm on my way."

"We've called the paramedics. Mrs. Kamlani, please stop by the school first."

My office was about an hour's drive from the children's school. I got behind the wheel of my car and sped on Highway 680, heading north. I was not far from my exit when I noticed a big brown car tailing me in my rear-view mirror. An arm stuck out from the driver's side car window and placed a manual blinking light on its roof. Ignoring the flashing light, I kept on driving, for this was a brown unmarked car, not a black-and-white police car. After a short pursuit, I pulled over my navy Honda to the shoulder. The other car pulled up behind me.

A tall, burly middle-aged woman in matronly clothing stepped out and walked up to my car. She flashed an identification badge. It looked official. Then again, how was I to know what an official one looked like? At first, I was hesitant to roll down the window for the woman wore ordinary clothes. Then I opened it a crack.

"You know you were speeding almost ten miles over the speed limit," she reprimanded. "The speed limit is 55 mph."

"I know I was speeding. My son was injured at school and has been rushed to the hospital."

"I've heard such stories before," she said in an intimidating tone.

"If you don't believe me, why don't you follow me?"

"Can I see your driver's license and registration?"

I was reluctant to hand over my documents to someone not in official police attire.

She displayed her police ID once more.

I rolled down the window a bit more and handed her my documents, grudgingly.

"You stay in your car. I'll be right back."

As she walked to her car, I wondered if I would ever see my driver's license again. I kept my nervous eyes fixated at my rearview mirror. Minutes later, the woman returned and handed me a speeding ticket to sign. "Now drive slow. Your son may be injured, but do you want to be another victim, too?"

I was relieved when she returned my driver's license, my registration, and my insurance documents. I took her advice and got back on the road, driving slowly in the right lane this time, allowing her to pass me by.

At the elementary school, the secretary informed me that Ari was back in the classroom.

"Back in the classroom?"

"The paramedics were called in. Your son was resuscitated and returned to his classroom. He's doing fine now. You may take him home, if you want."

I picked up Ari from his classroom and brought him home.

Summer of 1984 was at the door. The children were off from school, but I could not take time off from work. Babysitters were hard to come by this year. Once again we sent the children to spend the summer with my family in Bombay. I handed the passports and tickets to Minal, who was now nine while Ari was seven. Escorted by a flight attendant, they took a flight from San Francisco to New York, and then connected to an Air India flight to Bombay.

The children returned a week before school reopened.

One day Minal suggested we have family conferences to discuss what was on everyone's mind. Thus began our weekly after-dinner discussions at the kitchen table. Everyone got a chance to be heard. Ari loved to raise his hand as he had loads of things he wanted to talk about. Ranjit, who initiated the meeting, would say, "Ari, wait for your turn." However, as time went by, the conferences dwindled until they were held no more.

One day Ari asked, "Mom, how come we don't have family conferences anymore?"

I explained to him that life got hectic and some things just gave. "But Ari sweetheart, if there's anything you want to talk about, Dad and I are always here for you."

If there are any regrets I have in life, it is that of not continuing with these conferences. They had kept the communication channels open in the family. The children had always looked forward to them. The heart-to-heart dialogues gave them an opportunity to air their grievances, talk about anything that was on their minds, and even start planning for their next vacation. It gave them a voice in the family decisions.

I seldom had to discipline my children. They watched me study and they studied. They earned their weekly allowances by performing household chores. Ari mowed the lawn, watered the garden, and took out the garbage. Minal helped with dinner, dishes and household chores. During their elementary school years, I gave the children twenty-five cents a day for allowance, fifty cents in junior high, and a dollar a day in high school. Daily allowance was based on adherence to house rules: Twenty-five cents deducted if they did not make their beds or pick up their dishes after meals; a dollar deducted for uttering a foul word.

"Not fair," they cried when they lost their allowance, but soon they caught on. As teenagers, they also had to be home before dark and keep me informed of their whereabouts at all times.

When Minal slipped into her teens, she became a bit rebellious. She talked too much in her junior high class and received several detentions. A couple of times, I was summoned by the school principal to discuss her behavior. When she started smoking, I was both angry and worried, so I bought her a book on how to quit smoking. It took her a few years to kick the habit.

Despite the hurdles, the California sunshine prevailed.

California Cruising

When life became a bit challenging, weekend family jaunts were invigorating with daytrips to San Francisco. We took a trolley ride to Chinatown for dim-sum and then to Ghirardelli Square, where we browsed through eclectic boutiques and watched acrobats and fire-eaters perform. Then we ambled down to Fisherman's Wharf for fresh seafood with sourdough bread and ended the day with a cruise to the Golden Gate Bridge or dinner at the coastal fishing village of Sausalito.

Sometimes, we took the winding coastal Route 17 to Monterey Bay via Gilroy, then the garlic capital of America, where we stopped at a gourmet shop. It sold practically everything made of garlic, including garlic wine, except for the mixed-nut brittle, which I loved. Along the way, the children waved at the surfers who were heading to Santa Cruz Beach with surfboards on the roofs of their cars. Then they broke into the Beach Boys' surfer songs in the back seat of the car.

Other times, we took Route 101 from San Jose. Although it was a long but less winding road, it offered countryside scenes of strawberry fields in Watsonville, artichoke fields in Castroville, and lettuce and broccoli farms in Salinas. We drove past the oak orchards, the walnut groves and wayside fruit, nut and vegetable stands until we arrived at the coastal hamlet of Monterey.

We visited the Monterey Bay Aquarium and took the children for a paddle-boat ride at a nearby lake. After meandering down the scenic seventeen-mile drive, we stopped at the neighboring town of Carmel and took a stroll down Ocean Avenue to the warm waters of the beach. In the fading daylight, with the wind blowing through our hair and the ocean spray on our faces, we feasted our eyes on a Pacific sunset as the last golden rays gently slipped into the waters.

Some weekends, we sampled wine at Napa Valley wineries or picnicked with our friends at Big Sur, where rugged sea cliffs overlook the sandy shores. We walked through the camping grounds then sat on the rocks to eat our sandwiches and chat while the cool stream ran over our tired feet.

Christmas holidays were savored in Southern California. We stopped at the Hearst Castle in the San Simeon Mountains, at Disneyland, San Diego, Beverly Hills, and Universal Studios where the waters parted for us, as they had done for Moses in the filming of the *Ten Commandments*.

During summer, we piled into a car and left our troubles behind for the cooler air of Lake Tahoe or Yosemite, where we steered around the winding mountains up to the Glacier Point and reveled in the beauty of nature.

One summer, we drove up to the Redwood Forest all the way to the Oregon border, stopped for a break near a lighthouse along the Mendocino coastline, then cruised through the thirty-mile wooded *Avenue of the Giants*. There was barely any traffic on this long scenic drive. We passed a car or two every couple of miles. Driving in the shade of the giant redwoods was like plunging into Robert Frost's serene world of the lovely, dark and deep woods.

While I was at the wheel, Ranjit told the children stories about his childhood days and about his father, who worked as a Director for the Indian Railways. "Every couple of years my father was transferred, so I had to change schools. Then one day, my parents shipped me off to Oak Grove boarding school, so I would not have to change schools every time they moved."

Ranjit recounted the times when he came home for the summer holidays and traveled with his father on business trips. "My father was given a private salon attached to a train."

"What's a salon, Dad?" asked Minal.

"It is a train car . . . a coach. All the other coaches were black, but my father's salon was red. When our family traveled with my father, we had two salons — one for the family, and one for my father and his office staff. They were big."

"How big, Dad?" asked Ari.

"It had a kitchen, a large sitting area, a dining area, and four sleeper booths. Outside the booths was a long corridor. We had a cook and a bearer who served us meals. Sometimes people boarded the train to have a conference with my father."

Ranjit told the children about the time the train stopped in Calcutta (now Kolkotta) and their salon was detached from the train and parked overnight by the station. Some of his relatives who lived in the city came to visit them and spent the night on the train. The next morning, the salon was attached to another train and they took off.

"Did the train have a caboose?" asked Ari.

"Yes, it did." Ranjit then explained to the children that his father was in charge of the railroad tracks and the coal used in the locomotives. He described how his father went back and forth from the locomotive room, where he observed the workers pump more coal to keep the engine running, back to the caboose to make sure the train was not jumping the tracks.

"Jaya, did I tell you about the dearness allowance my father received from the railways?"

"Dearness allowance? No. What kind of allowance is that?"

"It's a British term for allowance given to someone for being away from his dear."

"Very funny." I laughed.

"No, really. It was only given to people who worked for the government."

"So did you read any books on the train?"

"Yes, I read *Mill on the Floss*, Somerset Maugham's *Of Human Bondage* and *Razor's Edge*."

"How come you barely read any books these days?"

"I'm done with reading books. I only like to read newspapers these days."

We drove past signs that read Eureka, a town where many movies of the late nineteenth century gold-rush years were filmed. We zipped by Arcata, once a mining center, where gravel and gold from the mountain ridges washed down into the rivers. During the Gold Rush years in California (1849-1854), people from all over the country came to pan for the yellow nuggets in the riverbeds.

We finally arrived at the thickly wooded Redwood National Park in Crescent City. There in the midst stood a three-hundred-foot tall redwood tree, with a twenty-foot wide drive-through cavity. Then we wandered in the cool shadow of the giants, some over two thousand years old, some with chewed-up trunks. Ari stepped into one of those trunks. Like a squirrel, he pretended to nibble on a nut. His wit often lightened up my day.

"Mom, Dad. Take a picture of me," he called out as we craned our necks to see the crowns of the trees that all but kissed the sky.

Click! We were the new generation of a Norman Rockwell American family.

Saudi Affair

October 1986. It had been six months since I had been working on the Royal Saudi Air Force (RSAF) logistics project in California. One of the company's managers, Marge, who had just returned from a trip to Saudi Arabia, called me to her office. She was the only female manager who worked on the large defense project. Although I did not report to her, we had a good rapport.

"Jay, what are you going to wear for Halloween?" she asked.

"To work? My regular clothes."

"Why don't you wear the black dress I wore to the Saudi market? I'll bring it in tomorrow."

"What about you?"

"I'll find something to wear."

Pointing to the ornate oxidized-silver trinkets that hung on the wall across from her desk, she said, "You can wear the black dress with that jewelry."

On Halloween Day, I went to work dressed in black: a long Bedouin-style gypsy dress, a chiffon headscarf thrown over my head and shoulders, and a face veil that hung from the bridge of my nose. Antique silver ornaments decorated my attire.

At the water cooler I ran into some coworkers, who were also dressed in Halloween costumes, when Earl, a senior project manager, stopped to talk with us. "Jay, I can see you're smiling under that veil."

"How can you tell?"

"From your eyes. They're smiling. I think you should go into the conference room and wish everyone a Happy Halloween."

"Who is in the conference room?"

"The managers. You know them all. Pop in and wish them a Happy Halloween." Turning to Jeff, another consultant on the project, he added, "Why don't you go along with Jay?"

Tall, brawny Jeff had come to work in a camouflage G.I. Joe shirt and a pair of jeans, with an army-green satchel slung over his shoulder. He wore a close-cut beard and dark sunglasses. He carried a rifle and sported the traditional white Arab headdress held in place with a black cord ring. The two of us made our way to the conference room and knocked on the door.

"Come in," said a voice.

We entered a room where a meeting of about twelve male managers was in progress. Bob, my manager, who had served as a navigator on fighter planes in the Vietnam War, was writing something on the white board. I took a bow in my veiled costume and lightly touched my forehead with my fingers, like I had seen Muslim women do when they greeted people in India. All but one face looked familiar, the one sitting directly in front of me. In a flash, Jeff raised his rifle. Pointing it at the managers, he told them to hand over the project.

What in the world is Jeff doing? Why is he pointing the gun at them? This was not part of the plan. We were only supposed to wish them a Happy Halloween.

All at once the mood in the conference room turned somber. Mouths hung open. My manager, who stood by the white board, looked as if he had seen a ghost. No one smiled or said a word. No one in the room had a clue it was Jeff and I under those costumes. Jeff brandished his three-foot rifle. The managers turned pale. He positioned the gun and placed his fingers on the trigger. I held my breath. Seconds ticked. Silence filled the room.

Thanks to Jeff, now both of us are going to be in big trouble.

Jeff pulled the trigger. Water spewed all across the room and on the tables. With hands on their chests, the managers heaved sighs of relief. A squirt of water was better than a spray of bullets, even if it wet their shirts.

I was infuriated at Jeff for pulling such a stunt. Why did he get me involved in his charade? Why didn't he inform me about his ploy? Without saying a word, I bowed out of the room. Jeff followed at my heels.

The meeting adjourned. The managers stepped out of the conference room and learned about our identities.

I ran into Earl in the hallway. "Jay, did you wish the president a Happy Halloween?"

"President? What president?"

"President of the company," said Earl, with an impish smile. "He was in the room, too."

Ouch! That was the only face I did not recognize in the room. Now I was in real hot soup. As a consultant, I could be shown the door right this minute. I was upset at Earl for sending me to the conference room, fuming at Jeff for pulling such a stunt, and angry at myself for having participated.

"Earl, why didn't you tell me the president was also in the conference room?" I asked.

He smiled, as if he had played an April fool joke on me. "But, Jay, did you wish them a Happy Halloween?"

"How could I wish them anything when Jeff pulled the gun on them? He's going to get us both fired."

"Why don't you go in there and wish them a Happy Halloween when they return from their break?"

Has Earl gone nuts? He may be the senior project manager, but he's asking me to commit hara-kiri. And all along I thought we had a wonderful rapport.

Fifteen minutes later, the meeting reconvened. I had to think fast, face management now, without my veil. I had to defuse the situation before it got worse. This was my first consulting assignment. Getting fired by my client could mean the end of my consulting career.

With frail nerves, I returned to the conference room, this time alone, without a veil, chanting a mantra under my breath. A mantra my mother had taught me to say if I was ever in trouble. Mustering courage, I knocked on the door.

"Come in," said a voice.

All eyes were on me as I walked in and confessed, "Now that I have unveiled myself, I want to apologize for interrupting your meeting once again. I want to wish you all a Happy Halloween."

The managers echoed "Happy Halloween" with a cheer.

"We needed that break," said the president.

Phew! One apology and my hands stopped trembling, my heart stopped thumping, and my fears evaporated.

Later that afternoon, as I walked down the hallway, I ran into Bob, my manager. Throwing his arms in the air, he grinned. "Here she comes in baubles, bangles, and beads."

Bill, a towering figure, joined us in the corridor. He and a few managers had recently returned from Saudi Arabia where they had spent a few months on the project. "We thought it was for real. When I saw you in the Bedouin dress, for a moment I was back in Saudi Arabia."

"Back in Saudi Arabia?" I exclaimed.

"We were getting ready to hide under the tables."

"Hide under the tables?" I fell back laughing. "Bill, this was no California earthquake."

Just then George joined us and let out a laugh. "We thought the Saudis were upset at the project delay and had sent the two of you to collect it."

"George, the Saudis would never send an American soldier to check on the project status, especially accompanied by a woman in a Bedouin outfit. They would have sent their officials. Male officials only."

The whole situation was so hilarious. But I could see how, with a gun pointed at them, the managers momentarily lost their sense of bearing. The office environment was also a buzzing rumor mill. Through the grapevine, I learned that the Saudis had extended the project deadline, but threatened heavy penalties for further delays. That explained the panic in the conference room when Jeff asked them to hand over the project.

Several retired NASA employees were brought on board the Saudi project for their knowledge and expertise on air force operations, including Bill, Bob,

Earl, George, and Sid. I learned much from them about planning and scheduling of sorties for flying missions, maintenance of warplanes, aircraft transfers between air bases, quick alert response, and much more.

Although George was usually cheerful, sometimes he broke into coughing spells at work. One day while we discussed the project, I said to him, "You need to see a doctor."

"Jay, I am seeing a doctor. I have lung cancer."

"I'm sorry to hear that."

George's cancer was at an advanced stage. During the Vietnam War, he flew on American planes that sprayed Agent Orange to deforest Vietnamese jungles, so they could locate the enemy. Contact with the chemical agent had contributed to his cancer. As he narrated his story, my heart went out to him.

Although the project was launched in Saudi Arabia, it was later transferred to Silicon Valley for the design and development phase. Several Europeans from England and Ireland had also accompanied the RSAF project from the Kingdom to the valley. Sometimes I joined them for lunch at the hamburger joint nearby. We sat on a bench under the shade of a tree and chatted over charbroiled hamburgers and beer.

From my European colleagues, I heard tales of their lives in the American housing colony in Riyadh: Stories of home-brewing beer parties, even though liquor is prohibited in Saudi Arabia. Stories of Friday afternoons at the town square, known as Chop-Chop Square among the Westerners, where criminals are beheaded for murder or rape, and lashed or jailed for robbery. One of our British colleagues was apprehended by a Saudi cop for speeding on the highway. He was told that the next time it would be jail time for him and his passport would be confiscated. Although women were not permitted to drive in the Kingdom, the Western wives drove within the confines of the American compound.

My two year Saudi affair had come to an end. The project was ready for implementation at all Saudi air bases, just in time for the 1991 Gulf War.

Polynesian Christmas

After a year of working seven days a week between two clients, I was ready for a rejuvenating respite. This year, when Ranjit suggested a Christmas vacation to Hawaii, the children and I could not wait to get on the plane. It would be seven nights in Maui, seven in Kauai.

At the Maui airport, a hostess clad in a traditional *pareau* — wrap around sarong — with *lei* around her neck and red hibiscus in her long dark tresses greeted us. "Aloha! Welcome to Hawaii." She slipped red *leis* over our heads.

We stayed at the Kaanapali Villas in Lahaina, a condominium with a private beach, where the children and I waded every morning in the tropical waters. Adjacent to the condo was the Royal Lahaina Hotel, known for its *luau*, a mini rendition of a Las Vegas style dinner-and-cocktail show. After a sumptuous roast pig dinner, exotic hula and fire dancers entertained the audience.

The following day, we browsed through Hilo Hattie's, a shop that carried a casual collection of traditional long *muu muus*, *pareaus*, capri pants and wide-brimmed straw sunhats. For the men, they had the lovely Hawaiian shirts.

A green grass skirt and shell *lei* caught twelve-year-old Minal's eyes. "Mom, I can wear it for Halloween."

The blond-haired lady at the register noticed our name on the credit card as she wrapped Minal's gifts. "Are you locals?" It was not the first time our last name had been mistaken for Hawaiian.

"No, I'm originally from India, but my children grew up in California."

"Have you been to a luau yet?"

"Yes. Last night we attended the one at the Royal Lahaina."

"You should also go to a traditional luau in town." She gave us directions to get there.

That evening, we went to the open-air luau at the Old Lahaina and joined dozens of people laughing, chatting, and drinking around a large pit, where a pig roasted in a traditional *imu*, an underground oven. After the pig was cooked, we took our seats at the picnic tables. There must have been over two hundred people at the event. Under a twilight sky and dimly-lit grounds, we feasted on a spread of Polynesian cuisine of roast pig and *poi* — taro roots mashed to a paste, *mai tai* cocktails, and much more.

After dinner, the Samoan fire and knife performers took the stage. Drums rolled. Ukuleles strummed. Feathered gourds rattled. Brass clappers clanked. Next, ebony-haired hula dancers in coconut-shell bras, grass skirts, and *leis* took their places on the platform. With a gentle sway of their hips to Tahitian music, their feet moved gently side-to-side and their hands flowed in harmony as they danced to the legendary tales of the islands and Don Ho's "Tiny Bubbles" and "Pearly Shells."

When the announcer requested hula dance volunteers to come up to the stage, Minal and Ari raised their hands, "My Mom! My Mom!"

"Shhh! Not me," I whispered.

The children ignored me and continued volunteering on my behalf.

The announcer looked in our direction. "Will the mom please rise?"

"No, not me," I declined. "I don't know how to do the hula dance."

"Don't worry. We'll teach you. Come on up here."

"Go, Mom, go," cheered Minal and Ari.

"Go, Mom, go," chanted the audience in chorus, thumping on their dinner tables.

Ranjit joined the cheer. I finally caved in, as they would not stop cheering. Weaving my way between the long dinner benches, I walked up to the elevated platform and joined the other hula dancers, where we were handed red leis and dry-grass skirts to slip over our clothes. As the drums rolled and the music played, hips and hands sashayed in tune to the gentle Hawaiian music.

Dear me, what we do to see a smile on our children's faces! We lose a board game to them intentionally and say, "I can't believe you're so smart." We play Santa Claus and eat up the cookies left on the plate for the man from the North Pole. We even perform the hula dance.

For Christmas week, Maui was decked in festive lighting, and carolers drew large crowds at the town square gazebo every evening. There was plenty to do in Maui besides shopping for Hawaiian shirts and hula skirts.

A road trip to Hana was a full-day venture. We made an early start, filled up our gas tank, and asked the man at the Hasegawa general store for directions. Along the forty-mile drive to the tropical paradise, we drove past pineapple and taro fields, bamboo forests, sugarcane and banana plantations. We snaked around the scenic coastal route and took in breathtaking views of the ocean and the sea cliffs, tropical rain forests and waterfalls, some that cascaded and emptied into the pools. The road to Hana was filled with spectacular landscapes, but it was narrow and steep and spiked with daunting hairpin curves, like the ones along Big Sur on Route 1 in California.

As the road leveled, Ranjit pointed to a large house on the beach. "That's Carol Burnett's house, the one the man at the general store was talking about. He said many movie stars have their second homes here."

Another day we took a cruise around the pineapple island of Lanai and the island of Molokai, where some eight thousand lepers had been shipped from China during the nineteenth century, to live out their lives on the Kalaupapa peninsula. The tour guide explained how the boats dropped off the lepers and food supplies for them at the shore. Although leprosy — now known as Hansen's Disease — does not pose the same threat today, he mentioned that the survivors' families continued to live in mountainside shelters in isolation, even though they were no longer contagious. Their only means of transport was by mule or on foot.

As the tour guide narrated the history of the Hawaiian colony, I recalled the lepers I had often seen as a youngster back home in Bombay. Even though they were covered from their heads to their toes, I could see large boils on the small exposed parts of their faces and hands. In front of them sat a metal bowl or a sheet of newspaper for alms.

"Always say a prayer for people who suffer," my mother said to me as she untied her handkerchief and dropped some change into their bowls.

I always admired my parents' compassionate nature. I am grateful it rubbed off on me.

After a splendid Christmas week in Maui, we took a flight to Kauai, where we were lavished with more leis at the airport. We spent a week at the Hilton Hotel on the private beach. We waded in the Pacific waters and drove by the verdant rain forests and the emerald green mountains. The island was blessed with passing showers almost every day during our stay. One moment it rained; the next hour the clouds had moved on. Some evenings, while I watched the children frolic in the shallow pool, I lounged with a Margarita and listened to music at the cabana. Instantly, I felt my stresses melt away. I am glad Ranjit had planned a Hawaiian vacation this year.

One crystal clear morning, we chartered a small aircraft. I had taken a scenic helicopter ride before, but this was my maiden flight on a private plane. Ranjit sat in the front seat with the pilot; the children and I sat behind. We flew over the coastal cliffs and the pristine blue waters of Na Pali Coast. The ocean appeared greener by the tropical forests. The pilot soared over Waimea Canyon — the Grand Canyon of the Pacific — the walls of which glowed in a spectrum of colors in the late morning sun. As we sailed through the skies, the pilot pointed to something in the distance, "That's the Haleakala volcano crater."

Another rise, another dive, another twist of the plane and my stomach churned. I could have taken in all the panoramic beauty of James Michener's Hawaii if only the pilot did not try so many aeronautical stunts. I tossed a glance at Ranjit, who chatted with the pilot. He appeared to savor every moment of the ride. With one arm wrapped around Minal who gazed out the window, another around ten-year-old Ari, who had his head in my lap, I prayed. The whole family was on the aircraft. Who was this pilot? Did he think he was a Blue Angel?

The man at the controls must have read the look on my face in his rear-view mirror. He steadied the plane and looked back. "You see there," he said, pointing to a range of remote mountains. "They are the Bali Hai Mountains where the *South Pacific* movie was filmed. Have you seen the movie?"

"Yes … yes, we've seen the movie," I replied, despite my frazzled nerves. "I can see the misty blue mountains. I can even hear the music of "Some Enchanted Evening.""

We had been in the air for an hour and a half when the pilot asked, "Ma'am, do you want to see any more?"

Did I want to see any more? "No thanks. Just land." The wild twists and dives had broken me into a cold sweat. I looked for a plastic bag in the seat pocket. There were none. I glanced at the children. Their faces were pale. They had not said a word on the plane.

The pilot took a sharp turn and pointed at the squares and rectangles on the sweeping terrain below. "You see those parcels of land down there? They belong to the farmers."

Yes, yes, I could see the farm and all. I wish he would land, even if it had to be on someone's farmland.

The two-hour daunting experience finally came to an end. As we stepped off the plane on the tarmac, I sighed with relief to feel the ground under my trembling feet.

"How was it?" Ranjit beamed.

"I'm never going to fly on a small plane again."

The next morning, after a passing shower, we drove north, past Hanalei Bay to the oceanfront golf resort of Princeville. After yesterday's wild and wacky plane ride, the road trip was a delightful welcome.

On New Year's morning, we drove south to the busy Poipu Beach. Over champagne brunch at the Sheraton Hotel, we watched beach lovers swim in the cobalt waters and others bronze themselves on the sun-burnished sands.

"Mom, I don't want a babysitter anymore. I'm almost twelve," said Minal. "The babysitters don't do anything for us. They're always talking on the phone or watching TV. Sometimes they call their friends over."

"They don't read to us like you do," Ari piped in. "They don't help us with our homework."

"Mom, you don't have to worry about Ari. I can take care of him."

"We can get them a dog," said Ranjit. "A German Shepherd will make a good bodyguard and the kids will have a dog to play with."

A dog? The children were so excited.

Upon our return from Hawaii, we drove up to see a breeder near San Francisco and brought home a six-week-old German Shepherd to look after the children while we were at work.

Ginger, our feisty little pup, played Frisbee with the children, yodeled to the harmonica, and dug a big hole under the backyard fence to play with the neighbor's dog. She drove Minal to tears when she chewed on her sandals, her new Swatch watch, and even her math paper.

Our little shepherd also knew how to win our hearts. She would pick snails from the backyard and drop them at Minal's feet as a gift for her. When Ginger was little, she stayed indoors and slept in the laundry room, and Ari would sit on the washing machine and sing her a lullaby until she was fast asleep. When she was six months old, she slept in a big doghouse in the backyard.

On Sunday mornings, the children and I took Ginger to an obedience class at the Menlo Park Schutzhund Club grounds, where police officers also brought their shepherds for training. She even walked with me at a dog show and won an Honorable Mention green ribbon. The judge said she could have fared better if only her coat were not so dry. So I took her to the vet, who prescribed mineral oil to be added to her meals. *Voilá*! In a couple of months her coat developed a lovely sheen.

"Mom, Ginger was the best Christmas gift we ever got," the children reminded me for years.

Don't Let Life Pass You By

Wake up to the bubble of the percolator,
Savor your coffee, read the morning paper.
Then take a walk in your primrose glasses,
If it rains, slip on your yellow galoshes.

If perchance the world gets under your skin,
You can always count on your kith and kin.
If on your journey you reach an impasse,
Remember, like all storms, this too shall pass.

Live every moment with dare and passion,
Like a river rushing to meet the big ocean.
Scale another mountain, sail another sea,
Follow your dreams, whatever they may be.

- Jaya Kamlani

A Closed Mind

Following the Saudi project, I consulted on two more. I worked long hours and weekends to bring in extra money for our dream house. We bought a small parcel of land on the Fremont hills, on which we planned to build a large custom home. While I looked for my next project, Ranjit suggested I look for a regular job, so I would not have to constantly look for assignments.

"Why don't you apply at my company?"

I took his advice and sent in my resume. While he worked for the networks division at one location, I applied for a systems job in the Sales and Marketing division at another location in the same town, Cupertino.

After interviewing for two full days at Tandem Computers, I got the job as a senior systems engineer to work on their new customer management system. During the interview, the director of the department informed me the job required 20 percent travel to the company's European offices. "Would that be a problem for you?"

"No. Not at all."

The company, known for its "NonStop" computer systems used by banks and stock exchanges, was also known for its Friday afternoon beer-bust parties and healthy employee culture.

A month after I was on board, a senior staff engineer of the company was scheduled to present the Magellan product to a large crowd at the company's cafeteria. I took an aisle seat. Rod, who was passing by, asked if the seat to my right was taken.

"No." I rose to let him in. Two days earlier, Rod had stopped by my cubicle to briefly introduce himself as my new manager. He had just joined the company that week, a month after I did. Until then, I was reporting to the director who had interviewed and hired me.

We exchanged some pleasantries and then he asked, "How long have you been with the company?"

"A month."

"Where were you working before?"

"I was consulting for the last few years."

"What college did you attend?"

"St. Xavier's College, University of Bombay. And you?"

"U.C. Berkeley." He paused, looked around the dining hall. "So you're from India?"

"Yes."

He stood up, glanced around as if he were looking for someone, then sat down and tossed some more questions at me. "What did you major in?"

"English Literature. Then I did a one-year course in advertising in New York. Later, I took many classes in computer science and manufacturing. And you?"

"Physics." He craned his head once more. "I once had an Indian professor in college."

"That's interesting. Berkeley had Indian professors back then?"

"Yes, but he and I did not get along well."

"I'm sorry to hear that."

"We had communication problems. After that, I did not take to Indians."

I almost fell off my chair. *Didn't the man hear me mention that I was from India?* Stunned by his unwarranted revelation, I pursed my lips, holding the urge to say something I might regret later. From that moment, I stayed on guard around Rod. There seemed to be something uncanny about the man.

In the weeks that followed, our department went through a reorganization. The director who had hired me was let go. I would miss reporting to him. John was brought in as the new Information Technology Director of the Sales and Marketing department.

One morning, Rod called me to his office. I walked in with a manila folder with copies of the systems design I had been working on. A couple of minutes into the conversation, he asked, "Jay, what are your future plans at the company?"

"I want to lead a piece of the project."

Brushing his four fingers horizontally across his forehead, he grimaced, "Jay, you don't have leadership written on your forehead."

I don't have leadership written on my forehead? Rod's hawkish colors were showing again. How did he know I did not have leadership qualities, when he had not even seen my work? He had no clue what I had been working on. The last time he spoke with me was in the cafeteria, when he said he did not take to Indians.

Why such hostility? Why brush me off at every opportunity? It is not that I had arrived from India yesterday. I had been living in America for almost twenty-five years. I did not have a heavy Indian accent. I dressed like any other professional woman and wore my hair in a soft bob.

With my hand on the manila folder, I said, "Rod, I'd like to show you what I have been working on."

He stood up, glanced at his watch and waved my words away. "Jay, I have to go to a meeting now."

In five minutes, the meeting was over. The folder with the systems design I had worked on with the user management team lay unopened on the table. Disappointed, I picked it up and left. *A closed mind is like a closed book, just a block of wood.*

Later that week, rumors swirled that John and Rod intended to bring in a project team of their own. Perhaps they were trying to cash in on the company's new recruitment policy. The company was growing in leaps. Signs posted outside the company's cafeteria and in the building corridors offered up to $ 7,000 bounty for referral of senior employees, who were hired.

A few days later, Rod put together a team of twelve members from the project group. They were to visit the company's European offices for two weeks for the global sales project that I was working on. My name was conspicuously missing from the list.

That summer of 1989, the team took off for Europe. I was the only senior member in the group left behind, other than a systems manager who sent a young woman on his behalf. She had no prior information technology work experience and had only recently graduated from U.C. Berkeley, Rod's alma mater.

When the group returned from Europe, John, the director, had a one-on-one meeting with all project-team members. During his conversation with me, he posed the usual management question: "Jay, where do you see yourself at the company a year from now?"

"I see myself as a project lead on the Customer Management system." The global sales-order management system included many sub-components. I had worked on such systems before.

"Have you spoken with Rod about it?"

"Yes, I have."

"What did he say?"

I worked up the nerve to cite my unpleasant meeting with Rod.

"I'll talk to him when he returns from Chicago," said the director.

A day after he returned from Europe, Rod left to visit the company's Chicago office. When he returned, he hired a young woman whom he referred to as "a lady friend I worked with at my previous place of employment." I sensed he had hired her to replace me, because this was also the week he had called me to his office and said, "Jay, you should look for another job."

Look for another job? Just like that, out of the blue. No warning. No explanation. This was only my second meeting with him in his office. He had still not seen any of my work and did not know what I had been working on. The nerve of him to ask me to look for another job when he had barely been with the company two months himself — one month of which he had been away on business trips, and the other he had spent planning for them and getting oriented with the company and the staff.

Undaunted, I marched up one flight of stairs and reported the matter to the personnel manager, who then had a talk with Rod.

Following a department meeting one afternoon, I found four male employees gathered in the hallway discussing Rod. A manager from our German office, who was visiting our project team that week, referred to him as "incompetent" for having suggested at the meeting that the company's reports be printed in California and shipped to each European office.

"The shipping costs will add up," said one employee.

"The information will be obsolete when I receive it," said the manager from Germany, who explained they had already been printing reports on site, as needed.

Bigot or incompetent, either way I was not happy with Rod. When he gave me bad performance reviews, I discovered I had company. Steve, the project leader, with more than ten years' tenure at the company, had his own barrel of grievances with management. Both Steve and I were senior members on the team. Many senior staff engineers at the company made more money than first level managers. Being a Silicon Valley technology company, it promoted a parallel growth path for software and hardware engineers as well as for management.

One afternoon, the director's secretary called to say he wanted to see me. I walked into John's office and found him sitting with folded arms and a grim look on his face. I had barely taken a seat when he asked, "How are things coming along between you and Rod?"

"Not good."

We talked a bit about the project. Midstream in our conversation, the director, who was usually self-composed, shot off, "Jay, you're making too much money." Then stroking his chin, he peered over his wire-rimmed eyeglasses and searched my face for reaction.

All at once, hostile silence filled the room. His remark had caught me off guard. I sat there stunned, for I had just bumped my head on the glass ceiling. Until that afternoon, I had no reservations about him. Now, my first instinct was to challenge him. *Too much money for whom? Too much money for an*

Indian? Too much money for a woman? Then again, I resisted the urge to say something I might regret later.

In a lighter vein I said, "John, I was making much more money as a consultant, before I joined this company."

"Then why did you quit consulting?"

"I got tired of looking for assignments. So I settled for a regular job that paid much less. But that was my decision."

The conversation continued in circles, at the end of which I realized I had fared no better with the director than I had done with my manager. If the commander and the general are no good, the soldier must still do what is expected of him, or her. I soldiered on into the next year.

I felt fortunate to be living in a valley of visionaries, innovators, and trailblazers in technology. A valley of the giants. A valley of the nerds. A valley where the first silicon chip was designed for computers and Apple and MAC personal computers were developed.

While the town of Cupertino, where I worked, was flush with campuses of Hewlett Packard, Tandem Computers and Apple, the city of Menlo Park was thriving with venture capitalists, such as Kleiner Perkins. At Xerox Parc, a research and development division of Xerox, Stanford University graduates and local companies jointly developed technology products.

A few years earlier, I had taken the APICS certification manufacturing classes offered by Foothill College of Los Altos, California. I learned about production, forecasting, shop floor control, inventory management and materials requirement planning. I learned about Bill-of-Materials required to build a product and about cost accounting. I learned about the Japanese just-in-time manufacturing concepts to prevent inventory build-up, about *kaizen* and continuous improvement and total quality control on the shop floor. For years thereafter, I held on to the manuals filled with my handwritten notes. They became my Bible and came in handy when I worked on manufacturing or purchasing systems.

The valley's innovative spirit and its culture of teamwork rubbed off on me. For a long time, I even toyed with the idea of creating a collection of entrepreneur cards, one for every founder of a Silicon Valley company. Like baseball cards, students could trade them and learn about the valley's great trailblazers.

On the opening day in 1990, I took the children to the "The Garage," now known as the San Jose Tech Museum. I remember that balmy day vividly. Having worked in a high tech environment, I wanted to expose Minal and Ari to the valley's innovations. I hoped the pioneering spirit would rub off on them at an early age.

To the left of the entrance was a semiconductor fab model room with demonstrations on chip-making processes. Adjacent to it stood a booth with exhibits of the Hubble telescope. I was disappointed the gene-splicing biotech workshop was closed, and we had to pass up the 3-D experience at the IMAX movie theater as the children were getting restless. After a snack break, I took them to the Children's Discovery Museum across the street, where they enjoyed participating in hands-on science and technology experiments.

Thus, life went on one day at a time; some days better than others.

One afternoon that December, I received a call at work that my father had passed away in Bombay. He was eighty-six. It had been six years since I last saw him. For days and weeks following his loss, my heart was flooded with memories of him and his caring ways. He always made sure we were well fed, well dressed, and did not fall back in our studies.

I remembered the evenings Kamal and I accompanied him when he ran errands for the home. Along the way, we often stopped by the Paradise Bakery where he bought us butter cookies and delicious French pastries; other times he treated us at the ice cream parlor across the street. This evening, we stopped by the *mithai* shop. While my father carried on a conversation with the potbellied *mithaiwallah*, my sister and I feasted our eyes on a colorful array of mouth-watering treats: milk and nuts *mithai*, tempting swirly *jalebies*, irresistible *gulab jamuns,* and delicious spongy *rasgullas* in syrup. My father bought us whatever our hearts desired. An array of Indian sweets would be dessert for the family tonight.

Later, when I visited home with little ones of my own, my father told me of the times he would save some of his lunch for me, so I would have plenty to eat when I returned from college. Touched by his revelation, I was lost for words. All I did then was smile with gratitude. Now, as I remembered my father, I wished I could turn back the clock, if only for a day, to bid him farewell and say, "Thanks, Dada. Thanks for everything you did for me."

The next day at work, the director stopped by my cubicle to pay his condolences. He probably heard about it from Steve, my project leader. He informed me that the company allows two days off for death in the family. I thanked the director for his kind gesture, but told him I did not need any time off as my father was to be cremated that day in India. As he sat there in the spare chair and lent me his ears, I don't know what came over me, but I talked to him about my father. That afternoon, I made the connection with John, the family man. For those few moments, he dropped his corporate guard and I saw a softer side of him. He told me about his daughters. On his way out, he reminded me again that I could take some time off if I wanted.

On the other hand, Rod never stopped by to pay his condolences.

In the weeks that followed, when I returned home from work in the evenings, I heard the latest news on the Gulf War on television, watched scud missiles fly from Iraq to Israel, and oil fires burn in Kuwait. All day long, I saw war: War in the Middle East, war at work, struggles at home. When Bette Midler's "From a Distance" played on the car radio, I got teary-eyed. My nerves were so frayed that anything and everything drove me to tears.

Disheartened by the hopeless situation at work, I called an agent who had placed me on a consulting project in the past. The following week, I interviewed with a client in Oakland. When the offer came through, I mentioned it to my husband.

"Jaya, don't take on a consulting assignment now."

"Why not?"

"Because of the war. Times are bad. What assurance do you have the project will not be cancelled once you start work? At least now you have a secure job."

"What secure job? Right now my job is less secure than a consulting assignment."

"I'm telling you, hang in there and fight it." He returned his gaze to the television, as he sat there in his favorite armchair with the remote control in his hand.

"Oh Ranjit, you're the rock of Gibraltar, but these big corporate honchos are waiting to chew me up."

As the fires raged in the oil fields of Kuwait, I tried to weather the firestorm at work. I followed my husband's advice and turned down the consulting assignment.

In late February of 1991, the Desert Storm calmed. A ray of sunshine peeped through the Gulf clouds and ceasefire was declared between the Arab neighbors. But here in my corporate world, hostility lingered. No truce. No détente. Even as I fretted and fumed, I could almost hear my father say, "Don't worry, Baby. This, too, shall pass."

Thus, life went on one day at a time, hoping better days were around the bend.

Early one morning, Steve and I met in Rod's office to review a complex design I had worked on. After reviewing the details that explained how the company's databases could be kept in sync with our European offices, Rod complimented me on my work.

The next morning, the Human Resources Director called me to his office and said my manager, Rod, had complained of his dissatisfaction with my job performance and asked that I be discharged from the company.

What insanity is this? A day after complimenting me on my work, he wants to throw me out of the company. In how many different ways is the man trying to skin me?

To my good fortune, I had a witness: Steve, my project leader.

Enraged by the turn of events, I suggested to the Human Resources Director that he confer with Steve who was sitting by me when Rod had praised my work only the morning before. I also proposed he talk to the business managers with whom I had worked on the system design.

When the truth unfolded, Rod's cesspool of lies put *him* in the spotlight.

I was further astounded by the project leader's revelation one morning as we stepped out of the small conference room called the "war room" where we had a one-on-one meeting. "Jay, if you think I am being tough on you these days, it's because John told me I was being too easy on you."

My mouth fell open. The director was trying to pit Steve and me against each other. I was furious. "Tell John he should come and see how tough you've been on me lately. I wondered why your attitude towards me had suddenly changed."

Steve walked into his cubicle, located across from mine, opened his desk drawer and pulled out the company's "Diversity at Workplace" poster. He then tacked it to the outside of his cubicle.

As I walked into the grocery store one weekend, I was struck with nostalgia when I heard *Walk Don't Run* playing over the store's music system. In a flash, I was back to St. Xavier's College in Bombay when tall, handsome Malcolm Mazumdar strummed on his electric guitar on the auditorium stage and mesmerized the audience with music by The Ventures. Wheeling my grocery cart between aisles, I savored the moment and hummed along. The fleeting escape to my carefree college days comforted me all day. If only I could bring back the magic of those days.

Weekends with the family helped me forget my miseries at work. Come Monday, the blues were back again. I wallowed in despair, seeking refuge in my cubicle, pretending all would be fine the next day. But wishing does not make ugly things go away. They would still be there the next day. If things had to change, it was up to me to make them happen. It was time for that Hail Mary pass.

I sent an email to the founding president and CEO of the company. It got his attention. He was known to be fair-minded. In the weeks that followed, he sent out a companywide online survey. When the department director revealed the survey results at a meeting, I discovered I was not alone. Several other employees from our project group had also lodged complaints against the management. A spark had kindled a fire, prompting an investigation by the company's CEO. The morale sank deeper as managers of another division interviewed my department staff for an entire week.

That summer, most employees in the department took an optional day off to extend their vacation that ran into a long weekend. A few of us came in to the office. While I worked on my project, I sent three pages of it to the printer located in a small room across from Rod's office. When I went to retrieve my printout, I found the laser printer spitting out reams of pages of a genealogy report. Just then Rod walked in. With a quick nod, he took the thick stack from the printer and left. The android continued to churn out more of *his* ancestral tree. I got tired waiting and returned to my desk.

Fifteen minutes later, I returned to the little room. Good Heavens! The man must be tracing his roots all the way to Adam and Eve. And for this he would be paid his wages for the day. I waded through the stack to find my three pages. There they were, wedged in the pile of paper. I recalled the time when he had boasted to some young women of our department that he could trace his ancestry to British royalty through genealogy software.

Aha! He thinks he has blue blood. Next, he might want to be knighted. Blue blood, huh? Bah humbug. I plucked a few leaves from his family tree and walked towards my cubicle. Along the way, I tossed his royal link in a trashcan, far from his office.

As I walked into the cafeteria for lunch on this Monday, I was surprised to find a jukebox playing oldies. The company was celebrating its tenth anniversary and a major business milestone that week. Later that afternoon, I returned to the cafeteria, scanned through the music list on the jukebox and played Ivory Joe Hunter's "Since I Met You Baby." I had not heard the song for decades. As the record slipped out of its slot and gently dropped onto the turntable, I took a seat at a nearby lunch table, sipped on my coffee, and let my heart soak in the melancholy notes. "Since I met you Baby, my whole life has changed. And everybody tells me that I am not the same. . ."

I fought back the tears and played my childhood song again. This time I let the tears trickle down my cheeks. Where had all those years gone? The struggles of life had become so overwhelming. I felt so alone, no one to tell my troubles to.

When the music stopped playing, I refilled my coffee cup, put on a Fats Domino record to cheer me up and hummed along, "I found my thrill on Blueberry Hill. . ." Then I went to the restroom, washed my face, pinched my cheeks, and returned to my cubicle.

All week long I visited the cafeteria, helped myself to some coffee and sat back and listened to the old melodies. Come Monday, the jukebox in the cafeteria was gone. I felt like a five-year-old who wakes up one morning and finds Frosty the Snowman is no more.

Days dragged by. Tensions between management and me continued to escalate. Rod did not include me on project meetings any more. When the situation became insufferable, I went through the company's official channels to file a complaint. Then I hit another snag. I learned that the entire chain-of-command — the director, the vice-president and the executive vice-president of the department — had all flown in from the same cuckoo's nest. No wonder my grievances fell on deaf ears.

Weeks dragged by. By now my spirits had sunk so low, I did not care what happened. I did not care how I dressed. For the first time I went to work in old clothes that I usually wore to wash out the garage or walk my dog.

One day I was asked to go through the company's arbitration process. I spent three half-days with a female manager from another department. I felt as if I was in a therapist's office as I told her my story, beginning with day one on the job at the company. Although I had no interaction with this manager before, she lent me her ears and put me at ease. I told her I had two binders of notes on the situation. She asked me to bring them in so she could make copies of them. "I will return the binders to you."

I did not respond. I had no intention of turning in all my evidence to her.

While she took down notes, at one point she said, "I'm glad he's not my manager." That was enough of a clue to tell me how she would report her findings.

One afternoon I received a call that the vice president wanted to see me in his office. Every time I was called in to see a company executive, visions of a pink slip danced in front of me. I wondered what the tea leaves would read today.

When I informed Steve about my meeting with the vice president, he dropped a hint: "Make sure Rod doesn't lose his job."

Rod, lose his job? And here I thought I was going to lose mine. Did Steve know something I didn't? A litany of thoughts raced through my mind.

My stomach knotted as I walked into the vice president's office. His friendly smile put me at ease. This was my second meeting with him on this matter. A few moments into our conversation he asked, "Jay, what changes would you like to see in your department?"

What changes would I like to see in my department? Was this a joke or a calculated move?

With Steve's words still ringing in my ears, I replied, "I don't want Rod to lose his job. He's a family man. Just reprimand him. I think he has learned his lesson. Give him another chance."

The vice president then sprang another surprise on me. "What else can I do for you to make you stay on at the company?"

I almost fell off my chair. That was two wishes in a row. Me, stay on at the company? What changes would I like to see? All this time they wanted to get rid of me. Now they wanted to accommodate me. I wondered if management was up to more tricks today.

All at once, a thought occurred to me. Since the door had opened a crack, I worked up the courage to say, "Everyone in my group got a raise, but me."

"How much of a raise are you looking for?"

I had split open a piñata and had no idea what would fall out. "I heard the average raise was four-percent this year. But, considering the circumstances, three-percent will do. Had I been given better opportunities, I would have proven myself and asked for more."

On my way out, the vice president said, "Jay, if you don't see the three-percent raise in your next paycheck, then you should see it in the following one."

"Thanks. I appreciate it," I said, still dizzy from the turn of events. It was not the salary increase that mattered. The three-percent did not amount to much, considering one-percent of it would go to Uncle Sam, but I felt vindicated. Although I had won this round, the real battle still lay ahead.

A couple of weeks later, I was called in by the department's executive vice president. He appeared to be in no mood to listen to me. In a few minutes, the meeting was done. He said he had another appointment. I wondered why he bothered to see me at all if he had less than five minutes to spare.

Soon Steve, my project leader, transferred to another division of the company, at a different location. Tired of battling his own troubles with management, he decided it was time to move on. With him gone, I was next on the hit list. Still, I was undaunted, for I could always bounce back as an independent consultant and select the projects I wanted to work on.

One afternoon, Rod called me to his office and asked me to turn over everything I had been working on.

"Everything?"

"Yes, everything. I also want you to write down the file names where your work can be found on the computer."

With all my assignments whisked away from me, I was a soldier relieved of my duties. I had no choice but to oblige, for he was my manager. Surely, he could not be acting alone. He must have the director's support.

It came as no surprise when Rod took credit for all my work. But his Machiavellian plot did not succeed. The business managers of several departments had been working with me for a long time on it. *How could he conveniently stamp his name on my work? Did he have no sense of ethics? Did he think he had a free pass to lie and cheat his way up the corporate ladder?*

Nothing uplifted me these days, not even my favorite songs. Disheartened, I dreaded to go to work. At the office, I walked to the water cooler for the third time, checked my email for the fifth time and looked at my wristwatch for the tenth time. The hands had barely moved. The pink slip appeared to be inching closer. Any day now, it would be at my door.

Then one afternoon, the director arranged a meeting between Rod and me at his office. As I knocked on the door, through the long glass panel I noticed the two men deep in conversation.

"Come in," said the director.

I took a deep breath and braced for the worst as I entered the room and slipped into the chair beside Rod. Save for a short stack of documents neatly piled on one side, the desk was bare. A white writing board on the wall was wiped clean. A large window offered a view of a few treetops and a crystalline sky.

The director broke the awkward silence with a faux smile, "Well Jay, …."

Rod leaned against the wall, arms crossed, with a look that said: *I dare you. I dare you to spill the beans.*

I felt his hostile eyes upon me. Any moment now, I expected fireworks. It was time to spill my heart or forever remain silent.

The exposé may have been too much for Rod's ears. He smirked, he snickered, and then he snapped, "Why don't you go back to consulting?"

His devious frown, his provocative remark, his audacity cut through me like glass. The air grew thick in the room. The match had been struck, the fires fanned, and I was one percolating cauldron. I had looked forward to an olive branch this afternoon; instead it turned out to be an all-out war. My jaws tightened, my ears burned, my cheeks felt flush. It was now my turn to let him know I was not intimidated by him.

Pulling myself together, I brushed aside my fears. Turning to Rod, I asked, "Are you telling me to leave the company *again*?"

He fell silent, but showed no remorse.

I summoned the courage to ask the director, who sat there with a poker face, "John, is this what *you* also want me to do?"

"Do what?"

"Do *you* also want me to quit the company?"

"No, I didn't say that. *He* said it. Don't include me." John shrugged his shoulders, pushed his eyeglasses up then folded his arms.

Sparks flew across the room. My eyes darted between the two men as if I were watching a ping-pong game. They exchanged esoteric glances. *Aha! They think this is a game, but I'm not going to roll over for anyone. I'm not going to let them break me. I can handle these honchos myself, if I must. I have nothing to lose but my job. If it comes to that, then I can always bounce back and return to consulting.*

"It's true. Rod said it, not you," I said to the director. "But he said it on your behalf as well. You've been in on this with him right from the start. I brought these problems to your attention from day one, yet you continued to side with him."

Outside the second floor window, the leaves on the treetops swayed gently under the California sun. Just then Rod rose from his seat, sulking. He excused himself and stepped out of the room, trying to avoid eye contact with me.

I slipped off my chair as well, but the director beckoned me to stay. "Jay, I want to talk with you."

I got that sinking feeling in my stomach again.

"Jay, if I asked you what is the one thing you do not like to work on, what would you say?"

Aha! This is a trap. Leaning forward, I rested my arms on the table, met his gaze and said, "I was hired as a senior systems analyst. If you assign me analysis and design work, I have no problem."

"I'm trying to figure what tasks to assign you. What if I gave you a programming task?"

Oh, he's rubbing salt on my wounds. But I'm not going to let him see me sweat. I had spent my time in the trenches. I did not have to stay there forever. Gathering courage, I let the words spill out. "Then I would tell you it's not the job I was hired for. When I interviewed for this position, I was assured it involved no programming. If it had, I would have not accepted the job. If you really must know, the one task I don't like being assigned is programming. I paid my dues long ago. I have no intentions to return to it and lose more sleep."

"Why? Did you lose sleep when you were a programmer?"

He leaned his elbow on the table and rested his face on his hand. How was the man to know what programmers go through? Although both my manager and my director worked for technology companies before, they had a business background, not a technical one.

"Yes, I had many sleepless nights. But those days are behind me. I have moved on to other things."

"Such as?"

"Business analysis and system design. John, we don't stay in the same position forever. We grow."

A soft gaze eased over his face, but I hesitated to let my guard down. The storm had abated for now. No olive branch. No pink slip either. I returned to my cubicle, sank in my chair, ran my fingers through my hair and stared vacantly at the computer screen in front of me. The emotional drama in the director's office had left me reeling. I longed for a generous portion of a luscious blueberry-topped cheesecake. I glanced at the hands on the clock. Oh, how slowly they moved.

As time passed, I noticed some changes at the workplace, as my management tried to get the house in order. The employee survey sent out by the company's CEO apparently had some impact. At a department meeting, the director recognized the only other Indian employee, a software engineer, for her work. This was the second month in a row he had acknowledged her. He had never done that before.

There was also a reorganization in the department. Much to everyone's surprise, a young Chinese woman named Charlene received a major promotion. She now had several first-level managers and some senior staff members reporting to her, including Rod and me. Even though I had been passed by, my heart sang for the two young Asian women. I am sure this was the result of my reporting the matter to the CEO, his companywide survey, and his involvement. Tables had turned. Roles had reversed. Derailed by his barefaced lies, Rod's authority was stripped away. I told Charlene if things did not improve for me at the company, I would report the matter to the Equal Employment Opportunity Commission (EEOC).

One Monday in October, the autumn winds whisked off more than the leaves on the trees. They had also blown a leaf off the corporate tree. The nameplate outside Rod's office was gone. His royal chambers stood empty. His peccadilloes had finally caught up with him. The man fell into the same bear trap he had set up for me. Through the grapevine I heard he had come in over the weekend and cleaned out his desk. The man who had heaped a plethora of misery on me was finally out of my life. I hoped our paths would never cross again.

To my chagrin, my euphoria was short-lived. Life did not improve for me after Rod's departure. The rising tide gathered speed. Now that John had lost his right-hand man, he was not going to forgive me. He stopped me from attending meetings with user management and sent someone else in my place.

This I learned from two business managers who told me they had specifically asked for my presence at the meetings.

One day the noose around my neck tightened. I was assigned junior-level programming work as if I were a college grad hire enrolled in a training program. All my previous years of experience were totally discounted. I was also asked to enroll in programming classes at a local college. No wonder my director had looked for my reaction when he asked me, "What if I gave you a programming task?"

I had great aspirations, and here my director was hell bent on sending me back light years and treating me like a rookie. It was naïve of me to think I could emerge from this corporate mess unscathed. However, I was determined to be the protruding nail that refused to be hammered down. I ignored the college-level program assigned to me. I called to make an appointment with an EEOC representative in San Jose, but they could only see me after the Christmas and New Year holidays.

I decided to look for a consulting project, but when I came in to work after the holidays I found someone had broken into my desk. I reported the matter to the personnel manager. That Friday, I met with the EEOC representative at her office and filed a complaint against my company. When I told her that my manager, Rod, had been let go, she looked me in the eye and said, "You had heads rolling? You single-handedly managed to get heads rolling?"

"I don't see it that way. Soon my head might be rolling, too."

The following Tuesday, before I could find myself a project, the inevitable happened. Charlene, my Chinese manager, handed me the pink slip. She cited the reason for my dismissal was that I had not complied with the programming task assigned to me, nor had I enrolled in a computer class at the local college.

Before handing me my final paycheck, she asked me to sign an agreement stating that I would not bring any legal action against the company, and would not pass on any confidential information to outside parties. I signed it for she was holding my paycheck in her hand. In exchange for the agreement, I received my paycheck and two weeks' severance pay. With the document signed, I was released of all my duties.

I did not harbor any ill feelings towards her, for she was only following the director's orders. I knew her to be a kind and accommodating person. I could see she was just as uncomfortable as I was about the whole affair.

I returned to my desk, sent an email to the president of the company thanking him for the opportunity given to me to work at his company. I also mentioned that he had many management challenges at the company. Before leaving, I distributed copies of the memo to the employees of my department. I was not going to take a silent exit. I was going to make a wave. I had been earmarked at the company from the start. I had exposed the ugly face of bigotry. I had stirred waters that were not meant to be disturbed. However, still waters need to be stirred sometimes else they can collect algae and become polluted with cronies and corruption.

I walked up to my car in the company's parking lot, rested my head on the steering wheel and let the faucet of my heart run until a gentle calm washed over me. Then, pulling myself together, I put on my favorite oldies station, KFRC, and drove home. This afternoon they played "Teach Your Children" by Crosby, Stills, and Nash. "You, who are on the road, must have a code that you can live by. And so become yourself because the past is just a goodbye. . ." The song always gets me teary-eyed.

I worked for Tandem Computers for two-and-a-half years, until January 1992. It was the only company that had treated me unfairly in my entire career. Five years later, it was acquired by another technology company.

While I looked for another job, I learned from an employment agent that I had been blacklisted by Tandem Computers. I reminded myself I had run into a bend in the road, not the end of the road. I was bruised, not battered. My spirits were dampened, not crushed. I was not going to let anyone run me out of town.

I called the EEOC office in San Jose and asked to speak with the representative I had met with six weeks earlier, but was told she was no longer with the company. So I set up a meeting with someone at their Oakland office. I met with a senior manager who took down my complaint. At the close of the meeting, he asked to whom he should forward the report. I suggested he send it to the CEO of the company, to my department director John, and to my former manager Rod, who no longer worked for the company. The EEOC officer asked for Rod's home address. I told him I did not know, but that he lived in the same town where the company is located. He said he would look it up and send him a copy.

As one door closed, another opened. That spring of 1992, I enrolled in a five-week Texas Instruments' Case tools class in Sacramento for business process and data modeling. Ranjit had been supportive of me through my entire ordeal. He took care of the household and the children while I was away. He took them out for dinner and movies and even drove up two hours with the children to see me one weekend in Sacramento.

When I returned from the technology boot camp, I was in Monet's world. Golden poppies were in bloom on the hillsides and in the fields. Jacaranda trees were budding with lilac flowers on my street. Red azaleas were flowering in my garden, too.

In a couple of weeks, I landed a consulting assignment.

Photo Gallery

1958, Bombay:
Sisters rehearse for social event with
friend Meena, dressed as Lord Krishna
(L to R) Kamal and Jaya Mirchandani

1965, Bombay:
Jaya Mirchandani
during teen years at
St. Xavier's College

1968, Bombay:

Mirchandani family portrait, taken before Kiku moved to USA

(Front L to R): Kiku, Mummy, Dada, and Mangha

(Back L to R): Kamal, Suresh, and Jaya

1970, New Jersey:
Jaya and Ranjit Kamlani at their
modest wedding reception

1970, New Jersey:
Jaya Kamlani
stepping out from
couple's first car –
Volkswagen Beetle

1970, New York:
Jaya enjoying a drink with Ranjit (L) and
his brother-in-law (R) at the Playboy Club

1972, New Jersey: Suresh's graduation at Stevens Institute of Technology, Hoboken (L to R) Suresh, Kamal, Jaya, and Ranjit

1975, New Jersey: Jaya taking firstborn Minal out for a ride

1976, Bombay:
Kamal with Mummy and Dada

1981, New Jersey:
Minal and Ari Kamlani

1983, California:
Celebrating *rakhi* with
brother Kiku's children
(L to R): Ari, Sarika,
Minal, and Kaajal

1985, Bombay:
The Shalimar Hotel, 20 years after the big brawl
Jaya (3rd from right) next to brother Mangha

1986, California:
Jaya goes to work on a Saudi
consulting project wearing a
Bedouin dress for Halloween

1993, California:
Jaya working as a
Technology Consultant
In Silicon Valley

1997, Bombay:
Mangha and Jaya dance
to *The Last Waltz*
at Wodehouse Gymkhana
Christmas party

1998, Delhi:
Siblings (L to R) Kiku, Hari, Jaya, and Mangha
at a family wedding

2002, Goa:
Jaya relaxing in hammock
at Taj Hotel in Sinquerim

2003, Florida:
Ari with Ranjit
at a South Beach bar

2012, Venice:
Minal, world traveler,
loves to jet to Europe

2013, Atlanta:
Jaya Kamlani,
author of *To India
with Tough Love &
Scent of Yesterday*

** Jaya's photo album may be viewed in color at jayakamlani.com **

PART IV

House of Tomorrow

With Minal now in college and Ari at prep school, life at home changed dramatically. The house turned into a barren fig tree; my heart empty, too. Every now and then I mailed a "care" package to them with their favorite cereal, fig cookies, dates, pretzels, granola, and health bars.

I missed driving Ari to his athletic events, watching him take those long strides to get to the finish line. I remember the summer of 1996 when he participated in the twenty-six mile San Francisco marathon. That morning, at the break of dawn, I drove him and his friend to the city to participate in the race.

With the children away, I became the sole companion of Ginger, our German Shepherd. I played the piano for her, even though I did not know C-major from C-minor. But our eight-year-old shepherd could not tell the difference. It was still music to her canine ears. She rested quietly on the doggie bed, but her ears perked up when I hit a sharp note. She missed the children, for she had grown up with them. Alas, with the children away at school, and Ranjit and I on traveling assignments, we had to find our dog a new home.

After graduating from the prep school, Ari left for Pennsylvania to study electrical engineering at Lehigh University. When the children came home for the holidays, the house was back to life again. Every morning, while Ari pumped up his muscles lifting weights, the theme music from *Rocky* reverberated through the house. After a workout, he came down to the kitchen for a drink of Gatorade.

"Mom, look," he would say, flexing his biceps and flaunting his well-toned muscles.

"Ari, what can I say? You have Sylvester Stallone muscles."

He savored the compliment. The rest of the day he watched sports programs on television, went biking or jogging, played basketball, or went to the gym.

Like most youth, he went through his share of fads: ear piercing, bungee jumping, tattoo engraving, goatee growing, even shaving a *Nike* symbol on his full head of hair. I did not find out about his little ventures until after the deed was done.

Once he called from college to say he had completely shaved his head. "Ari, what made you do that?"

"I feel lighter, Mom. Got too much workload at school."

"After your exams, grow it back. Otherwise, no girls will look at you."

"What girls, Mom? This is an engineering college. There is no time for girls. They give us way too much homework."

Kojak may have been a trendsetter, but within a couple of years I saw many more shaven heads on television and on the streets. It became a trend among men with thinning hair.

When Minal came home for the holidays from Indiana University, we took daytrips to San Francisco, Carmel, or to Napa Valley for wine tasting. Although her energy helped me feel young, her battery could run all day long, whereas mine needed periods of rest and caffeine recharge.

We often played Scrabble. One afternoon while we played, we talked about women losing their identity when they got married. I told her about my Sindhi friends who had not only lost their last names after marriage, but also their first names. The in-laws ask the priest who performs the wedding ceremony to select a name for the new bride, a name he believes will be auspicious for the family.

Placing a few letters that spelled 'DOWRY' on the Scrabble board, Minal said, "Mom, I can't believe they still have the dowry system in India."

"Yes, it is common practice for arranged marriages." I noted her word score. Going for double and triple score, Minal often outwitted me. Using the open letter 'O,' I placed a few letters of my own on the board to read 'WOMEN.'

"I wish they would do away with the dowry system," I continued. "No matter how much dowry a bride brings into her marriage, it never seems to be enough for the in-laws. . . Go, Minal, your turn."

She put on a Madonna CD then picked up some tablets from the alphabet pool. Using an open letter 'E' on the board, she spelled the word 'GREED' for another big score.

"India is a male-dominated society," I explained to my daughter. Sometimes the bride is abused and even burned alive if she does not bring enough dowry into her marriage."

"Burned alive?"

"Sad but true. It still exists, even among the rich and educated."

While Madonna sang *La Isla Bonita*, I hummed along, placed my tablets on the Scrabble board and explained to my daughter that sometimes the bride's parents have to borrow money for their daughter's wedding. My parents had to sell their seaside apartment to come up with the money for Hari's dowry and wedding related expenses. I recounted the things my sister took in three suitcases to her new home: gold-gilded silk saris, lingerie, linen, cosmetics, purses, sandals, and jewelry. She also received lots of money as part of her dowry. My parents had to give clothing, gold coins and money to the groom and to every member of his family. Today, dowries include expensive honeymoon packages, household appliances, a car, even a condominium. That is one reason Indian parents prefer to have sons rather than daughters, and many women are compelled to abort their female fetuses.

I explained to Minal that traditionally in India a son inherits his parents' property and family business. The daughter gets none of that. Instead, she receives jewelry, which the parents believe she can pawn in case of an emergency. Sometimes, the in-laws use it to get their own daughters married.

Minal won this round of Scrabble. We wrapped up the mother-daughter hour, watched *The Color Purple* movie and then prepared her favorite stir-fry chicken and vegetables.

Minal helped me around the house. Helping others is second nature to her. During her school years, she had volunteered for a charitable organization. She called people in the community to ask them to donate clothes and household things for the needy. The packages were then picked up from their doors by a truck. She befriended a hundred-year old woman at a senior citizens home, helped her get around when she visited her, and kept her company.

During her college years, she volunteered for the Big Brothers, Big Sisters organization. She became a big sister to Amber, a young girl who came from a low-income broken family. Every week Minal met with her, helped her with her studies, and took her out for treats and to visit her relatives. Amber accompanied Ranjit and me to Minal's college graduation ceremony.

Over the years, Minal encouraged her to complete her schooling before looking for a job. Often she passed on her hand-me-down winter clothes, scarves, and accessories to Amber so she would have something good to wear.

Two decades later, Minal is still a big sister to Amber, who is a mother now. "A very good mother," says Minal.

The children helped me stay young at heart. When they returned to college, I missed them. I missed *Rocky* music. I missed playing Scrabble. I looked forward to their next vacation.

Two to Tango

Oddly enough, despite its innovations, in the mid-nineties California was plagued by four years of recession and consulting assignments were hard to come by. As a result, Ranjit and I were compelled to take on out-of-town projects. The hefty mortgage and the children's college tuitions and expenses had to be paid. We lived gypsy lives, each out of our own suitcases in different towns. We dined solo in unfamiliar places, talked each night on the phone, and came home for a weekend or two each month. Over time, the traveling assignments took a toll. It created a distance between us.

In 1996, Ranjit took a yearlong project in Copenhagen, Denmark. Each month, he came home for a week. With him in Europe, and the children away in college, I worked long hours on a consulting project for a client in San Francisco. On evenings and weekends, while I buried myself in office work or reading technical and business books, the house echoed with silence.

One Saturday, I opened the *Yellow Pages* and looked for a place that offered dance lessons. I wanted to learn to tango. So I signed up for a package of ten Saturday afternoon dance lessons at the Fred Astaire Studio in Santa

Clara. After an hour of dancing with bold flowing steps in high-heels to "La Cumparsita" and "Blue Tango," my feet were sore, but my spirits high.

Once when Ranjit came home, I told him about my newly acquired talent. "When you're done with your assignment, you can take tango lessons, too. It's been a long time since we went dancing."

"Jaya, you can take whatever lessons you want. Don't ask me to do the same."

"But, it takes two to tango."

After ten weeks, my tango lessons came to an end. As time went by, without a partner to dance with, I forgot my tango steps.

Often when he came home for the week, I surprised him with theatre tickets to hear Luciano Pavarotti or the Boston Pops, watch the *Cabaret* and the *Nutcracker* Christmas shows. I would purchase the tickets and tell him later that I could not waste expensive tickets. He dragged himself to the show. All through the event he sat there suffering in his seat, showing no signs of enthusiasm or interest. I could talk to him all day long about business, technology and politics, but not about any art form. He was not into music, dance, or the theatre.

Over the years, I had consulted for large and medium-sized companies. While many major technology companies in America were trying to shed their formal dress code, EDS (Electronic Data Systems) office in Virginia upheld its long standing policy. I was brought in at the company as a consultant to train three different groups on how to facilitate business process and data modeling sessions. People were flown in from the company's different sites across the country to work on the project.

Usually I wore a jacket over a blouse and skirt to my client site. But that day during lunch break, I was to move from the hotel to a corporate apartment and did not want to get a run in my stockings dragging my baggage. Unaware of the dress policy, I went to work in my navy-and-white polka dot silk pants. Then, I noticed the stares.

An employee pulled me to one side and informed me of the company's dress code. Men were required to wear a dress shirt with a tie, and a blazer or a suit jacket. Women were required to wear dresses or skirts to work. No jeans. Business-casual slacks were permitted once a month, only when the dress-down day was announced over the intercom, or a company telephone message left for employees. One month, there were no messages on the intercom or the telephone. Instead, a note was posted on the outside of the side door exit, which I happened to miss as I had worked through my lunch break.

The dress-down day also varied from month-to-month and was usually announced the day before, so no one could plan ahead for it. Having lived in California for many years, where casual wear was the norm, my client's dress policy struck me as rather strange. Then I learned that its California office did not observe any dress code.

Consulting assignments took me to New York, Chicago, San Francisco, Atlanta, Virginia, Minneapolis, and Montreal. In the winter of 1998, it took me to the state of Indiana, in the heartland of America.

Due to flight transfer and delay, it was past midnight when I arrived at the Dayton International Airport in the neighboring state of Ohio. The auto rental agency at the airport was out of midsize cars, so the agent upgraded me to a sporty white Mustang. Wheeling my carryon, I walked to the car in the parking lot, slipped into the low bucket seat, and familiarized myself with the buttons on the dashboard and the door panel. Over the years, I realized each rental car had a personality of its own; some with quirky brakes, others with temperamental ways. I had never driven a sports car before, but there's always a first time for everything. Turning on the ignition, I slowly pulled out of the parking lot and headed towards the highway.

Wow! This auto baby on high octane took off with such fire power, it got me nervous.

Disoriented after a long flight, I struggled to stay awake behind the wheel. After ten minutes, I realized I had coasted down the wrong highway. Taking the next exit, I got myself back on Route 70, put on some music and rolled down the window to keep from falling asleep.

It was a two-hour drive to Richmond, Indiana. As I hummed along to Willie Nelson's *To All The Girls I've Loved Before*, I was startled by a jarring honk. I looked in the rearview mirror and noticed a monstrous truck flashing its big bright headlights at me. Easing over to the slow lane, I let Goliath-on-wheels be King of the Road that night. Soon I found myself wedged between more honky-tonk trucks. I weaved my way between them in the small hours of the morning.

When the coast was finally clear, I heaved a sigh of relief. Now it was just the long stretch of road and I, with an occasional car that passed me by. My mind wandered. Only a few days earlier I had returned from a trip to India, where I had attended a couple of family weddings in Delhi along with my daughter. A flurry of wedding scenes flashed by me as I drove down the dark and lonesome road: the henna ceremony, the groom arriving on a white horse, the seven rounds around the sacred fire, the naval band playing music at the farmhouse reception by the bonfire, the relatives I met, the day-trip Minal and I took to see the renowned Taj Mahal. The white marble mausoleum built by the Mughal Emperor Shah Jahan as a tribute to his wife, Mumtaz Mahal, gleamed in brilliant hues, from a golden glow in the afternoon to a peach blush in the evening. This was my second visit to the Taj Mahal, one of the Seven Wonders of the World.

It was almost two in the morning when I staggered in with my baggage into the Holiday Inn in Richmond. I was worn out and famished. Besides a paltry packet of pretzels on the flight, it had been more than fourteen hours since I had eaten anything.

I asked the man at the reception desk if there was any food left in the kitchen.

"Only bread, ma'am."

"I'll take some."

He went to the kitchen and returned with a plate of two bread rolls and butter. I thanked him, dragged my baggage to my room, ate the bread, and then slipped under the covers.

For the next three months, this hotel would be my home.

When I returned from work one evening, I heard Van Morrison's *Brown Eyed Girl* song streaming into the hotel lobby while this brown-eyed girl waited for the elevator. I walked in the direction of the music, "Sha la la la la la la la la la la te da. . . la te da" and found a live band playing in the restaurant, with the singer strumming on his guitar.

It would be a pity to call in for room service this evening.

"How often does the band play here?" I asked the waitress who seated me.

"Every Thursday."

And so on Thursday evenings, whether it rained or snowed, I stayed warm in the hotel's dining room, entertained by good music over filet mignon dinner and a glass of Cabernet Sauvignon.

Three months later, when my assignment ended, I thanked the singer for the weekly entertainment. "I won't be coming here any more," I said.

"Why?"

"I'm headed home."

"Where's home?"

"California."

He pulled up a chair and sat me beside him. "What song would you like to hear?"

"*Maggie May.* You sing it so well, like Rod Stewart himself."

Turning to the audience, he announced, "This song is for our friend from California."

I was deeply moved. Forever after, the song reminded me of my days in the quiet hamlet of Indiana, where simple pleasures filled my thirsty Thursday evenings.

Although out-of-town assignments were tiresome, they gave me a chance to see America. On weekends that I did not go home, I visited local museums and historic sites. Sometimes, I visited friends and relatives in nearby towns, even in neighboring states.

Over the years, I got accustomed to traveling alone and living alone. I found comfort in the solitude.

The Roads I Traveled

Born by candlelight in India's civil war,
never dreamed I would travel so far;
goodbye my land of sages and spice,
hello America, my pleasant surprise.
With passing years, many miles I rode,
in search of the "Yellow Brick Road,"
saw rugged coastlines, hairpin bends,
tricky forks, and some dead ends.
Through all my travels, far and wide,
I searched the alleys and countryside,
from New York City to Napa Valley,
in the Golden State, on a green trolley.
Time and again, I took the high road,
found myself at more crossroads;
what I gained as the years unfurled,
a pound of knowledge of this world.

- Jaya Kamlani

Alien No More

As on every Sunday morning, Ranjit sat in his favorite cozy armchair in the bedroom, reading the *San Jose Mercury News*. When I walked into the room he asked, "Jaya, have you thought about where you want to retire?"

"Retire? No. We are a long way from retirement."

"But we have to plan for it now. How about India?"

"Why India after all these years?"

"The dollar goes a long way there."

"Ranjit, what will I do in India?"

"You'll not have to work anymore. You can retire."

"After thirty years in America, it would be difficult for me to adjust to India. If I retire, what would I do with my time there?"

"Change your lifestyle, Jaya. Find a hobby. Learn to play *Bridge*. Do what other women in India do."

"You mean I should spend half my day telling the cook what to prepare for the three meals of the day, keep an eye on the servant who cleans the house, attend luncheons, gossip tea parties and card sessions. Ranjit, you know that's not me. I've lived a working woman's life in America. I cannot suddenly change my lifestyle."

"Then become active there. Join a club or something to keep you busy."

For a fleeting moment, it was as if Archie Bunker was sitting in his armchair, directing my life. But, I was no Edith Bunker. I was not going to dance when he tells me to dance. Not anymore.

I held my ground. "But it's not the same Bombay where I grew up. Even its name has now changed to Mumbai. The living conditions are not good there. We will have to face harsh realities."

"Such as?"

"Water shortage. Pollution. Slums everywhere."

"So? You saw it all when you were growing up."

"But it's hard to go back and adjust to it after thirty years."

"You think there are no slums in America?"

"Not to that extent. . . And don't forget about the corruption in India."

"You think there is no corruption in America?"

And so, the conversation danced in circles.

A few months later, Ranjit broached the subject again. "I still think India is the best place to retire."

"Ranjit, since our visit to India last year you've been feeling homesick. When we go there on a vacation, we visit friends and relatives. We are wined and dined. We go sightseeing and shopping. But it will not be the same if we retire there. We'll have to cope with everyday hassles."

"So we'll cope with them. But you'll have servants and a chauffeur to drive you around."

"Ranjit, I have fond memories of India, too. But that was then. Our children are here, in America. I don't want to be living eight thousand miles away from them."

"Jaya, you've got to face it. Now that the children are away in college, they're not coming back. They're grown up. They will find their own lives. You can visit them once or twice a year."

"What if they run into some emergency?"

"Then they can call us in India."

"Ranjit, even in an emergency, it will take a few days to get to America."

Once again, our conversation ended in stalemate. However, my mind was made up. Much as I cherished my childhood memories of India, America would be my home for the rest of my life.

Another day, while Ranjit read the *India West* newspaper in his armchair, he looked towards me and said, "It says here that many Indians of our age are returning to India."

"So? Let them go."

"You know, America is for the young. We're no longer young."

"Ranjit, you're too young to retire. What will you do in India?"

"Start a business. Technology is booming in India."

"America may not be a bed of roses, but it's a whole lot better than India. Women are not treated well in India. They have no say. The problem is that India is still a male-dominated society."

"Jaya, you don't know what's happening in India these days. Things are changing. Women there are as independent as women in America. Many of them are professionals."

"You are talking of a small percentage of women living in the cities. Most women in India have a long way to go. I still prefer to live in America. . . One of these days I'm going to apply for my US citizenship."

Ranjit did not look too pleased at the mention of my citizenship. "If you become a US citizen, you'll still be treated as a second-class citizen."

"Aren't women treated as second-class citizens in India? So what's the difference if I'm treated as a second-class citizen in America because I'm an Indian, or if I'm treated as a second-class citizen in India because I'm a woman? Either way, I'm a second-class citizen."

The air got stifling in the bedroom. I stepped out on the balcony of our hillside home and looked out to the city twinkling in nightlights. Leaning on the balustrade, as I wrestled with my emotions, I recalled what Ranjit had said to me over the years, "Jaya, don't give up your Indian passport. . . Jaya, you never know what tomorrow brings. . . One of us should retain our Indian passport." Yet, decades ago he had exchanged his Indian passport for an American one to sponsor his younger brother to migrate to the United States.

I remembered our trip to India the year before in the winter of 1997. Usually Ranjit dropped me off at my family home in a cab, but that evening he walked me home after tea at the Taj Hotel. That's when I learned about what had puzzled me for thirty long years: the reason for my family's objection to our marriage. He told me about Mangha's business dispute with his brother-in-law, a dispute that had taken place years before I had even dated Ranjit. Since that time, the two men had not talked with each other. When the truth unfolded, I was both angry and sad. To think I could have lost the opportunity to come to America because of my brother's business dispute.

"When did you learn about it?" I asked Ranjit.

"When I was in Germany."

"You've known about it all these years and you did not tell me?"

He did not respond. After almost thirty years it was good to finally learn the truth, but I felt let down by the men I trusted in my life. On the other hand, as they say in India, when you marry a man, you marry his family. Perhaps my brother Mangha had been over-protective of me and thus did not want me to marry Ranjit.

We walked in silence most of the way home. I was lost in a mélange of emotions, but I understood Ranjit's predicament. He did not want to get involved in a quarrel between his two brother-in-laws. However, I was now even more determined never to return to India, even if Ranjit refused to talk to me for months. I did not want to be part of the family circus.

It had been almost three decades since my arrival in America. The first year I was a student, the next twenty-eight a permanent resident — a Green Card holder. I reflected over my life in America and wondered if becoming a US citizen would change my life. This is where I had married. This is where our children were born. Although life had sometimes been a little rough around the edges, this is where I was given sterling opportunities.

I had given business and technical presentations to all levels of management and even managed projects. Clad in a white bunny suit, I had walked through a semiconductor plant where silicon wafers were spliced, polished, etched with logic design, and processed into computer chips. To understand manufacturing processes, I had visited dairy, cosmetic, auto and other industrial plants, computer and peripherals assembly plants. I had walked through warehouses to understand how companies managed their inventories. I had even worked on an Air Force logistics project. Here in America is where I had found my confidence. I had learned the spirit of teamwork. I had learned to persevere. I did not know I could fly so high. Why would I consider myself a second-class citizen in a country that had offered me so much growth?

My mind was made up. America would be my home forever.

Despite Ranjit's objection, in the spring of 1998 I applied for US citizenship. While preparing for the citizenship exam, I studied the nation's history: Christopher Columbus who discovered America in 1492; the Pilgrim Fathers who came to America aboard the Mayflower in 1620 to flee religious persecution in Europe; George Washington, the first President of America; Thomas Jefferson and the Declaration of Independence; President Abraham Lincoln and the Emancipation Proclamation.

I read up on the Civil War of America, the Bill of Rights, the three branches of the US government, and the thirteen American colonies represented on the US flag. I learned about President Thomas Jefferson's purchase of Louisiana from Napoleon Bonaparte of France for fifteen million dollars in 1803, and the Lewis and Clark expedition from Missouri to the Pacific Northwest.

As I read about the Boston Tea Party episode, I was back to an evening when my business colleagues and I dined at a seafood shack in Boston. A museum boat named "Boston Tea Party" was anchored across on the Griffin Wharf. While savoring the jumbo shrimp, I recalled from my high school history class about how the British had once traded in spices, cotton, silk and opium with India. The opium from India was exchanged for tea with China. The Chinese tea was then sold by the British in Europe and America. I sat there gazing at the museum boat and mused. It must have been this bartered Chinese tea that was dumped into the Boston Harbor during the Boston Tea Party episode of 1773.[8]

I looked out at the wharf where Paul Revere, Samuel Adams, and the New England patriots, dressed as Mohawk Indians, boarded the ships on a cold December night. They dumped hundreds of tea chests into the Boston harbor to protest the British taxation on tea.

A pattern emerged. Could it be that Gandhi's non-violent "Salt March" from Sabarmati to the coastal village of Dandi in Gujarat was modeled after the success of the Boston Tea Party?

The British monopoly on salt trade in India dictated that sale or production of salt by anyone but the British government was a criminal offense, punishable by law. To protest British salt taxation, on March 12, 1930, Mahatma Gandhi, staff-in-hand, peacefully shepherded the Indians on a twenty-four day march to the Arabian Sea, to produce their own salt.[9]

Lifting a handful of salt from the seashore, he said, "This salt is made in the Indian Ocean. Let every Indian claim it as his right."

In December 1998, after a written examination on American history and an interview with an immigration officer, I attended the naturalization swearing-in ceremony at the Masonic Auditorium in San Francisco. It was packed with about a thousand other immigrants like me. While I waited in line in the registry foyer, I was reminded of my visit to the Ellis Island Museum in New York, where scores of early European immigrants had once walked up the "Stairs of Separation" to the Registry Room (1880–1924). The long flight of stairs separated the ones who were directed to take the train to their US destination, from those who were ill and were returned home by sea.

The clerk checked my name against a roster and handed me my citizenship certificate, signed by President William Jefferson Clinton. After the ceremony of speeches in the auditorium concluded, the newly naturalized citizens pledged allegiance to the flag of these United States of America. That week, I applied for my American passport.

It was a week of mixed emotions. I looked back to that snow-packed day in February 1969, when I arrived in America at the age of twenty-one, in an oversized brown velvet coat. After three decades, with one foot in America, another in India, I finally felt a sense of belonging. I had earned my stripes. At fifty-one, I was granted the right to vote. But, where were the fireworks?

Yin and Yang

If we only knew about *Feng Shui* and its Indian twin, *Vastu*, before we built our home, we could have saved ourselves a lot of grief.

For several years after the children left for college, our California home stood empty or with one resident. Ranjit and I were away on assignments. The children sometimes came home for the holidays but also joined us on location or stayed on their campuses. Despite the four of us living in different time zones, we stayed in touch over the telephone.

After graduation, Minal and Ari found jobs on the East Coast. Ranjit's prediction had come true. The children were not coming home. We put our house up for sale, but did not receive any good offers. Silicon Valley was then recovering from four years of recession. Upper-end homes were difficult to sell, unless you wanted to give them away. We held on to our home hoping better days were around the bend.

One Sunday morning, while Ranjit sat in his favorite armchair reading the *San Jose Mercury News*, I said to him, "Many Chinese fall in love with our home but decide not to buy it. Do you know why?"

"Why?" He continued to read the paper.

"Because the front door of our house faces the back door."

"So?"

"Chinese believe money comes in through the front door and goes out the back door."

"How do you know that?" He threw a quick glance at me.

"That's what our Chinese real estate agent told me. She said it would be no problem if the doors were a little offset and not directly opposite each other."

"It's too late for that now."

"She suggested we block the view of the back door with a couple of ficus trees. She insisted they should be live trees."

In the 1990s, Fremont was home to many Chinese and Indians. One day when a Chinese family came to view our home, I noticed the elderly woman point to the front and rear doors of our home and say something in Chinese to her family. From her gesture, I understood her concern.

A few days later, we had two eight-foot ficus trees delivered to our home to give it a Feng Shui touch. In a few months, they grew tall and full, almost blocking the view of the oak-trimmed, double French doors. Still no good offers for our home.

The next time I brought up the subject about the rear doors, Ranjit said, "We got the ficus trees as the agent suggested. That's it. I'm not going to knock down those French doors and put up a wall because of some silly Chinese superstition." He returned his gaze to the television set and continued surfing through the channels.

"Ranjit, the Chinese also don't buy a house in the center of a cul-de-sac street."

"You believe in all that mumbo jumbo?"

"No, not until now. Not until the house across the street on the cul-de-sac was bombed."

I recalled an evening when I was on an assignment in New York City. Ranjit called to inform me that he was spending the night at Kiku's.

"Any particular reason?" I asked, considering there was still some distance between my family and him.

"The FBI stopped by our home and asked me to leave the house immediately."

"Why did the FBI come to our house?"

"Because the house across the street at the cul-de-sac and the one up the hill under construction were bombed."

"Bombed?"

"Yes, bombed. FBI was afraid there might be other bombs planted on our street. They got everyone out of their homes and asked them to spend the night with friends or relatives. Then they went through all our homes."

Gees! A few years ago, our street did not even exist on the city map.

There was also another problem with our home, as I would later learn. Chinese and Indians generally do not buy a home facing south because it brings bad luck.

One day I said to Ranjit, "All the homes on our street have an address beginning with number 44. Our agent said the Chinese believe 44 is an unlucky number. But, she said 8 is a lucky number, especially 88."

"Well, we can't do anything about the street address, can we?"

"No, we cannot. But, we can do something about the back door. You've been saying that money has been flowing out faster than it has been coming in. Perhaps there is some truth to the Chinese superstition about the back door facing the front door."

"I said I'm not going to knock down the French doors."

And that was his final word.

Several months passed. We changed real estate agencies. This time Ranjit hired an Indian agent, hoping she might bring in some Indian clients. Still no good offers.

Disappointed by the few frivolous offers we had received for our home, I said to Ranjit, "We should do what our Indian agent suggested. She said we should hang some wind chimes outside the door, because it brings good tidings. She also suggested we place a water fountain in the foyer. Running water implies life, she said."

"Then do as she says."

So I bought a pair of antique-blue copper wind chimes from a garden shop and hung them on either side of the front porch of our home on the Fremont hills. The wind chimes swayed gently with the breeze and produced an enchanting melody.

That weekend, I dragged Ranjit to the garden shop and we brought home a large terracotta statue of a country girl holding a water jug in the fold of her arm. We placed the statue by the ficus trees in the thirty-foot long marble foyer. He connected the mechanical pump while I poured water into the jug. As he plugged the cable into the outlet, a cascading stream of water flowed from the urn. The soothing sound of flowing water was rhapsody to my ears. We had added another touch of *Vastu* — the Indian Feng Shui — to our home.

"Ranjit, the Chinese say that having water flowing in our home or garden is good chi."

"What is this chi thing you keep talking about?"

I reminded him about our visit to Chinatown in San Francisco and we looked for a chi sign to hang on our doors, because I had read the Chinese believe it brings good luck. "Ranjit, remember what the old Chinese shop-keeper said. 'I no heard of chi sign, but I have good luck, good health, and triple-happiness signs.'"

So we bought some triple-happiness signs and a red-tasseled rosewood-and-jade carving, hoping they would bring us good luck and our home would sell.

"Get to the point, Jaya."

"I found out that chi is a positive energy that moves around our home. Not a sign we can buy at a Chinese store."

Now that we had triple-happiness signs hanging on the inside of all our exit and balcony doorknobs, and the rosewood-jade carving on the family room wall, we waited for a miracle to happen. Then one day, I noticed the carving from the family room wall was gone.

"Ranjit, did you take down the rosewood carving?"

"Yes, I put it away. I don't know if that thing is bringing us good luck or bad. We haven't received any good offers for the house as yet."

The carving was put away for a few weeks, then back on the wall, then off, and on again. Still no good offers.

"Oh Ranjit, those real estate agents have brought out the worst supersti-tious streak in us."

My mind was inundated with wind chimes and flowing water, chi, and ficus trees. I went to the bookstore and leafed through the Feng Shui books, hoping they would put my mind at ease. They confirmed chi as a life force, a cosmic energy. For the energy to flow freely, the center of the foyer should be clear of furniture and things and the rooms clutter-free, so positive energy could flow through our living and work space.

I also looked into what number 44 represented and was told that Chinese believe it brings very bad luck or death.

A few days later, I asked Ranjit, "Have you heard of yin and yang?"

He rolled his eyes then turned his gaze to watch a political debate on television. He was not interested in any yin-yang stuff today or any day. I did not know which was worse, not knowing about these superstitions or learning about them and wishing I had not.

In the last few years, there had been many bizarre happenings on our street: a break-in at our home by the town's teenagers that brought twenty-two cars to our house while we were out of town; the bombing of two houses that brought the FBI officers to all the homes on our street; a large landslide along the ridge of our hillside street; fortunes of some neighbors that had turned sour; even death and divorce. At the time, no more than a dozen families lived on our street. Each one of them had experienced some dilemma or personal tragedy.

Murphy's Law governed our street. Anything that could go wrong did. It was time to call in the ghost-busters or move out.

"I think this street is cursed," I said to Ranjit. "Look at all the spooky incidents that have occurred here. I wonder if Ohlone Indians are buried under these hills."

"Jaya, you imagine too much."

"No, I'm not imagining. After all, Ohlone Indians lived on these hills over a century ago."

Before the turn of the century, our home was sold and we left California. By now, Minal was working in the advertising industry in New York, and Ari was a telecommunications engineer in Pennsylvania. Since Ranjit was traveling on assignments, I moved into an apartment in Bronxville, New York, to live closer to the children. Only after I had signed the lease, I realized that while Avalon was located on Parkway Road, my mailing address was 44 again! 44 Millburn Street. But, I was willing to set aside silly superstitions.

PART V

Pound of Knowledge

Of late, my health had not been up to par. The arthritis in my back often flared up. So I decided to retire from my two-decade long technology career. No more living on the road. No more designing business and data models. No more drawing process flowcharts. No more working on enterprise supply chain management systems.

Oddly enough, at this time information technology jobs were being outsourced to my old country, India. Ranjit had been right all along. The technology boom was gaining momentum on the other side of the globe.

I had arrived at another crossroad. It was time to do all the things I wanted to do when I retired. Time to read and write. What better story to pen than the story of my life? I typed a few pages and read them back. The writing was pitiful, nothing like the novels I had read. I enrolled in a creative writing workshop at Sarah Lawrence College in town.

It was tart cold outside. It snowed. I stayed indoors and read Anne Lamott's *Bird by Bird*, a witty book that encouraged me to feed my passion for writing. I started with a small anecdote, built on it bird by bird, and did not give up. I let the words spill from my heart and memory onto the keyboard and did not stop until the story was told.

I read *Sound Shadows of the New World*, a memoir by Ved Mehta, who had come from India to the United States as a young teenager, to study at the Arkansas School for the Blind. His handicap and hardships did not stop him from his aspiration to become a writer. He wrote his book on a Braille type-writer. I was inspired by his determination, his perseverance, and his positive attitude. A year later, I would meet Mehta in person in New York City, at a reading of his new book *All for Love*.

January 2000. Late one Friday evening, I was in bed reading Frank McCourt's *Angela's Ashes* when the phone rang. It was Ari. The night before, he had taken a flight from Philadelphia to San Diego to interview for another job. He told me about his flight woes — the delay, the cancellation, the rerouting and connection, and finally a shuttle to San Diego. When he finally arrived at his destination at five-thirty in the morning, he could not collect his baggage.

"Why?" I asked.

"The conveyor belt was shut down. They said it would restart at eight o'clock. My suit was in my bag and my interview was at eight-thirty."

"Don't tell me you went to the interview in your jeans."

"No, Mom. When I checked in at the Wyndham Hotel, there was this bellhop in a black suit. I asked him if I could borrow his suit and tie for my interview."

"You did what?"

"I borrowed his black suit for the interview."

"Did it fit?"

"No. The pants were short. The coat sleeves were short, too. Luckily, I was wearing a white shirt I had worn to work the day before."

I burst into laughter then pulled myself together. "What color was his tie?"

"Red."

"Short pants. Short coat sleeves. Ari, all you needed was a top hat and a cane, and you'd be walking like Charlie Chaplin. . . What about your shoes?"

"I was wearing the black leather shoes I had worn to work the day before."

"I'm glad you were not wearing sneakers, or you would have had to find another bellhop for your shoes. If you could not fit in this dude's suit, how could you fit in his shoes?" By now, I was hysterical.

"Mom, don't laugh. Just hear me out."

"Okay, go on."

"The pants were so tight I had to skip lunch. I only had orange juice at the hotel that morning. When I sat down for the interview, my coat sleeves went up even higher."

I tried to hold back my laughter even as I lent my ear. Ari has a way of telling the funniest stories.

"I finally told one of the guys who interviewed me that I was wearing a borrowed suit."

"What was his reaction?"

"He laughed."

"What time did the interviews wind up?"

"At four-thirty. When I got back to the car, I unzipped my pants so I could breathe."

I tried so hard to keep from breaking into another laugh. "Poor you. No suit. No breakfast. No lunch. Let me know when you hear from the company."

A few days later, Ari called. He did not get the job.

"I'm sorry to hear that. Don't worry sweetheart, there are many fish in the ocean. Next time, I think you should apply for a software job, not a hardware job. There are many more software jobs out there."

That summer, Ari got a software job in the telecommunications industry. He moved to Atlanta. Both Ari and I had been at crossroads that year. We acquired new skills and forged new career paths for ourselves.

I read. I learned. I wrote. I wrote about my family's hardships during the Partition of India, as I wanted my children to learn about their roots. I wrote about my coming to America, as I wanted my children to learn about my own endurances and aspirations.

Memory Lane

In the summer of 2000, I learned from Mangha that my mother had taken a fall twice in the bathroom. Due to her old age and weak knees, the doctor had confined her to bed for the rest of her years. So I decided to take a trip to see her. En route, I stopped in England and spent a few days with an old college friend, whom I had not seen in years.

On the evening of my birthday, I arrived in Bombay, which had been renamed to Mumbai. Since Mangha's birthday had been the day before, he had bought a luscious chocolate cake to celebrate our special days together. My mother, the cook, and the maid joined in.

It had been ten years since my father passed away. I felt his absence as I slept in the spare bed by my mother. I was saddened to see her bedridden. She used to be so active. Her smile, her laughter had always been infectious. Back when I had pulled all-nighters studying for high school exams, she had stayed up with me removing grit from rice kernels, keeping a vigil on me so I would not fall asleep over my books.

She used to make beautiful handkerchiefs for my sister and me, each of them embroidered and crocheted along the edges. She tailored café-style

curtains for the many windows of our home and clothes for the family —
pajamas for everyone, school uniforms and dresses for Kamal and me. From
the leftover fabric, she sewed pretty clothes with ribbons and lace and bows
for the children of the less fortunate. I always admired my mother's big heart
and caring ways.

Now at eighty-six, bent with age, despite the yawning gaps in her teeth
and her pronounced high cheekbones, her dark eyes still had that old sparkle
and she could still tell stories of yesterday. Sometimes when she reminisced
over her own childhood years, she got teary-eyed, took her white tunic and
wiped the corners of her eyes. My mother wore white — white sari and
white pajamas — ever since my grandfather had passed away. She was then
thirty-two.

Despite being confined to bed, her spirit was strong. When the cook
served her evening tea and cookies, she offered them to me before she had
any. "Here, dip your biscuit in my tea," she said, like she used to tell me when
I was a little girl.

To please her, I did.

When the cook brought her dessert at night, she told him, "Serve Baby
first." Still that same caring mother who always made sure there were homemade snacks for us when we returned from school and home-prepared dessert
every night after dinner.

Being the peak of the monsoon season, the first week of my vacation was
confined to home. Mangha and I spent the time watching replays of cricket
matches, reminiscing over bygone days, and listening to oldies. I sang along
with Frank Sinatra to *Strangers in the Night* and with Paul Anka to *Diana*.
"I'm so young and you're so old, this my darling I've been told. . . Oh, please,
stay by me, Diana."

Over tea and cookies he told me about how our father was conned by
his company management when he worked overseas. One day my father's
employer, an Indian businessman whose textile business he managed in Japan
for over a decade, offered to make him a partner at the company. When it
came to compensation time, he paid my father his regular salary, but not his
partnership dues.

"Why?" I asked.

"Because the deal was made on a gentleman's handshake. That was how it was done in those days. There were no documents signed. So Dada quit the company and joined another. That employer also pulled the same scam on him. Not once, but twice Dada was conned, because he was very trusting of others."

"How much money was involved?"

"Forty-eight thousand rupees from one employer; fifty from another. With that money we could have bought a large lavish flat in the city. Perhaps even two."

One hundred thousand rupees was a truckload of money in the late 1940s and early 50s. I was saddened to learn how people had taken advantage of my father's kind and trusting nature.

While Mangha and I talked, I was reminded of the time when I was in tenth grade and my father loaned six thousand rupees to his bachelor friend, Shyam. He told my father that he needed the loan for only three months, as he was short of cash to finish producing a movie.

One evening while I was studying, I heard my mother, who was ironing clothes in the adjoining room, say to my father, "Don't you see your friend has been feeding of us? When you gave him the money, didn't you think about your six children? That Shyam is a crook. He is no movie producer. He always shows up here at mealtime. I can read him well. Just you wait and see. You are not going to see the six thousand rupees ever again."

In 1962, six thousand rupees was a substantial sum of money. It could feed our family of eight for at least three months. It had been quite a few years since my father had retired due to illness. Since then the family's finances had taken a turn for the worse. The little money that supported the family came from Mangha's sales job and Hari's job as a railway clerk. Kiku, who had graduated from engineering college that year, had just started working. In the past, we had borrowed money from relatives for household expenses and Kiku's college fees.

Mummy's prediction had come true. My father's friend never returned the money.

One evening, my mother dispatched our cook to his home, with a note demanding that he return the borrowed money. But the man could not be located. It turned out that he had given us a fake home address. He had always visited our home, but my father had never stopped by his place.

One day Mummy said to Dada, "Let me manage the money. You are going to land us in the poorhouse."

Weak with age and feeble health, my father did not argue. From that day on, my mother managed the purse strings. She steered a tight ship while my father had more time to read the newspaper.

∽

To escape the Bombay monsoons, I visited my cousins in Delhi for a week. It was always a pleasure to see them and reminisce over fun-filled childhood days. When I returned to Bombay, the skies had cleared and the storm clouds held back their fury. A car service picked me up from the airport. On my way home, I asked the driver to take a detour by my old childhood neighborhood of Mahim.

Old memories returned as I drove past St. Michael's School, a boy's school that my brother Suresh had attended. I remembered the times when our girl's school, Canossa High School, was invited for a viewing of *The King of Kings* and *The Ten Commandments* movies at its auditorium, and how I cried. On its grounds stood the church that I once visited on Good Fridays, Easter Sundays, and Wednesday morning Novena services with my classmates.

About a mile down the road by the train station, we came upon the dilapidated half-a-century-old, four-story building. My eyes traveled to the corner flat on the third floor, my childhood home of twenty years. I asked the taxi driver to stop for a few moments. The old balcony was now fenced-in with an iron grille. The balcony from where I had once watched the kite flyers, the snake charmers, and the gypsies do their one-act performances. My old friends no longer lived there. Sheila, my next-door neighbor, was long since settled in Massachusetts, while Meena lived in London.

I recalled the days when we walked to school together, sprayed each other with colored water during the Holi festival, and from our balconies we watched the effigy of evil King Ravana go up in flames on Dusserah night. I glanced around the neighborhood. The four-story building where the Parsee families once lived was still standing; so was the two-story bungalow where two Christian families lived.

The family on the bungalow's main floor always had Christmas parties. When I was twelve, I was invited. That's when I met Santa Claus for the very first time. While the couples danced on the mosaic tiled floor, Santa went around the large hall and handed gifts to everyone.

The second floor was rented out to another Catholic family. One day, I was saddened to learn their older daughter, a school teacher, was swept away by the tidal waves at the beach. Some nasty boys in our building used to call her Blackie because she was dark-skinned. I wondered how they felt about her tragic untimely death. Although I did not know her, I was moved when the pallbearers placed her black casket inside the hearse and the convoy, all dressed in black, headed for the funeral parlor. About a year later, the family moved out of there.

As the taxi driver drove around the block and turned at the bend, I noticed how the provincial town had aged. The streets looked narrower than I remembered. The stores, the tea cafés, the sweets shop, the buildings were all still there, only jaded with time. As we drove past the park where I once watched the three-ring circus and town fairs, I asked the driver to pull over outside the old convent school and wait for me.

Through the teacher's gate I entered the school building. "Can I help you?" asked the school secretary who sat behind a desk in the gray-veined white marble lobby.

I introduced myself as a former student. Noticing the empty corridors on a weekday afternoon, I asked, "Where is everyone — the children, the teachers, the nuns?"

"The school is closed today. It's a holiday."

I was disappointed. I had expected to see children in blue uniforms playing on the school grounds or in their classrooms. I requested to see the principal or the vice-principal and was informed that the principal was out that day. The secretary then talked to someone on the phone and directed me to the nun's parlor on the fourth floor, a forbidden floor for students during my schoolgirl years.

This was my first visit to the convent since my graduation in 1963. I remembered a distant morning as I walked up the wide marble staircase. After assembly as we walked up the stairs in a file of two to our classes, Mother Trezzi pulled me from the line. She had me kneel in the lobby to check if my blue uniform touched the floor. It did not.

"Your uniform is too short," she scolded and had me open the hem while she watched. She also reprimanded us if a button or school badge was missing from our uniforms, our tennis shoes were dirty or our long hair was not braided.

Mother Trezzi was my nudging conscience, yet she was also one of the kindest. Like the other missionary nuns at school, she spent her weekends trying to improve the lives of the city's poor, who lived in the slums. She was instrumental in starting an evening education program for the children of the less privileged.

At the fourth floor landing, a middle-aged woman approached me. "Can I help you? I'm Veira, the school custodian."

Thirty-seven years had passed and Veira had not changed much — the same lean figure, the long braided hair, the soft-spoken persona. The custodian whose matronly dress I had to wear one distant morning when my uniform got soaked in the rain. I asked to see the vice principal. She seated me in the parlor and then disappeared. The room with two windows looked out to the street and was sparsely furnished: a sofa, two light armchairs, a coffee table, and a large easel-style magazine rack with religious literature.

Moments later, a nun in a pastel blue dress and a matching bonnet walked in wearing a smile. She reached out to shake my hand. "Hello, I'm Sister Flory D'Souza, the vice-principal. Will you have some tea?"

"No thank you, Sister. I have a car waiting for me."

We chatted for a while then sang the old school song, "C.H.S" (Canossa High School). I had forgotten the lyrics, but once she got me started, the words just fell on my lips. I felt like a schoolgirl again. Sister Flory, who had graduated from the same convent a year before I did, filled me in on the news. The school uniform had not changed in all these years. It was the same royal-blue uniform with a blue belt, three large white buttons, and a white collar.

I learned that Mother Trezzi had passed away a few years ago.

"What about Mother Edna?"

"She is very old now and is living out her years at our facilities in Belgaum."

Mother Edna was a very kind nun. She had nicknamed me Jaya. She taught us history, geography, and Moral Science during the last three years of our high school. She trained us to be very logical and showed us techniques to remember our class material in the form of bullets and tables. It was those skills that helped me remember my school work and improve my grades. Her modus operandi stayed with me forever.

On my way out, Sister Flory handed me some school memorabilia: the school centennial magazine, a pastel-blue rosary, and pins of Mother Mary and Saint Bakita of Sudan, who was to be canonized by the Pope the following month.

As Sister Flory saw me off at the elevator, I noticed a tuft of hair sticking out from under her headdress. Instantly, I was back to a distant day when I heard from a classmate that the nuns had shaven heads.

"You mean they are bald," I exclaimed.

I wanted to verify the rumor for myself. One morning during recess, I tiptoed up to the fourth floor to take a peek at the nuns' living quarters. As I walked down the corridor, I found an open window. My eyes fell upon a nun in white, who was reading a piece of paper in her boudoir. She wore no head-dress and had no hair and was unaware of my gaze upon her. I saw what I had come to see.

Eureka! The nuns really are bald.

I scurried down the stairs before I got caught snooping around on the forbidden floor. For a while, every time a nun in white passed me by I pictured her bald under her headdress. I am glad the nuns could not read my mind or they would have reprimanded me for such evil thoughts.

Times have changed, I mused, as I stepped out of the elevator and walked to the rental car. Now that I had met Sister Flory, I realized the nuns were not shaving their heads any more. On my way home, I was spilling over with emotions as my childhood days flashed by me.

❧

That week, I also visited my alma mater, St. Xavier's College. It had been thirty-three years since I graduated from there. Walking through the arched portico and the campus foyer, I found myself in the large open quadrangle where I had once hung around with my friends. The square was now used as a basketball court, but no one was shooting hoops at this hour. They were all in their classes. I stopped at the canteen, which had been relocated from the clock tower building to make room for more classes. After replenishing my energy with vegetable-stuffed samosas, I took a stroll around the campus and talked to some students who had just emerged from their classes. Then I wandered into the college library, where I had once spent hours doing research on the works of western authors and poets for my English Literature classes.

The college had come a long way. It was no longer merely a College of Arts and Sciences. With the passage of time, new structures had mushroomed to accommodate the College of Business, College of Communication and Mass Media, and College of Management.

I walked up the familiar wooden stairs and found myself outside the registrar's office, once my French classroom. Instantly, I was transported to my freshman year, when the boys in the back of the class got a little rowdy and stomped their feet on the wooden floor. Then, one by one they dropped their books with a thud. The French teacher would have none of that. She had the entire class stand until the bell rang, and *Tartarin de Tarascon* went unread that morning. It was the last time the troublesome boys pulled a stunt on the pretty but austere French teacher.

I trudged up another flight of stairs and stood outside the large classroom where the European rector in white cassock taught us economics in our sophomore class. His monotone voice and the dry subject could put me to sleep. One morning, after he took the roll call, he turned to write something on the board. In a flash, three of my friends and I ran out the back door. Later that afternoon, we learned from our classmates that the rector caught a glimpse of us dashing out of the classroom as he turned around to face the classroom. He took the roster again. Some students answered for us. But the rector was not one to give up easily. He went around collecting slips of paper from every student with their names on it. Now he knew who had walked out of the class. The following day, my friends and I apologized to him.

Next, I stopped to see Principal Joseph Dias. During my conversation with him, I asked about the annual College Day program.

"We don't have College Day anymore. We now have *Malhar*. It's an intercollegiate arts festival held here every August on our college campus. Many colleges participate in the event. Next time if you're here in August, you must come and see it. It's a big festival."

I had missed the festival by a couple of weeks.

On my way out, the principal handed me the centennial magazine and two keepsake college calendars: one depicting the history of the college founded by European pastors, another with college sketches illustrated by an alumni member.

A lump rose to my throat as I walked down the stairs and evergreen images of bygone years scrolled by me. Bringing my fingers to my lips, I kissed yesterday goodbye.

After three weeks of walking down memory lanes, I returned to New York.

⟨≈⟩

Upon my return from India, I decided to visit the town of Hoboken in New Jersey. I was back to 1969 as I drove down Washington Street then up the hill on Ninth Street and onto the campus of Stevens Institute of Technology.

I parked my car, walked up to the old MSA building and rang the buzzer. A student passing by let me in. Scurrying up three flights, I knocked on the door of apartment 503 that had been my first home in America some thirty years before. No response. Not that I expected one on a weekday morning. The students were all at school. Standing there, I recalled a distant April morning when I left the dorm with one suitcase to start a new life with Ranjit.

I walked over to the student center next door, where Suresh had once taken me to a dance. We danced the evening away with disco music blaring, psychedelic lights flashing, a large mirrored ball revolving in slow motion from the ceiling, sparkling in a kaleidoscope of colors. Suresh was then seventeen while I, twenty-one.

Lost in thoughts, I wandered around the center. *Dear me, where had all those years gone? I now have children older than twenty-one. If only I could turn back the clock. If only I could be twenty-one again, for one long, long weekend. Then I would not care if my car turned into a pumpkin and my dress into rags.*

At the college store, I picked up the campus newsletter and bought a sweatshirt for Suresh, who now lived in California. Then I drove down the hill and parked my car on Washington Street from where I had once taken the bus to my school in New York. It was a beautiful day. I took a stroll downtown, where an array of bistros and upscale restaurants had replaced yesterday's dime stores and street-corner taverns. It was past lunchtime and I was famished. After a sumptuous meal of pasta and shrimp in creamy garlic sauce and a glass of Cabernet Sauvignon, I was energized for the afternoon.

I walked down several long blocks to the PATH station from where I had once taken the weekend train to Newark to meet Ranjit. We were new arrivals to the country then — both of us young, both of us with larger than life dreams. Some of those dreams had come true, but at great sacrifice.

"How much is it to Newark?" I asked the man at the ticket booth.

"That'll be a dollar."

Hmmm! Fifteen cents in 1969.

"Do you know the bus fare to New York?"

"A dollar sixty-five."

Hmmm! Forty cents in 1969.

I moseyed down the waterfront promenade. Once known as the Riverside Street, it was renamed Sinatra Drive, after Hoboken's celebrated son, singer Frank Sinatra. On the other side of the Hudson River stood the Twin Towers, shimmering in steel and glass in the afternoon sun. Who could have imagined that a year later the twins would be missing from the New York City landscape?

I returned to my car. Cruising around downtown, I could appreciate how the industrial college town of Hoboken had morphed into a yuppie town. Even the pre-World War II brownstone row houses on Washington Street, the town's main street, had received a charming facelift. In the neighborhood where Lipton Tea plant had once churned out truckloads of tea bags, waterfront lofts now rented for $2,600 and two-bedroom apartments for $3,000 a month. Gone were also the

Jell-O and My-T-Fine pudding plants, Bethlehem Steel plant, warehouses, and the shipyard where many ships were built during World War I and II. Luxury condominiums and shopping arcades had sprouted on these sites.

Driving down on Hudson Street, I found myself in front of the Maxwell House coffee plant, where coffee beans had once come down the Hudson River on barges. The beans were emptied into a silo, then roasted, ground, and packed in coffee canisters produced by its neighbor, the American Can Company. Since the Depression years of the 1930s, both the plants had kept the local residents employed. Their parking lots now stood empty. The plants had been shut down. No coffee aroma wafted in the air and perked me up as it had done thirty years before. I pulled over at a Starbucks Coffee bar down the street for a café latté for midday break.

Then I pulled up to the gate of the Maxwell House plant, parked my car in the empty lot and walked over to the security office. A guard, who sat behind a long counter, was engrossed in a book. We chatted. He informed me that he had once worked for the coffee plant, but today he worked for the new property owner who planned to tear down the plant and build riverfront condominiums at the site. He spoke about the day in 1992 when the coffee plant that once employed more than 650 locals had closed. "It was a sad day. I remember it well. Many of the town's folk who worked here have not yet recovered from it."

❧

The following month, I visited Ari, who had by now settled down on his new job in Atlanta, as a telecommunications software engineer.

"Mom, you like my apartment?"

"Very nice. Very clean."

"I cleaned it last night since you were coming," he grinned.

I returned his smile. He was blessed with a good sense of humor. I also appreciated my children's honesty. I recalled how he had kept his room clean, even as a kid. He had no choice or else it would have cost him a day's allowance.

I browsed through the memorabilia that decked the living room wall of his apartment: a montage of photographs of Ari with his high school and college friends and a white fabric wall-hanging with his San Francisco Marathon number "3033" embossed in bold red. Adjacent to it hung a picture of him running with his friends at the marathon, wearing a placard with his number around his neck. All at once, I was transported back to the summer of 1996, when I drove Ari and his friend Andrew to San Francisco at dawn for the twenty-six mile race.

Ari was born with a minor deformity. His feet turned left, parallel to each other at 45 degrees. When he was a month old, I took him to see an orthopedic doctor who said he had 'windswept" feet. As a result, all day and all night long he had to wear special orthopedic shoes held together with a metal strip, so his feet would grow straight. Every month, I would tighten the nut-screws on the strip a notch, so his toes moved closer to the center. A year later, his feet were normal.

During his high school years, he ran long distance and participated in many inter-school meets. Running a marathon was a major milestone for him. He reminded me of Forrest Gump. "Run Ari, run," I would cheer.

The next morning at his Atlanta apartment, Ari asked, "Mom, what are your plans for today?"

"I've brought along a book to read. Why? What do you have in mind?"

Handing me a two-inch thick black hardcover book, he said with a puckish smile, "You may want to read this book during your spare time. In the evening, when I return from work, we'll go out to dinner."

I glanced at the title: JAVA Black Book Comprehensive Problem Solver – A how-to-program in JAVA language computer book.

"Very funny, Ari. You want your mother to read a computer programming book when she is visiting you? Wait 'til I get you, you *Gingerbread Boy*."

As a budding teenager, he would tease me while I cooked, "Nanny, nanny, nanny, you can't catch me."

Spatula-in-hand, I would chase him around the kitchen's center island, calling out, "Wait 'til I get you, you *Gingerbread Boy*."

He would respond with a belly laugh, which made his day and mine.

That week in Atlanta, Ari and I reminisced about the day the two of us went to see the *Malcolm X* movie for a school report he had to write. We talked about the times I watched Super Bowl football games with him. The times he quizzed me on the basketball and football players and I got the names of players and teams all mixed up and he got such a kick out of it.

A couple of years later, Ari had to undergo ankle surgery. It marked an end to his running days. He then redirected his energy, discipline, and passion to his engineering career. In his spare time he tinkered with electronics, built a desktop computer from scratch, and programmed it to make it work. The computer lasted a few years until it was time to upgrade it.

Looking back in the rearview mirror, I remember the times when the children were young. I lent them my ears when they were sad or disappointed, put cold compresses on their foreheads when they came down with fever, gave them homemade carrot and orange juice when they came down with a cold. I played board games with them, read bedtime stories to them, helped them with their homework, and even carved Jack-o'-Lantern with them for Halloween. They had come a long way. I was proud of them.

Ashes to Birch

In the spring of 2001, Minal moved to downtown New York. With Ranjit away on assignment, I leased a condominium in Guttenberg, New Jersey. When Minal stumbled upon the rental property, she said "Mom, the view will inspire you to write, and we can visit each other on weekends. It's only fifteen minutes away from New York by bus."

Minal was right. The view from the condo was breathtaking, by day and by night.

The towering fifty-story condominium stood above the New York skyline with the Hudson River flowing at its feet. The Hudson is no meandering Mississippi River where you might see a paddle wheeler come coasting down playing Dixieland music, but rather a commercial waterway with boats and barges carrying timber, barrels of goods, even freight boxcars.

As I threw open the blinds of my wall-to-wall windows in the mornings, I watched a new day dawn on the other side of the river. Along the cascading skyline rose the Empire State Building. To my right was downtown, with its stately Twin Towers.

When the sun climbed high, the shimmering waters twinkled and a barge or two sometimes anchored outside my window. When the sun came easing down, the city glowed peach and a sailboat or cruiser dotted the scene.

The early spring blizzard turned the river to a long white sheet, pristine and peaceful. When the snow melted, the boats and barges returned to the scene.

On stormy days, the New York skyline vanished behind a misty curtain. When the clouds lifted, the skyline emerged and a swollen river ran to meet the ocean.

I soon settled down in my new abode, read Scott Fitzgerald's *The Great Gatsby*, Tracy Chevalier's *Girl with a Pearl Earring*, and Amitav Ghosh's *The Glass Palace*. I also worked on my memoir. In the afternoons, I soaked in the hot tub at the building's clubhouse, pampered myself in the steam and sauna rooms, attended Book Review Club meetings and spent weekends with Minal in the city.

This Tuesday morning in September is forever etched in my mind. The sky was spilling over with sunshine. While I fixed myself muesli breakfast and coffee the phone rang. It was Minal, on her way to work. After some small talk, I put the receiver back in its cradle.

Some fifteen minutes later, Ranjit, who had only days ago returned from his travelling assignment, called out from the living room where he watched the television news. "Jaya, come and see this. The World Trade Center is on fire."

I looked at him with disbelief, but seeing the shell-shocked expression on his face, I walked over to his side and watched the news unfold on CNN. My jaw fell as I looked out the living room window. To my right, a blanket of dense dark smoke hung over downtown New York. Only minutes before, all was well on the other side of the river.

As the news unfolded, another jet crashed into the south tower. The Twin Towers were ablaze. Instantly, my thoughts rushed to our daughter Minal, who now lived close by there. A few months ago, she had moved to One West Street by Battery Place, a short walk from the World Trade Center. I called her on her cell phone. No answer. I watched a bit of news, looked out the window and called her again and again. Still no answer.

I dashed out of the apartment and walked down Kennedy Boulevard for a closer view of the towering infernos. The locals were out on the promenade with their binoculars, cameras and tripods, fear and anxiety written on their faces. Across the river stood two tall black square candles, burning, discharging dark plumes of smoke.

Fifteen minutes later, when I returned to the apartment, news flashed on TV that a jet had crashed in Shankesville, Pennsylvania, and another at the Pentagon in Washington D.C.

Goodness gracious me! What is happening out there? Is it a war on America?

My eyes danced between the living room window and the horrific scenes on television screen. The Twin Towers burned helplessly. Flames thrashed. Smoke billowed. Icons of steel and glass, how they shuddered and imploded. All at once, a giant white cloud of soot arose and chased people down the alleys with such tsunami force.

Just then a reporter announced, "Rector Street Station has caved in."

My blood ran cold. It seemed the sky was falling. My daughter was out there somewhere. But where? She usually took the train from Rector Street Station to midtown, around the time the jets crashed into the Twin Towers.

I dialed Minal's cell number and received a recording, "All circuits are busy. Please try again later." I hit the redial button frantically. The same message played like a broken record. I called BBDO advertising company, where she worked. No answer. I called the concierge's desk at her apartment building. No answer.

A lump rose to my throat. "Ranjit, what's happened to all of New York City? Why isn't anyone answering anywhere?"

"Keep dialing, Jaya," he said, without shifting his gaze from the television set.

Once again, I stepped out to the promenade on Kennedy Boulevard. The scene had changed. The twin towers were no more. Only dust clouds left behind. It had all happened so fast.

When I returned to the apartment building, I found a woman in the lobby sobbing. The concierge told me her husband worked at the World Trade Center. I was about to go and console her when he held out his hand to stop me from disturbing her. Many people in our building worked in New York's downtown financial district.

Still no word from Minal. For the thirtieth time, I dialed her number. The same recording chewed on my ear. My stomach churned. I feared the worst. I prayed as relentless stream of tragic news continued to unfold. Replays of a jet slicing the tower, the enormous fireball, and the mammoth white cloud chasing people down the streets flooded the screen. Still, I could not tear myself away from the television set. I listened to Mayor Rudolph (Rudi) Giuliani talk about how he had escaped the tragedy. I listened to President George W. Bush address the nation.

All at once, it dawned on me that Minal had mentioned she had a focus group session in Connecticut that day. What time? Morning? Afternoon? I hadn't asked. There was no reason to ask. It was supposed to be another workday in September. I called my sister Kamal in Connecticut to inquire if she had heard from Minal. She had not.

Around 3:40 that afternoon the phone rang. I rushed to answer it. "Minal, thank God it's you! I was so worried about you."

I was relieved to hear she had taken the earlier train that morning to attend the meeting. "Did you hear about the World Trade Center?"

"Yes. First the World Trade Center then the Pentagon." She explained that nobody in the back room knew how to interrupt the focus group and inform them what had happened. They sat there in shock waiting for the session to end. "Mom, I had planned to go to the Windows on the World restaurant [at the World Trade Center] last night, but it was pouring."

We were unable to pick up Minal that day from Connecticut. Due to bomb threats, all bridges and tunnels were shut down in New Jersey and New York. Even the New York primary elections scheduled for that day were postponed. She wound up spending the night with my sister.

That night, sleep did not fill my eyes. As gray clouds hung over the city, I kept a vigil on the Empire State Building across from my window. The city's icon was in the dark. It was reported that it was also a terrorist target.

For many nights before, everything looked fine along the cascading New York skyline. The moon hung high, the river flowed gently, twinkling like sparkling wine. But on this night, the city was in the dark, the people in a fog, and the world was in mourning. The man in the moon did not smile. The river, too, seemed to have stopped flowing. I stayed awake thinking of the last moments, the last emotions of the fallen. The last words they may have uttered before they joined the Milky Way in heaven. Many dreams now lay buried under warm ashes, as ashes mingled with other ashes.

When daylight streamed in, I jumped out of bed, looked across the river, hoping last night was just a nightmare. The Empire State Building was still standing. Sadly, the twins were no longer on the scene.

The next morning, we drove up to Connecticut to pick up Minal. The highways were deserted. She spent the next couple of weeks with us in New Jersey. Her office was closed for the first week. The second week she took the ferry to New York and then a cross-town bus to work. For many months thereafter, she was terrified to take subways or a bus ride through Lincoln Tunnel.

On Friday night when she returned from work, Minal and I chatted after dinner, and she broke down. I let her cry, purge her pain, as she recalled the times she went to eat and shop at the World Trade Center. It was her neighborhood.

"One of them had a big friendly dog. Mom, I wonder what happened to the dog and the lady. I wonder how many people in my building did not make it."

"Say a prayer for them, Minal."

Sunday, September 23, 2001: Twelve days after the terrorist attacks, Ranjit and I drove Minal downtown to pick up some of her personal belongings from her apartment. At the Lincoln Tunnel tollgate, searches of taxicabs, trucks and minivans brought the traffic to a crawl. While we inched our way through the traffic, my eyes traveled to the tunnel rooftop where four armed guards stood in full deployment mode, with rifles pointed towards the tollbooths.

When we got to the other side of the tunnel in New York City, we found the traffic had been diverted. West Side Highway, the usual route to Minal's home, had been cordoned off and would remain closed for several months.

Only two weeks before, the mighty Twin Towers had stood there proud and tall.

We parked our car at a parking lot by Canal Street station in Chinatown, beyond which all roads were closed to traffic. Pulling out two empty suitcases from the trunk, we crossed the street and took two subways to our destination: Bowling Green Station. Although Minal lived only about five miles away from our home, it took us over two hours to get to her apartment that day. Before crossing the street, we slipped on our surgical masks for protection. It was reported that the air by the World Trade Center was contaminated from chemical spills, asbestos dust, and charred structures.

Except for the state troopers and national guards in camouflage suits, the streets of downtown were deserted. Army vehicles, barricades and checkpoints marred the scene. A delightful neighborhood had been transformed into a war zone by one morning's tragedy.

We took off our surgical masks outside Minal's apartment building. The acrid smell of carnage and chemicals seemed to have been contained for the moment. Standing there by the barricades at One West Street, we looked towards the World Trade Center grounds, referred to as Ground Zero. All at once, I got an urge to visit the site I had seen over and over again on television for the past two weeks.

Presenting my New York driver's license to the National Guard, I told him we have come to collect my daughter's personal things from her apartment, and asked if I could visit Ground Zero. The man in the camouflage suit let me through. Some of the guards securing the area were provided temporary lodging in the building where Minal lived. That may have helped, as no one was permitted entry beyond the barricades on West Side Highway.

Before Ranjit and Minal could stop me, I took off like a cheetah, wheeling an empty carry-on behind me that Minal needed for packing. I did not look over my shoulder. I did not respond to Minal's calls. There was no one there but me on the deserted highway. One morning's tragedy had turned downtown into an eerie ghost town. The skywalk ahead of me was also blown out.

As I got closer to the ill-fated site, the guards stopped me twice for my identification papers. I learned from Officer Cordova that he and other officers had been working twelve-to-fifteen hour days. When I told the officer I wanted to get a closer view of the site, he directed me one short block up along the side street. And there on Rector Street I saw the appalling ruins of the 110-story twins, the skeletal remains of an architectural dream. A dream that had taken more than a decade to conceive and seven years to build had been destroyed in an hour. Some fifty feet away, a massive haunting smoldering pit with steel girders was gaping at me. At the foot of the girders was a mound of mud and debris.

Standing there, I felt a void. With the ashes still warm and no one there but me, I closed my eyes, clasped my hands, dropped my head and said a prayer. I did not know anyone buried under the rubble, but I felt their loss, as if they had been my neighbors.

From ashes to ashes; from ashes to birch, to healing, to new beginnings.

I thought about the families with empty chairs at dinner tables, of children who had lost a parent, and of those who were laid to rest with unfulfilled dreams. In those few moments of silence, I was overwhelmed by emotions. In those few moments of reflection, I was forever changed.

Brushing away my tears, I returned to my daughter's apartment. The Venetian-style lobby of the century-old landmark building was gracefully decorated with a fresco-vaulted ceiling. In the past when I visited Minal, the concierge sat behind a desk and a doorman in brass-buttoned red jacket, white cotton pants, white gloves and hat helped us unload our things from the car. The man in the red jacket was not there today. A young lady sat at the reception desk in the long lobby. I introduced myself to her. She said she was a building resident and was filling in that day for the concierge.

"Your daughter is waiting for you in her apartment."

"If she calls again, tell her I'm on my way."

"The electricity is still out in the building. Only one of the six elevators is working on a generator." She pointed out to the one in service.

I took the elevator to the twenty-fourth floor. Minal answered the door. She was a little peeved at me. "Mom, we are only allowed twenty minutes to pick up our things and you took off with the carry-on I needed for packing."

I apologized and helped her finish packing. Within minutes, we were out the door with two packed suitcases, a large paper bag filled with shoes, and a toiletries bag.

We stopped to talk to the young lady in the lobby. When I asked her why only twenty minutes were permitted to collect our things, she explained, "Today is the first day residents are allowed to return to their apartments. For safety reasons, I can allow only four residents in at a time."

"Did the building suffer any damage?" I asked.

"No. But it has gone through many days of intensive cleaning. There was thick dust and smoke in the corridors. Tenants who had left their windows open that morning returned to find a two-inch thick layer of soot on their windowsills today. Their furniture, their carpet, their belongings were all covered with dust."

"Must be asbestos dust. Did the tenants have renter's insurance?" I asked.

"I don't know, but I bet now they wish they did."

Minal heaved a sigh. "I'm glad I shut my window the night before. It was pouring. Did anyone from this building die?"

"Unfortunately, some of them who worked at the World Trade Center did not make it."

A sad look crept over Minal's face. "I wonder which ones I had met on the elevator who did not make it."

Just then a group of men and women carrying cleaning equipment entered the premises. "That's the cleanup crew," she said. "Today is their last cleaning day here."

Wheeling the suitcases behind us, Ranjit, Minal and I took the subways back. As we walked towards our car parked by Canal Street, we were alarmed by a thunderous explosion and saw a big dust cloud rise from Ground Zero. We were ready to run for shelter, when a passerby seeing the anxious look on our faces said, "No need to run for cover. They're demolishing one of the other World Trade Center buildings that was damaged."

With the leveling of seven buildings scheduled that week, a Herculean cleanup task lay ahead for the city. With sirens blaring all over New York City, it felt safer to be living on the other side of the Hudson River.

It had been an emotion-packed morning. Ranjit got behind the wheel. We were all silent in the car as we drove home. I reflected on John Lennon's beautiful lyrics of "Imagine." Yes John, what a beautiful world it would be if there were no countries, no wars, no religion, but people living as one, in peace. "You may say I'm a dreamer, but I'm not the only one. . ."

The following week, Minal returned to her downtown apartment. I urged her to stay with us a while longer, but she was determined to move on with her life. She also wanted to look around for another apartment in midtown, closer to where she worked. Since the Rector Street station had caved in, she had to take the bus to work.

With fires still raging, spitting fumes of paint and plastic, and the demolition of buildings kicking up mounds of asbestos dust at Ground Zero, in a matter of days Minal developed a respiratory problem and had to go see a doctor.

All month long following the tragedy, we kept our windows shut as the stench of the carnage and chemicals traveled across the river and seeped into our New Jersey apartment. It must have been difficult for the New Yorkers to breathe.

Night and day, patrol boats policed the river and military helicopters with strobe lights circled around the Empire State Building, all over the city, and up and down the river. At times the copter came so close to my building, I could see the pilot inside. Any closer and the rotors would have rammed through my window. I also lived in a two-dimensional world. The condominium we had leased had a wall of mirrored closet doors in the bedroom that reflected the New York skyline. And if a green chopper circled outside my window, there was one reflected in the mirror, too. I drew the window blinds on the peeping tom and returned to my reading. Books had become my refuge from the turmoil outside.

Monday, October 1, 2001: I went to Manhattan with Ari, who was visiting us from Atlanta. We stopped at St. Patrick's Cathedral on Fifth Avenue, as I usually do when I am in the neighborhood. The church was packed that afternoon. All seats were taken and there was barely any standing room. From a police officer at the door, I learned that a memorial service was in progress for the fire chief, who had died in the line of duty at the World Trade Center on

9/11. I paid my respect, lit a candle and left. Television news stated that fifty funerals were held each day of the month in the city for victims of the tragedy.

Concerned for Minal's persistent cough and news reports warning of contaminated air downtown, I insisted she spend a few nights with us.

Saturday, October 6, 2001: Three weeks after the ominous day, Minal found herself another apartment near Columbus Circle. I helped her pack for the move. As I took down the pictures from the wall, I saw the red-tasseled, rosewood-and-jade Chinese wall hanging staring down at me; the one that hung in our California home and was meant to bring us good luck; the one that was off the wall and then on again. Only now, I grew skeptical. I wondered if this good luck charm had saved Minal from worse harm or brought her to the door of this tragedy.

"Minal, what do you want me to do with this Chinese wall hanging?"

"You can throw it away. I don't want it."

With the ornamental rosewood hanging in my hand, I walked up to the trash compacter room in the hallway. The garbage chute was backed up. Next to it sat a stack of packing boxes and a pile of trash bags. I left the pretty Chinese wall hanging on top of a box and walked away. No more would I worry if it brought good luck or bad.

With most of the packing done, we visited Ground Zero. It was practically in Minal's backyard. The light rain earlier in the day had muted the smoke stench and toxins in the air. A small crowd had gathered there this evening. Some clicked their cameras; some had sadness written on their faces; others were in shock as they took in the tragic scene.

We walked up a side street and found a car cloaked in white dust parked by the curb. "Is this asbestos dust?" I inquired from a security guard standing nearby.

He confirmed my fears. "Yes ma'am."

In a flash, haunting images of the dust cloud that chased people down the streets on the ill-fated morning returned. I grabbed Minal's hand. "Let's get out of here. We don't want any of that white powder on our clothes or up our noses with a gust of wind."

Pinching our noses, we crossed the street. On West Side Highway, we stopped to talk to an officer whose nametag read Priola. About a hundred feet away, a mammoth construction crane was spraying a stream of fluid over the rubble at Ground Zero.

"What is it spraying? I asked the officer.

"Embalming fluid ma'am," he explained, "to preserve the bodies under the rubble and keep the stench down."

Embalming fluid. Makeshift mortuary at Brooks Brothers store. Minal was living by a mass graveyard. I was glad it did not take her long to find a new abode.

We crossed the West Side Highway to Battery Park City — a waterfront condominium community located on the banks of the Hudson River. At the entrance, a security officer checked our ID and let us through. A short distance away, a handful of officers chatted around a small garden table while another hosed down the dusty tires of vehicles exiting Ground Zero with a detoxifying rinse. At another table sat Officer Jean Pierre. We briefly joined him and exchanged some notes.

It was Minal's last stroll in her neighborhood. In a few days, she would be moving out of her downtown apartment. As the evening faded and colors of the sunset spilled into the sea, we ambled down the promenade along the riverbank. And there in the midst of the surging waves, stood Lady Liberty bold and tall, holding high the freedom torch for us all.

A garden trail led us to an alcove. "Mom, some evenings I come here and feed the ducks. It's so quiet here."

Standing there on a canopied boardwalk in mellow lighting, we watched the ducks frolic in the waters. For a few peaceful moments in the twilight hour, we leaned on the wooden banister and watched the nightlights dance on the lapping waves as they kissed the shore.

Thursday, October 11, 2001: A month after the tragic day, the fires were still burning at Ground Zero. That morning, Ranjit and I drove into New York to help Minal move to her midtown apartment. The night before, the FBI had put out a security bulletin, which triggered the country's security alert code to be moved up from yellow to orange. The drive was a nightmare. Security checks slowed the traffic to a crawl. Traffic to the financial district was restricted to residents and employees.

At one checkpoint, a police officer asked for Minal's telephone number and called her to verify if she was expecting us. At another checkpoint, we were pulled off the line. Although we showed our documents and a copy of the moving company's papers to the officer, he had us take an exit, sending us away from our destination. We turned around and joined the traffic line again. This time another officer at the checkpoint pulled us off the line. After reviewing our documents, he let us through. As we took off, the previous officer, who had refused us entry, waved and yelled for us to stop. We did not. Instead, we quickly merged with the moving traffic and finally made it to Minal's apartment.

The movers also had a difficult time getting to Battery Park downtown. A police inspector escorted them in their truck from Jacob Javits Center in midtown to the apartment building. The officer did not release the truck until he met in person with Minal. Every van, every truck, every taxi going downtown was inspected, for fear they could be carrying a bomb. Later, news reports revealed that New York's financial district had been the target of another potential attack that day. No wonder the alert code was reset to orange and extra safety measures were taken by the officials.

The movers loaded the truck. While Ranjit and Minal drove in the overloaded car, I accompanied the movers in the moving truck. I could not wait to get to Minal's new apartment in midtown. However, due to security checks and traffic bottlenecks, it took us over two hours to get there.

The 9/11 tragedy had not only caused loss of lives, but also livelihood for many. It delivered a crippling blow to New York City's economy. Some companies moved their operations to other states. Since the air downtown was still unsafe to breathe and asbestos clung to the exterior of the buildings, many merchants and tenants vacated their premises. Some residents moved out of the city, others moved out of state. But, Minal's heart belonged to New York.

Saturday, October 20, 2001: I took the bus into the city. As I walked up 8th Avenue to Minal's midtown apartment, I noticed a small crowd gathered around a wagon on 44th Street. I stopped to take a peek. There on the cart were three life-size bronze plaques, gifts from an Italian company: a fireman on bent knee holding his helmet in his arm, another of a fireman leading two children by their hands, and a plaque engraved with lyrics of "America the Beautiful."

Further up on 48th Street, bouquets of flowers and miniature US flags lay on the sidewalk outside a firehouse, a sign above which read: Engine 54, Ladder 4, Battalion 9. Next to the offerings, a memorial book lay open on a wooden pedestal. Inside the firehouse, two men were at work, buffing the fire engine.

I approached the older one, who was polishing a fist-size round brass item in his hand. "Excuse me, Sir. Did your crew make it through on September 11th?"

He shook his head without looking up at me and continued to polish the brass.

"You had casualties at this firehouse?"

"Yes."

"How many?"

"Everyone who reported to work that day." He spoke so softly I had to strain my ears.

"How many reported to work that day?"

"Fourteen or fifteen."

"You lost them all?"

"Yes." He opened the fire engine door and placed the brass item on the seat.

"I'm sorry to hear that."

Head bent, he walked into a small office. I wished him luck. On my way out, I signed the memorial book. I was choking with emotions as I walked up to Minal's apartment on 56th Street, the one she had moved into only days ago.

With security alerts and anthrax scares, people in the city were gripped by paranoia. They were afraid to check their mail for fear some white anthrax powder might jump out at them when they tore open the envelope. Their emotions ebbed and flowed with the FBI alert color code.

Sunday, November 18, 2001: I had set the alarm clock to wake up at 3:30 that morning to watch the meteor showers. In the early hours, as I looked out the window, I saw a few sprinkles of stardust, a pause, and then it was raining stars over the Hudson River and New York City. Stars spilling from the Milky Way, showering us with blessings — courtesy of asteroid Comet Tempel-Tuttle and its trail of Leonid meteor showers.

I slipped into a coat and stole out of the apartment to watch the star-spangled pageant from the building terrace. A handful of stargazers were already there. Standing there in the open-air theater, I feasted my eyes on the celestial magic as hundreds of stars zipped through the sky; some with tails, others that left fine trails. A burst of shooting stars, wishing stars, morning stars lit up the sky — falling, blessing, healing. My eyes traveled to where the Twin Towers once stood, as I remembered another surreal morning. Stars of hope now fell into that space of void. Wounded and blessed this year were we.

The pit at Ground Zero burned for months until old man winter arrived and blanketed the void with white.

Over the years, I stopped by to see the construction progress of the *Freedom Tower* at Ground Zero. On the Viewing Wall fence were bulletin boards with 2,792 names of the fallen and a chronology of September 11 events. A silver-haired, bearded piper in soiled clothing and a baseball cap usually played "Amazing Grace" and "Glory, glory, Hallelujah" on his flute for the visitors. I crossed the street to say a prayer at the historic St. Paul's Chapel, which was set up as a staging place for relief operations on 9/11. Cots used by first responders on that day were on display at the church. After signing my name on the patron's scroll of paper, I walked around the garden to reflect a bit and then took a stroll in the neighborhood.

On April 21, 2009, US President Barack Obama signed legislation to officially designate September 11 as a federally recognized National Day of Service and Remembrance.[10] It also prompted me to connect with a larger community for the greater good.

Mother Becomes Child

After the heartrending 9/11 tragedy, it was time for another long respite. That December, Ranjit and I took a seven-week vacation to India. Over the years, our traveling assignments and the stresses of life had created a distance between us. It was time for us to reconnect and see our families again, before it was too late.

During this visit to Mumbai, Ranjit stayed with his family while I stayed with my kin. It was good to see my mother again, although like autumn leaves she was withering away with time. The only glimpse she got of the outside world was the tall apartment building outside her window, some two hundred feet away at Cuffe Parade. Confined to bed, she had aged faster, but she still had that twinkle in her eyes. At eighty-seven, she suffered from memory lapses. She repeated herself for the fifth time, but I pretended I heard her story for the first time. At times, she unleashed her troubles on the live-in maid. But it was not my mother's fault. She was in her tender years. In her heydays, she used to run an efficient household with six children, servants, and constant guests.

However, on this trip I was shocked to find my sixty-six year old brother, Mangha, in frail health and dampened spirits; not the bold stalwart I had known him to be. He looked very pale and had grown incredibly lean. None of my siblings had informed me he was so ill.

When I inquired about his health, he confessed, "I have a kidney problem."

"How bad is it?"

"I go to the hospital three times a week for dialysis. They hook me up to a machine for four hours to clean out my kidneys. The other two days I go for physical therapy for my legs." The aneurysm surgery he had undergone two years ago had not brought much relief. In fact, the surgery had only complicated the problem.

"How long do you have to continue with the dialysis?"

"Until I can find a donor. But the doctor said that at my age the transplant is not always successful. I went for dialysis early this year. After six months I felt better, so I stopped the treatment. Then my lungs got infected. The doctor said the bile had retreated to my lungs. They flushed out my lungs and put me back on dialysis."

I was at a loss for words. Last year my mother had taken to bed; this year, it was my brother. During my visit the year before, he would join his friends at the Wodehouse Gymkhana Club in the evenings and chitchat over a couple of drinks of Scotch whisky. My brother had many friends, but no partner in life to help him through the rough patches. He was once married. It was an arranged marriage, but after a year the couple parted. He never remarried.

When Mangha returned from his dialysis treatment, he felt nauseous and drained and stayed in bed all afternoon. Watching him waste away, I felt the weight of his suffering. I felt his pain. Sometimes, I warmed coconut oil and gave his back a gentle rub. Other times, I had him sit in his chair and exercise his arms and legs, but he would tire soon.

On weekends when he did not visit the doctor or the hospital, we chatted or watched a cricket match on television in his bedroom. Then we listened to songs from yesteryears.

When Dean Martin's "Sway" played, I said, "Mangha, remember you taught me to waltz to it when I was barely ten? And you taught me to fox trot and jive and cha-cha."

A soft smile crept upon his face and that old spark returned to his eyes. But his pain overshadowed his smile.

Another Sunday, Mangha called me to his room to listen to tapes and CDs of old music. I opened the window to let in some fresh air. The room reeked of tobacco. Despite the air conditioning unit, odor from his last cigarette lingered. Although he did not smoke or drink much these days, every once in a while when he lit a cigarette I reminded him that it was not good for his health.

"To heck with it. I'm going to die anyway one of these days," he would say.

We basked in the vintage tunes of the fifties. I was drenched with nostalgia as I hummed along with the Platters to *Only You* and *The Great Pretender.*

I tapped my feet, snapped my fingers and clicked my tongue to Bill Haley's *Rock Around the Clock* and *See You Later, Alligator.* I wished Dave Brubeck's *Take Five* music would not stop, and my heart danced to Glenn Miller's *In the Mood* rhythm.

That morning, I think my brother almost forgot he was ill while I felt like ten years old again. Over lunch, we listened to soothing music by Yanni.

Some evenings, I met Ranjit for tea at the Taj Hotel's Sea Lounge. We sat by the window looking out to the Arabian Sea, watching gondolas and cruise boats sail by, and crowds in vibrant clothing stroll down the Gateway of India promenade.

Every night at my family home, the lights were turned out before the clock struck ten. With my inner clock still ticking to New York time, ten hours behind, I was not ready to turn in for the night. So I sat in the living room and read until my eyelids grew heavy.

As I slipped under the covers on the twin bed in my mother's room, Mangha broke into a coughing spell in the adjoining room. I rolled out of bed, went to his room and gave him a tablespoon of honey. It calmed his throat and I returned to bed. But then the dogfights outside broke the silence of the night and kept me awake. Half an hour later, my mother pressed the buzzer by her bed to summon the live-in maid. The maid walked into the room, turned on the lights, rubbed the sleep from her eyes, and attended to my mother. Fifteen minutes later, the lights went out. At times, it was almost four when I finally fell asleep.

At half-past six, the doorbell chimed. The live-in cook answered the door. It was the milkman. Soon the maid and the cook were bickering, Indian music was blaring from the kitchen, pots clanking, crows cawing, dogs barking, and the building watchman yelling at someone in the compound a couple of stories below. A new day had dawned in the busy city of Mumbai. Fortunately, my family's apartment building was set away from the road and the balcony overlooked a park, else the street clamor and the constant honking of cars would have driven me out of my mind.

Confined to bed, my mother's legs had become stiff and bent at the knees. I offered to rent a wheelchair and take her out for fresh air and sunshine, but she turned me down. She said she could not straighten her legs. I told her I would make her outing comfortable, but that did not sway her mind. Guilt pangs nudged at my heart. I had not been there for her during her difficult years while she had raised us with such loving care.

When the day wore heavy on her, I opened the cupboard where I kept the large box of assorted liqueur-filled chocolates I had bought for her from a duty-free shop at the Amsterdam airport. "Mummy, which one will you have today?"

Like a child, my mother's eyes lit up as she gazed at the chocolates wrapped in colorful foils. Picking one, she carefully peeled the gold foil wrapper, bit into the neck of the chocolate bottle and blissfully slurped the liqueur until the nectar was gone. Then she put the empty bottle in her mouth and she was one happy camper. A gentle calm slowly washed over her face. Moments later, she smiled baring her teeth. The maid gave her a quick wash and change. Once I even trimmed her nails before the liqueur effect wore off.

Since my mother did not let the live-in maid comb her hair, it became matted. She only let the part-time maid, who stopped by to launder the family clothes, comb her hair and attend to her bedsores.

While I combed my mother's scanty long tresses one morning, I asked the live-in maid to tell her a story. Engrossed in the tale, my mother did not realize I had cropped her hair short. Peter Pan short. The maid had to keep extending the story to hold her attention until I was done clipping.

It was not until sundown that my mother realized her long gray locks were gone. A sad look crept upon her face. "Baby, did you cut my hair?"

"Yes Mummy. Now your hair will not get tangled."

She moved her fingers slowly through her short hair.

"Mummy until I am here, I will give you oil massage and your hair will grow back fast."

To cheer her up, I broke into an old Indian song by Mukesh that called out her name, Radha, and sang of the two sacred rivers of India: the Ganga and the Jamuna (Yamuna). "Mere man ki Ganga, aur tere man ki Jamuna; Bhol Radha bhol sangam hoga ki nahi?" With the Ganges of my heart and the Jamuna of yours; Pray tell me Radha, will our hearts ever meet?"

She hummed along. I held up her chin, looked her in the eyes and repeated, "Bhol Radha bhol sangam hoga ki nahi?"

The merry song lifted her sagging spirits and she conceded with a smile, "Hoga, hoga, hoga." It will happen, happen, happen.

Watching my mother being cared for like a child took me back to a distant day, when Suresh made his debut in the family. That afternoon, I found my mother propped up in bed with a little baby in her arms: fair of face, dark hair and bright charcoal eyes. I thought she was holding a neighbor's baby. Instead she said, "God gave me this baby brother for you when I went to the terrace for the *puja* this morning." That week, a religious event was held on the rooftop terrace.

At age four, how could I have known anything about babies or storks? I believed my mother. I always did. Mothers went to the rooftop terrace and prayed, and God gave them a gift: a baby. My mother had received six gifts from God. He must like her a lot, I thought. The ceremony on the rooftop lasted all week. I remember trudging up two flights everyday and bringing the blessed fruit, *prasaad*, to share with my family. That is the earliest memory I have of my mother.

Pearls of Life

They bring sunshine and love tarts,
Leave tender trails in our hearts.
For them we build castles of dreams,
Thru' them we appreciate what life means.

They shower us with hugs and kisses,
Turn our worries into a basket of blisses,
Weave their stories with a magic brush,
Fill our lives with music and mirth.

Then one day we wake up and find,
Our young ones have left their nest behind,
They have gone to fend for themselves,
For they are no longer the size of elves.

Now caring for young ones of their own,
They look back at the years that have flown,
Share pearls of wisdom with their offspring,
Laugh with them and count their blessings.

-Jaya Kamlani

Southern Escape

When we planned this vacation to India, we had included time for a side trip to the south. Only now I hated to leave my mother and brother when they needed me most. On the other hand, Ranjit had already purchased the three-week tour package. Flight and hotel payments were made. He would not understand if I asked him to cancel the plans. It was not his family.

The day after Christmas 2001, we took an early morning flight for Bangalore (now Bengaluru), the technology hub of India. Across the West End Taj Hotel, where we spent a couple of nights, was the racetrack. It so happened that upon our arrival, I fell ill from food poisoning. The next day, while I stayed in bed, Ranjit wound up going to the races alone. That evening, he attended a wedding party on the hotel grounds.

When he returned, he was in mighty good spirit. "Jaya, you don't know what you missed. A real nice wedding. The couple was so handsome."

"But you don't know these people, Ranjit. How could you attend?"

"So? I gate crashed. I went around and introduced myself. Met a lot of nice people."

"Have you had dinner?"

"Yes, I had dinner with them. It was a wedding reception."

"I'm sure you charmed them, too."

The following day, when I felt better, a chauffeured car drove us around the city's Cubbon Park. In the afternoon, we took a walk through the sprawling botanical gardens and did some shopping in the evening. Bangalore and Mysore are two cities to shop for beautiful silk saris.

We drove to the city of Mysore. En route, we stopped at the Tipu Sultan Palace built in the eighteenth century. The structure with scalloped Moorish arches was weathered by two centuries of neglect. Tipu Sultan, ruler of Mysore, was defeated and killed by the British in 1799.

The next day, we visited the Mysore Palace, once home to the former royal family of the Wodeyars for five-and-a-half centuries until India's independence in 1947, when all 562 princely states had come under the jurisdiction of India. Nestled on sprawling grounds, the palace had opulent halls and carved redwood doors inlaid with ivory. It also included a museum that showcased royal armory, sedan chairs, coronation robes, and antiques. Its walls were graced with murals depicting war scenes from the Indian epic, *Mahabharata*. Later that evening, we visited the Brindavan Gardens, which boasted colorful dancing fountains on the banks of the Cauvery River. We had to wait in a long winding line to view the fountains.

On New Year's Eve, we set out early for a day-trip to the hills of Coorg. Mile-upon-mile we passed tropical forests, coconut groves, and wayside villages. We drove past coffee plantations and peppercorn and cardamom groves, where the scent of coffee and exotic spices wafted in the air. Two hours later, at the misty height of five thousand feet, we arrived at the Orange County Resort Hotel and took a stroll around the hotel grounds. The lodge was fringed by rosewood and mango trees, coconut palms, Dubare Reserve Forest and Lake Thadakam. A lone man had anchored his boat and was enjoying the day fishing on the lake with his dog. The rustic setting provided a peaceful ambiance. I wanted to indulge in a nice hot oil ayurvedic massage at the spa, but it was closed for the day.

We could have spent the New Year's night here, but we were not dressed for the occasion. That morning, we had checked into a hotel in Mysore, left our belongings there and had planned to attend the New Year's party on the hotel grounds.

Upon our return from Coorg, I rushed to bed and slipped under the covers. The rickety drive on the country roads had unsettled my stomach. Once again, Ranjit wound up going to the party alone.

Next morning, we took a flight to the islands of Kochi (formerly Cochin) in Kerala, located along the southwestern coast of the Indian peninsula. According to legend, centuries ago Lord Parasuraman, the sixth incarnation of Lord Vishnu, stood on a mountain peak and flung his axe across the seas. The land that emerged from these cobalt waters was Kerala — a land of tropical rain forests and wildlife sanctuary, mountains and lakes, bordered by the Arabian Sea to its west and forested hills to its east.[11]

A car picked us up from the airport and drove us through a long stretch of a palm tree-lined country road. We passed a busy seafaring town until we pulled up at the Taj Malabar Hotel on Willingdon Island.

With terraced grounds overlooking Lake Vembanad, the lakefront hotel with its high ceilings, mahogany wood beams and paneling revealed old colonial charm of the British era. That evening, we joined the hotel guests for a sunset cruise. As the boat cut through the lake waters, the tour guide brought our attention to the fourteenth century mechanically operated Chinese fishing nets. They were all done with their catch and pulled up for the day.

"Long ago, Chinese merchants from the court of Kubla Khan traded on this island," he explained.

As we sailed past colonial bungalows and the elite clubhouse once patronized by the British, he reminded us of the days when under the colonial rule, Indian citizens were not permitted entry to this or any other social club of India. As daylight faded, the skipper turned off the engine, and we watched a crimson sun cast its last rays for the day as it slowly dipped and melted into the lake.

The cruise was followed by candlelight dinner on the lakefront terrace. An elaborate buffet of delectable Southern cuisine: fried fish, chicken curry, Goanese shrimp curry in coconut cream, *sambhar* (lentil curry), *idli* (steamed rice puffs), *masala dosa* (rice crêpes with potato stuffing), and much more. The spicy, savory spread of dishes kindled our taste buds. For dessert, an assortment of mouthwatering delights: semolina *halvah,* wheat *payasam,* cakes and custard pudding. If Kerala was God's own country, then this was ambrosia, food of the gods.

The next morning, after a therapeutic ayurvedic massage and breakfast, we went into town. The hotel chauffeur let us off by a narrow street lined with shops that carried sandalwood carvings, teak furniture, curios, and spices. The scent of cinnamon spice wafted in the air. Kochi, once an epicenter of international trade for coffee, spices, and handicrafts, was still bustling.

Nestled in the corner of the street was *Pardesi* synagogue, a white-washed structure with a bell tower dating back to 1568. Inside the temple, under Belgian chandeliers, lay Hebrew inscriptions and long scrolls of the Old Testament under a glass case. A man there told us that the town was once home to hundreds of Jewish families, but now only six families remained.

Next, we drove up to Santa Cruz Basilica, a Roman Catholic Church and then on to St. Francis Church, the oldest European Church in India, built in 1503, where the body of the Portuguese explorer Vasco de Gama was originally laid to rest, then later moved to a monastery in Lisbon, Portugal. The Catholics in Goa, Cochin, and Mumbai are of Portuguese descent. As I stepped out of the church, I was drawn to a tablet on a wooden post that read, "This tablet is erected as memorial of the visit of her majesty Queen Elizabeth of Great Britain on 17th October 1997."

In a flash, I was back to my ninth grade class in 1961 when the teacher announced the Queen of England was coming to town. Her carriage was to drive past the main causeway, one short block from my school. Although India was no longer a British colony, that afternoon, along with hundreds of other students, I waited to catch a glimpse of the queen as her motorcade passed by. I remember to this day how beautiful and graceful young Queen Elizabeth looked as she sat in her black carriage and gently waved to the spirited crowd. I waved back. The Queen was then thirty-five while I, thirteen.

Earlier that month, a coloring contest of the queen was held in the city. I bought myself a set of paint brushes, a tray of watercolor paints, a few mini jars of assorted metallic paints, and ten black-and-white posters with an outline of the queen in her royal attire. For the next fortnight, I spent many play hours painting lovely portraits of Queen Elizabeth in an opulent evening gown and sparkling crown jewels. Even though I did not win the competition, I enjoyed painting the pictures.

After two memorable days in Kochi, a speedboat ferried us to Kumarakom – a coastal hamlet in Kerala fringed by rubber plantations, rice paddies, banana and coconut groves, and mangrove-lined shores. Bouncing with every wave, tipping its tail end into the lake, the speedboat sent my adrenalin pumping. There was no seat belt. I prayed I would not fly off the boat with the next wave for I cannot swim. Twenty minutes later, I heaved a sigh as the feisty ride came to an end, a little mechanical gate opened, and the boat glided through the canal and entered the private blue lagoon of the Taj Garden Retreat Hotel.

The 120-year old two-story historic colonial bungalow was once home to three generations of the Bakers, a missionary family from England. Nestled in the shade of the coconut palms were several chalets and a houseboat moored in the lagoon.

With terracotta floors, high ceilings, crown moldings, European paintings, and a masonry fireplace, our charming suite upstairs with colonial ambiance was inviting. Outside the six suites was a large lounge with rattan furniture where I sat and read the newspaper. A middle-aged man by the name of Bogle joined me for some light conversation.

In the evening, when the sun disappeared behind the mangroves, we savored a cuisine of grilled chicken, fish curry, tofu-style *paneer* cheese curry, *idli sambhar*, rice pilaf, noodles, and more. For dessert, we indulged in the pistachio soufflé, rice pudding, and fruit salad with ice cream. Afterwards, under a canopy of stars we tuned into live classical music on the *sitar* and *tabla*, and feasted our eyes on the traditional *Bharat Natyam* southern dances.

The next morning, we took an overnight cruise on a motorized houseboat to Lake Vembanad. The boat was equipped with two bedrooms with attached baths, a kitchen, and a lounge furnished with a divan, a round glass-top dining table, and wicker chairs. Orange life preservers hung from the ceiling and a large Carom board leaned against a wall.

Our crew included two navigators and a cook. The cook was also our tour guide. Sporting a curly moustache and blue plaid loongyi wrap, the mahogany-toned skipper turned on the ignition. The engine roared. The seagulls flapped their wings and soared. Not a cloud in the sky.

Sunlight filtered through the mangroves as our boat snaked around the emerald canals, known as the Backwaters of Kerala. Skirting leisurely around the waterweeds that spilled from one village to the next, we glided past rice paddies and mud houses with palm-thatched roofs.

We passed the coastal town of Alappuzha, where holy statues of Jesus and Mary were enshrined in alcoves along the water's edge. The Christians who live in Kerala are of Syrian descent. The town was bustling with activity. Children returning from school waved to us. Women pounded soiled clothes on the rocks as soapsuds floated down the river. Overloaded double-decker commuter boats ferried workers to the rice fields; canopied cargo boats were headed for the market.

When the sun grew bold, the pilot turned off the engine and walked to the rear of the boat. It was lunchtime. The young cook in white cotton pants served us vegetable club sandwiches and fruit for lunch. While we ate, he filled us in on the local news.

"Did you finish school?" I asked.

"Yes. It is compulsory. Everybody here has to go to school."

"Everybody?"

"Yes, everybody. We have to pass twelfth class. Everybody in Kerala speaks English."

"How about college?"

"I wanted to go to college, but it is too far. All colleges are in the city. It takes more than two hours to get there. After school, I started working."

"What kind of jobs do you have here?"

Stroking his chin, he smiled. "Fishing, pulling coconuts from trees, working in the rice fields and rubber plantations. I worked in the rice fields. The government gives land to everybody in the village to grow their own vegetables." He cleared the table. "You must come again in August."

"Why August?"

"That's when everybody in town comes out to see the boat race." His teeth gleamed against his mocha skin as he smiled.

After lunch, the skipper's mate took the over the wheel and navigated through the meandering canals. Like most Keralites, he too wore a dark mustache, but his was long and curled at the ends, like an army Brigadier's. When the sun peaked, the cook lowered the bamboo shades in the lounge and served us tea and cookies.

After tea, Ranjit placed the big Carom board on the glass table and sprinkled it with talcum powder. In the center of the board, he arranged the mini beige and black discs around the red queen. Then he gave the large striker disc such a flick on the board with his two fingers that it hit a couple of mini discs and sent them flying into the side pockets of the board, just like when you play pool and you send the balls to the billiard table pockets with your cue stick.

After beating me in three of the four rounds, he boasted, "See, I won again."

"So? It doesn't prove anything except that you're good at Carom."

Had it not been for the skipper at the wheel sitting some thirty feet away, my husband would have beaten his chest like Tarzan. Oh yes, he would. He has done that many times before. While I put away the discs in the box, I let him bask in his moment of glory. We put away the Carom board, sank into our lounge chairs, took turns to read aloud a few pages from *The Inscrutable Americans*, and enjoyed a few laughs. The skipper, who had by now folded the umbrella and slipped on a khaki safari hat, turned his head and smiled, as if to say, "I got the joke, too." After reading a few pages, I put the book away. It wasn't funny anymore.

The sun eased down. The cook rolled up the shades and the skipper took off his sunhat. A couple of commuter boats teeming with villagers passed us by. They were returning from their day's work on the rice paddies.

By now, we had passed the meandering canals and were entering Lake Vembanad — a freshwater lake where the emerald Backwaters of Kerala converge. There, sitting on the divan sipping on our coconut drinks, we drank in the peaceful scene. At six o'clock, the skipper turned the boat around to face the sun and dropped the anchor. Along the palm-fringed shores, the seagulls and blackbirds flocked home as the tired sun surrendered to the lake.

Twilight set in. The cook walked in with two mosquito coils. He lit them and placed them under the dining table, to keep the buzzing insects at bay. The mosquitoes were on an offense that evening. After serving us dinner of fried fish, vegetables and chapattis, the crew retired to the stern of the boat for the night.

Ranjit turned out the lights to keep the mosquitoes away. We lay on the divan as evening morphed into the night. Under a crescent moon, a handful of houseboats were moored in the distance. Laughter streamed in from one direction; music and singing from another. Before long, the lights on the other houseboats were out and we were plunged in the thick of darkness on the lake. We weaved our way to the bedroom. It was time to retire for the evening. In the hush of the night, the gentle sway of the boat lulled us to sleep.

The next morning, I was up before the first blush of dawn. I stepped into the lounge and found a chain of four houseboats anchored in the distance. *Must be the party caravan from last night.*

As the skipper turned the boat around to face the rising sun, three fishing boats rowed in our direction. One of them pulled up by our houseboat. The fisherman in a white vest and plaid *loongyi*, folded above his knees, threw a large fishing net into the lake. While he waited for his catch, he hummed along to the *Malyali* music coming from the other boat anchored some two hundred feet away.

Moments later, a smile lit up his face as he pulled up a heap of mussels and emptied them into his dinghy. He looked up at me. I gave him my nod of approval. With a small metal can, he collected the water from the bottom of the boat that had accompanied the mussels and emptied it into the lake. At eight o'clock, the three fishermen put away their fishing nets and turned their boats around.

"They're going to the market to sell the mussels," said the cook.

Our skipper, too, pulled up the anchor and turned around. We had been moored on Lake Vembanad for fourteen hours.

When the boat docked, two little boys, about seven or eight years old, ran up to meet us. "Do you have pens?" they asked.

"Pens? Yes of course." I dug into my purse and handed them the only two pens I had.

Where there is writing, there is learning. No wonder Kerala is the most literate state in the country, with claims of ninety-nine percent literacy.

We returned to the hotel, where I replenished my supply of pens to journal my journey. A chauffeured car then drove us to Thekkady.

It was a weary, four-hour drive through the winding hills and country roads of Kerala, to the hillside hamlet of Thekkady. Along the way, we passed tropical rain forests, rubber plantations, peppercorn trees, and pineapple and papaya groves. As we got closer to our destination, we came across signboards that read, "Tiger Land — No Horn Please."

We pulled up at the Taj Hotel nestled in a quiet rustic setting. Once a coffee plantation, now only a few coffee plants sprouted between peppercorn trees on the hotel grounds. The manager, who gave us a tour, pointed to a tall tree. "That's the only papaya tree left."

"What happened to the others?" I asked.

Handing me his binoculars he drew my attention to the two lean tan monkeys with long tails sitting on the tall fruit tree. "You see those two *langurs* up there? They're the reason we don't have papaya trees any more. We once had plenty, but the *langurs* ate up the fruit. Now we buy papayas from the market for our hotel guests."

The next morning, I woke up as fresh as the morning daisy, when my ears caught the sweet chirping of magpie robins. Stepping out into the enclosed veranda of our second-floor cottage, I drew in the crisp mountain air. My eyes swept across the horizon. The morning mist veiled the hills. The sun was in no hurry to rise this morning.

We sat on the porch reading the newspaper and had breakfast delivered to our cottage. An hour later, the sun leisurely crept up from behind the hills and burned the early morning fog, revealing breathtaking views of the rolling green knolls, just across the street from the hotel. I could have had a whole pot of Kerala tea and let the magpie whistle a happy tune for me. I could have curled up all day on the porch and read a book, but a busy schedule awaited us.

Later that morning, escorted by a guide provided by the hotel, we got a private tour of the eighty-acre Atapallam Spice Ranch in town. He explained the ayurvedic medicinal purposes of various spice plants: basil, cardamom, cinnamon, clove, cocoa, coriander, cumin, ginger, nutmeg, peppercorn, star anise, turmeric, and vanilla bean.

Stopping by a palm tree, he craned his neck and pointed to the coconuts. "We use the whole coconut. Herbal hair dyes are made from coconut shell. The fiber maintains moisture around the trees. The fruit and cream are used for cooking; the trunk of the tree for furniture."

He shook the coriander seeds off a shrub. "If you soak these overnight in warm water and drink it in the morning, it will help with your digestion and acidity. Fenugreek seeds boiled in water is good for diabetes, blood pressure and small intestines."

Bringing an aromatic cinnamon stick up to my nose, he let me sniff it. "Cinnamon powder mixed in warm water cures cholesterol."

He bent down and snapped a piece of a root, the inside of which was yellow. "Turmeric is good for bones. It must be cooked with food as it is very potent."

We walked past a bed of tiny white, pink, and magenta flowers. "You see these little forget-me-nots? They are also used to cure diabetes and stomach ulcers."

Then we came upon a tree with green peppercorns. "Peppercorns — red, white or green — grow on the same vine. Only their picking and processing times are different. The white ones are good for eyesight." He ushered us up a short flight of steps to a small terrace where green peppercorns were laid out on a newspaper to ripen in the sun. "This sun-drying process changes the color of the peppercorns to red or black, depending on how long they are left to soak in the sun."

I now understood why Europeans had been coming for centuries to India to trade in spices not just for their flavor, but also for their natural cures.

That evening, we took a safari cruise on Lake Periyar to catch a glimpse of the endangered animals at Periyar National Park — a wildlife sanctuary and tiger reserve in the Cardamom Hills. A French couple, who sat behind us on the boat, lent us their spare binoculars. Through the lens I spotted a menagerie of antelopes, bison, boars, deer, elephants, and other four-legged creatures that emerged out of the thick woods to the water's edge for a drink. In the afternoon sun, alligators basked on the banks, sea otters frolicked in the lake, and rare birds perched on the trees. And the tigers? Forty of them were known to have made their home in this neck of the woods, yet not one sighting. I wondered if they kept them at a different location, away from the public, since this endangered species has always been hunted down.

After a two-night stay at Thekkady, we proceeded to Munnar. The road climbed and climbed, then coiled around a chain of verdant rolling knolls. We drove past sprawling tea plantations of the Cardamom Hills where scattered groups of men and women wove their way through a sweeping maze of shrubs, plucking ripened tea leaves and stuffing them in gunny sacks slung over their backs.

After a four-hour drive, we arrived at the Best Western hilltop hotel in Fort Munnar — a small hotel with plenty of flora and fauna and no other structures around. The windows of our room opened to captivating views of luscious green hills and cobalt waters of Lake Anayirangal, over six thousand feet below.

We washed up, had samosas with tea, then Ranjit and I walked down the hill for a countryside stroll. Ah, the rustic setting, the intoxicating mountain air, the silence of the hills. I now understood why the British loved to vacation at the hilltop tea plantations during the colonial era.

"I wish Minal and Ari could have taken this trip with us," I said to Ranjit. "They would have enjoyed it. I wonder how they're doing back home."

"You can send them an email from the next stop. There is no internet facility here."

That evening, we joined the hotel guests for an informal south Indian dinner and then chatted in the reception area with a couple of women from Hyderabad, one of whom was a lawyer.

The next day, we drove down the same range of Cardamom Hills, lunched at the Tea County Hotel in the foothills, and then went on a scenic drive. To our left, rose an army of eucalyptus trees. I rolled down my window to draw in the scented air. A few sniffs and my sinuses cleared up.

After a brief stop at the local dam we drove down to nearby Echo Point at Mattupetty Lake, where a handful of hawkers sold eucalyptus oil and coconut drinks. The man from whom I purchased two small bottles of eucalyptus oil for my sinus headaches told us, "Shout and you will hear your words echo in the hills. Everyone comes up here and shouts." Ranjit and I tried to clear our lungs and let our voices reverberate. It did not work for us.

Then we indulged in a boat ride in a canopied *shikara*. The man in the gondola paddled through the calm waters that looked up to the towering wooded Idduki Hills. The blue skies, the drifting clouds, the soaring black-birds and sweet serenity helped me forget yesterday's worries. In those few blissful moments, I was lost in paradise.

That evening, Ranjit and I shared a few laughs over some rounds of carom, chess, and table tennis at the hotel recreation room. This time, I made sure he did not win all the games. Despite being a novice at table tennis, I gave him a run for every ping-pong point.

"Oh Ranjit, you sure are a hard-hitter. But, I know how to position the ball. . . right by the net and not where you are expecting it."

However, chess is one game I have not mastered. Every now and then I indulge in the game after someone explains the moves to me. In a few days, I forget all the rules until someone comes along, like Ranjit did this evening, and asks, "Jaya, want to play chess?"

"Sure. But first you have to explain the game to me."

He explained the cardinal rules of the game: the hop, skip, and jump moves on the board, even the four-step waltz performances by the knight. After the game, the king, the queen, the knights, and the pawns were all returned to the same box.

That evening in the dining hall, the hotel hostess in a silk sari asked us to join her on the terrace after dinner. We rushed through dinner and went to the terrace where a small crowd had gathered around a big bonfire. It was a bit nippy, but the fire kept us warm and the evening was filled with music and merriment.

"We're going to dance around the bonfire," said the lively hostess.

Joining hands, we circled around the kindling flames. There under a nocturnal sky, we partnered up and danced the evening away to vintage western music from the 1950s and 60s.

The following afternoon, we took an overnight train for Margao Station. The train whistled past a few village stations and stopped at others. We passed villages, plains and wilderness, but no rolling hills or soaring mountains, no scenic rivers or lakes. Several peddlers boarded at stations: *chaiwallah* with a hot teapot and disposable cups, someone with a tray of snacks, another with packaged meals. We did not buy anything for fear our stomachs might get upset. On our way to the train station, we had stopped to pick up dinner-to-go and two large bottles of water from a restaurant.

It was very noisy in our overcrowded second-class, air-conditioned compartment. The only train with a first-class coach had left for the day. There would not be another headed for our destination until the next day. As evening fell, the train crew came around to distribute blankets, freshly laundered white linen and pillows. Soon the lights dimmed.

"You want to take the upper berth or the lower?' asked Ranjit.

"I'll take the lower. You take the upper. I might fall off from up there with a big thud if I fall into a deep sleep."

At dawn we arrived at our whistle stop, Margao. The hotel's chauffeured car picked us up and drove us to a red-tiled roof villa with a peach-stucco façade. Nestled in thick foliage at the beachfront resort of Sinquerim in Goa was the palm-fringed Taj Hotel. By the entrance stood an imposing three-hundred-twenty-year old Banyan tree with a very wide knotty trunk, entwined like Medusa's hair. Sweet-smelling quesquila tree with red blossoms and a willingtonia with white buds welcomed us as we drove up the long driveway. A rambling vine with scarlet flora scaled the sidewall, and white flowering maria exotica, pink ixora and red hibiscus dressed the front garden.

A young receptionist in a colorful silk sari at the front desk greeted us and checked us in. "You missed the 'Good Golly Miss Molly Rock n' Roll night.' We had live band and dancing last night at the beach house."

"Are there any events planned for tonight?" I asked. Surely there would be some activities planned for Friday evening, even if we had missed the rock n' roll night. After all, this was Goa, the Club Med of India.

"Yes," she beamed. "We have live Indian music here at the beach house and Salsa night at our new Fort Aguada Taj hotel."

"How far is your other hotel from here?"

"Only a few minutes away. You can walk there or take our shuttle bus." She handed me a copy of the activities and entertainment schedule for the week.

Wheeling our bags across the terracotta floor, we walked down the brick path to a seaside cottage with Moroccan windows that welcomed us with exotic blossoms at its entrance. The rear of the chalet backed up to the sea wall. Opening the sliding glass door to the porch, which was walled on two sides, I threw myself in the hammock that hung between two palm trees. There, caressed by the tropical sea breeze, I dozed off.

Feeling refreshed after a siesta, I browsed through the hotel's activity schedule, and noticed "Salsa lessons." *But what good would that do? Since Ranjit had refused tango lessons in the past, he might not volunteer for salsa.* Still, I tried.

"Ranjit, want to take salsa lessons today?"

"Jaya, you can take whatever classes you want. Don't ask me to do the same."

"You miss half the fun of life if you only watch television or read the newspaper."

If he wants to play Mr. Grinch, let him. Slipping into my khaki shorts, I sauntered down the brick path, passed the lush red and white bougainvilleas and to the calling waters of Calangute Beach. At the beach, past parasailers glided over me, sun-lovers bronzed themselves on blue chaises while children built sandcastles with mud pails. I came upon a snack stand with British and Swiss flags flying over its thatched roof, where young Europeans chatted over drinks. I talked to the man behind the counter who said the flags were gifts from the regular visitors.

The next hour belonged to me as I watched the sun slip into the warm waters. The tropical breeze, the whispering waves, the seductive waters that caressed my feet. When twilight set in, I left the beach with footprints in the sand. With salt from the ocean still on my lips, I strolled back to the cottage past the yellow orchids.

The Salsa Night by the poolside was a gala event. Live band played music from yesteryears while salsa dancers performed on stage for an audience of a couple of hundred people. The candlelight banquet included a smorgasbord of Italian pastas and Chinese stir-fry, stuffed crêpes, meat kebabs and tandoori chicken, local catch from the Arabian Sea and spicy Goanese shrimp in coconut cream. There was food for every palate and dessert for every sweet tooth. A grand delightful fiesta it was.

The next morning, after sending emails to Minal and Ari from the hotel, we joined the hotel guests on a sightseeing tour. We strolled through the 17th century sprawling church of St. Francis of Assisi, the walls of which were decked with murals depicting the life of the saint. Across the street stood the Basilica of Bom Jesus, also known as the Church of St. Francis Xavier, which holds the remains of the saint. Walking through the corridors of the church I was back to my youth years at St. Xavier's College of Mumbai, which was named after the Portuguese saint who had brought Christianity to India.

For the next couple of days, I indulged myself at the Calangute Beach, soaking in the sun, wading in the waters, and watching the wind kick up the surf.

After four heavenly days on the beaches of Goa, when we checked out of the hotel, the receptionist said, "Next time, you must come in February."

"Why February?" I asked.

"That's when we have the Carnival. Four days and nights of celebration."

"That's when we have Mardi Gras in New Orleans."

It had been a memorable winter vacation to Southern India. I am glad we visited Goa when we did. No monsoons. No summer heat. No mafia. No drug lords. Simply Paradise.

Farewell

When I last spoke with Mangha from Goa, he did not sound good. Upon our return from the south, I found that his physical condition had deteriorated. He had developed a persistent cough, and the occasional smile had left his face. He shuttled between the hospital and the doctors. It hurt to see my brother and mother confined to bed.

That weekend, Mangha's friend invited us to his daughter's bridal dance party. Due to his illness, my brother could not join us, but he urged Ranjit and me to go. I had known my brother's social crowd since I was a teenager. He had often taken me to social events in town. At the party I ran into Mangha's old friend, Kishu. We chatted awhile about my brother's health and exchanged news on what was happening in our lives. Then he asked, "Do you remember the Shalimar incident from many years ago?"

"You mean about the dance and the fight way back in October 1965?"

"Yes."

"How could I forget that? Gosh, I was only eighteen then."

"Do you know that your brother Mangha and I were asked not to return to Shalimar for a whole year?"

"A whole year? No, I didn't know."

"You have a nice brother, Jaya. He has always been very protective of you."

I was touched by his revelation.

The next morning, I teased Mangha. "So you and your friend Kishu were banned from Shalimar's for a whole year?"

"Who told you that?"

"Kishu. He was at the party last night. He said it used to be your favorite hangout place."

A smile escaped my brother's pale lips.

In a matter of days, I was to leave for America. So I spent all my waking hours with my family. All week long, when Mangha broke into a coughing spell at night, it woke me up in the adjoining room. I rolled out of bed and gave him a tablespoon of honey to calm his throat. The night before my departure, he did not sleep well. He also refused the spoonful of honey.

The next morning, he did not look good at all. Still, he stepped out for a couple of hours to take care of personal affairs. That evening, I gave him homemade chicken soup. Then I put on Herb Alpert's CD for him. When "A Taste of Honey" music played, his eyes grew misty while my heart heavy. It sunk deeper than the Indian Ocean. Leaving my family in the care of servants, in their hour of need, was my saddest moment. I was torn between my two worlds.

The doorbell rang. It was my husband's family driver. Time to say goodbye to my family. I went to my brother's room, wanted to hug him, stroke his hair, and touch his face to heal him. I wanted to kiss his forehead and bless him. But tonight, I was afraid to even shake his hands. Afraid I might catch the contagious cough. Afraid I might break down and not be able to pull myself together.

Standing a few feet from his bed, I almost choked on my words. "Mangha, the driver is here. I have to go now. Thanks for everything."

"I didn't do anything for you this time." He spoke so softly that his lips barely moved. He lay on his side in bed, wilting away in pain.

"You don't know how much you've done for the family and me. You sent us all to America while you stayed behind and took care of Mom and Dad."

A few tears trickled down his face and onto his pillow. I tried hard to fight back my tears, even though it was raining in my heart.

"Talk to the doctor about your cough. Maybe it's bronchitis or pneumonia, not the bile backing up to your lungs this time," I said. "Don't go anywhere by yourself. Take the servant with you wherever you go." I waved a kiss at him by the door. "I love you. Get well soon. I'll call you when I get to America."

Bringing his hand slowly to his mouth, he returned my kiss.

For a few painful moments, an awkward silence filled the room. Deep inside me I had this gnawing feeling that this might be our last reunion. Standing there in the doorway, I felt as if my heart was breaking. I was back to that day in 1954, when Mangha had a motorcycle accident. He was then nineteen while I, seven. He lay helpless in bed then, as he did now. I played music for him then, as I did now.

I went to my mother's room and hugged her frail body. "Mummy, I have to go now. The driver is here."

"You'll be back tomorrow? In the morning?" she asked, holding her hand to my chin.

Dear me! It would do no good to remind her that I lived in America, half-a-world away.

"You'll come tomorrow?" she repeated, beckoning me with her soft eyes. A mother's heart always full of hope.

"Yes Mummy, some day soon. Until then, take good care of yourself. Don't skip your dinner."

"Pray to God before you leave," she reminded me as she pointed to the mini cupboard across her bed, a remnant of the shrine from my childhood home with a few portraits and little statuettes of Hindu Gods.

I lit an incense stick and prayed. Cupping my hands with blessings from the Gods, I gently brushed those hands on my mother's head and face, like I used to do when I was young. "God Bless you, Mummy." Then giving her a kiss on her cheek and forehead, I tore myself away from her embrace.

I stopped by the kitchen to say goodbye to the cook and requested him to look after my family. The maid was on her evening break. I had already bade her goodbye and asked her to attend to my mother's needs. "Treat her like your own mother," I said to her. "Ignore anything unkind she says to you. She does not mean it."

I had dinner with Ranjit and his mother that evening and then we left for the airport.

On the plane, memories from the past flashed by me. I remembered fondly the Christmas dance with my brother four years before at the Wodehouse Gymkhana Club. As the band played *The Last Waltz,* Mangha said, "Baby, straighten your arm."

He's still teaching me to dance, I mused.

The morning after my return from India, I received a call from Kamal. "Mangha had a stroke yesterday and was rushed to the hospital," she said. "The infection has spread to his lungs."

The prognosis was not good. I prayed for a miracle. Meanwhile, Suresh, who had remained a bachelor, took a flight home from California.

Then I received the chilling phone call. My brother Mangha was no more. The sad news tore at my heartstrings. Still, I took comfort in the thought that we had spent his last moments together, reminiscing and listening to oldies music. I stood by the window and watched the ripples in the Hudson River while a vintage Indian song by Talat Mahmood played in my heart. "*Meri yaad mein tum na, aansoo bahana. Na dhil ko jhalana, mujhe bhool jhana.*" Don't shed tears in my memory. Don't grieve, forget me dear."

A month later. . .

Late one evening in March 2002, a bright glow in the sky caught my eye. Twin beams radiated from Ground Zero, fused into one and almost touched the heavens. The *Tribute in Light* illuminated the sky for a whole month, heralding hope and peace on this great land.

That month, when the apartment lease came up for renewal, we pulled up stakes once more. Now that Minal was settled in New York City, we moved to Atlanta to live closer to our son, Ari. A year later, he received another job offer and moved out of state.

My mother passed away on August 26, 2007, five years after Mangha's death. She died on Mother Teresa's birthday. In many ways, my mother was much like her: unassuming, loving, and caring. She was the bond that held the family together. I had plans to see her later that year before my humanitarian trip through India, but that was not meant to be.

I can still see her smiling today. I can still hear her say, "Baby, what will you have for breakfast? . . . Baby, can you pick up my medicine on your way back from college?"

"Always walk with humility," she would say. *Namrata sa haljain.* Her words continue to resonate with me.

Acknowledgements

I owe all that I am to my loving and caring parents, the nuns and teachers at Canossa Convent High School, and the rectors and professors at St. Xavier's College of Mumbai.

I am grateful to my family for their immense support, especially to my daughter, Minal, for her creative and strategic direction. Many thanks also to my friends at the Writers' Circle of Georgia Perimeter College for their valuable feedback.

DISCLAIMER: This book is my journey through life. The events portrayed in the book are to the best of my memory and the notes I had taken down in my journal over the years. While all the stories and names in this book are true, names in "A Closed Mind" chapter have been changed to protect the privacy of the people involved.

Notes

1. "Indian History," http://deepak-indianhistory.blogspot.com/2011/05/lord-mountbatten-last-viceroy-of-india.html; Wikipedia *s.v.* Partition of India, http://en.wikipedia.org/wiki/Partition_of_India; and Wikipedia, *s.v.* Radcliffe Line, http://en.wikipedia.org/wiki/Radcliffe_Line. Sir Cyril Radcliffe was commissioned to carve out the territories between India and Pakistan. Pakistan was further divided into West and East Pakistan, its two wings separated by six hundred miles of Indian terrain. Twenty-four years later, East Pakistan would go on to become the sovereign state of Bangladesh.

2. "Partition of India." http://postcolonialstudies.emory.edu/partition-of-india/ and http://www.english.emory.edu/Bahri/Part.html and
"At the time of Partition there were 1,400,000 Hindu-Sindhis living in Pakistan," Wikipedia *s.v.* Partition of India, http://en.wikipedia.org/wiki/Partition_of_India; and Lata Jagtiani's *Sindhi Reflections*, Page 8-9:
Of the 14 million who crossed borders – both Hindus and Muslims – 1,225,000 Sindhi-Hindus migrated out of Sindh province, and doors of Hindu homes were marked with a red cross.

3. "A million casualties," Sindhishaan, 5th anniversary magazine; and Somini Sengupta, "Potent Memories From a Divided India," New York Times, August 13, 2013, Preserving Partition: A 1947 Partition archive of oral histories of those who lived through the violent split of India and Pakistan, http://www.nytimes.com/2013/08/14/arts/potent-memories-from-a-divided-india.html. Watch New York Times video of trains overflowing with people and many sitting on train rooftops as they fled to cross the new India-Pakistan border. According to the Times, it could have been as many as two million who may have been killed during the partition.

4. K.R. Malkani, "The Sindh Story," originally published by University of Michigan, then Allied Publishers Pvt. Ltd. in 1984, Digitized August 29, 2008. He is also author

of "The Midnight Knock," a book about the 1947 partition of India; and Lata Jagtiani, "Sindhi Reflections," published 2006, Jharna Books, Mumbai.

5. Lata Jagtiani, "Sindhi Reflections," Page 289. There were lootings and murders of Hindus by the Mohajirs in Hyderabad on December 26, 1947, and in Karachi on January 6, 1948.

6. Meena Menon, "Leader Who Brought Ethnic Politics to Mumbai Melting Pot," The Hindu, November 18, 2012, http://www.thehindu.com/news/national/leader-who-brought-ethnic-politics-to-mumbai-melting-pot/article4105715.ece; "Milestones in the Life of Shiv Sena Chief Bal Thackeray," Thackeray arrested first time, Hindustan Times, November 17, 2012, http://www.hindustantimes.com/India-news/Mumbai/Milestones-in-the-life-of-Sena-chief-Bal-Thackeray/Article1-960556.aspx; "Summer of '69: Reading the "riot" act with the Shiv Sena," Indian Express, December 30, 1998, http://expressindia.indianexpress.com/ie/daily/19981230/36450594.html; 397-page book was published by Viking.

7. Apollo II, July 8, 2009, http://www.nasa.gov/mission_pages/apollo/missions/apollo11.html#.UreBfrSmao8.

8. Wikipedia s.v. Opium Wars, http://en.wikipedia.org/wiki/Opium_Wars#The_Growth_of_the_Opium_Trade_.281650.E2.80.931773.29; and "Boston Tea Party," http://www.history.com/topics/boston-tea-party.

9. During the British era in India, the Salt Tax made it illegal for workers to freely collect their own salt from the sea. The Gandhi Salt March 1930, http://www.then-again.info/WebChron/India/SaltMarch.html; and Wikipedia s.v. Salt March, http://en.wikipedia.org/wiki/Salt_Satyagraha.

10. "United We Serve," http://www.serve.gov/?q=site-page/september-11th-national-day-service-and-remembrance; "How You Can Volunteer To Commemorate 9/11," 9/8/2011, http://www.huffingtonpost.com/2011/09/07/how-will-you-remember-sep_n_953037.html; and Good Deeds "I Will" http://www.911day.org/.

11. Kerala Tourism guide.

Made in the USA
Charleston, SC
20 March 2014